Fritz Baumgart

A History
of Architectural Styles

Pall Mall Press · London

Translated from the German by
Edith Küstner and J. A. Underwood

Pall Mall Press Ltd.
5 Cromwell Place, London SW 7

First published in Great Britain 1970
© 1969 by Verlag M. DuMont Schauberg, Cologne
English translation © 1970 by Pall Mall Press Ltd.

ISBN 0 269 02639 8
Printed in Germany

Contents

On the Meaning and Essence of the Art of Building

Any attempt to arrive at a definition of architecture as art (the art of building) in terms of the twentieth century is going to run into difficulties. A simple one-family house need not differ in its formal elements from a huge office block, a library, factory or museum, etc. For these are all, even down to the cheapest tenement building, shack or stable, a part of architecture. But at what point does art begin?

Until the beginning of this century, architects and the general public shared a fairly precise concept of what constituted the artistic element in building. To warrant such an evaluation, a building had to have an institutional or representative role, and had to use a richer variety of forms than a purely utilitarian structure. The state was represented by parliament buildings and ministries; the town by the town hall; the Law by the law-courts; the arts by museums in their role of temples of art and by theatres in their role of centres of ceremonial entertainment; knowledge and education by universities, schools and libraries; progress by international exhibition buildings and railway stations, and so on. All such external indications as to the nature of a particular building are to a large extent lacking today. It would seem that after five millennia of architectural practice we must search for new terms to define building as art, but it is not until the final chapters of this book that we shall attempt this.

The concept of the institutional or representative building (implying both representation and substitution) is central to any examination of the history of architectural styles. Every architectural item of any note that has been preserved or discovered since building began has this quality of representing a particular human institution. It might be assumed that these beginnings go back to prehistoric times and to man's first attempts at artistic expression, but this is in fact not so. For many millennia before the first building was erected, the role of representing man's situation in the world and his interpretation of that world was assumed by painting and sculpture. Architecture, in the sense of anything more elaborate than the construction of a simple shelter, began only in the fourth millennium B.C. with the emergence of the earliest high cultures of Mesopotamia and Egypt, when the nomadic existence of hunters and shepherds gave place to the settled life of farming communities. The creation of new types of community in turn led to the building of cities and the establishment of states. Man's whole conception of the world around him necessarily underwent a fundamental change. New gods were revered who demanded permanent places of worship, and so temples were built. At the same time, the new community required a new order such as could not be guaranteed by distant and invisible gods, and so rulers emerged who were god, priest and king in one person, and temples were followed by palaces.

Death was as important as life. The dead also demanded a fixed abode, so tombs were constructed which were monuments at the same time. As the settlements grew, new building problems arose, and prominent among them was the need for defence. In this way a rich field of architecture came into being, distinguished by its use of particular forms, which gave expression to the community's desire for order. This meant that the buildings which we may in this context regard as architecture not only took into account the exigencies of everyday, material existence, but also acquired a special significance by virtue of the fact that they institutionalized man's interpretation of his religion, his state and his community.

We should not, however, overlook one factor inevitably omitted from the present study, and that is that painting and sculpture almost always played an integral part in any institutional building, not as mere aesthetic adjuncts, but as essential elements of the building's significance, thus creating a total work of art which united every aspect of the artistic expression of man's desire for order.

But this quality of a total work of art does not in itself determine the particular essence of architecture. A building, considered as an object that encloses and defines space, stands in a closer relationship to reality than do painting and sculpture, and this involvement in reality implies a higher degree of functionalism than is the case with other art forms. Temples, churches, palaces, etc. were in fact conditioned by their function, not only in respect of their institutional role, but also in respect of the practical use for which they were intended. In addition to this, they were conditioned by the materials which lay to hand, and which placed limits upon the possibilities of construction. An architect was never able to give free rein to his fancy, as a painter could, as long as he was dependent upon natural building materials such as clay, tile, stone and wood. The wider use of iron and glass as artificial building materials, which began in the late eighteenth and early nineteenth centuries, and the steady increase in new artificial building materials since the end of the nineteenth century, presented undreamt-of possibilities. During the nineteenth century such materials were only really exploited by engineers; architects brought them to the service of their art only in a reticent manner. The fact that there is now no longer any essential difference between engineering and architecture has given rise to the situation to which we earlier alluded.

It would be possible to discuss Western architecture from the eighth century onwards in isolation, along the lines indicated above. But such a procedure would be inadequate, for the origins of that architecture, the key to our understanding, derive from the late Holy Roman Empire and the art of Byzantium, which themselves developed from the architecture of the late Roman period. Roman architecture is in many respects derived from Greek architecture, which in its turn drew inspiration from Egyptian, early oriental and Creto-Mycenaean architecture. So we must devote the first few chapters to an examination of these pre-occidental cultures, and their conception of form and construction.

Characteristics: A feature common to all the early civilizations of Egypt, the Middle and Near East and Crete were complexes of tombs, temples and palaces. From the exterior, these appeared to be solid but inside they contained a number of open spaces of varying sizes, and a larger number of closed, concealed rooms. These were mostly very small.

In all except the Hittite and Cretan civilizations, these units were usually laid out according to a very regular pattern.

Materials: Freestone, brick, clay tile, wood.

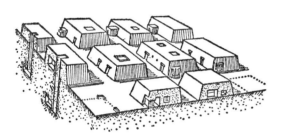

Group of Mastabas, Fourth Dynasty (after A. Badawy)

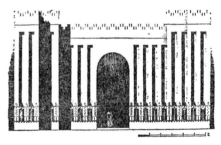

Warka, Inanna Temple, reconstruction of the southeast façade

| a | b | c | d | e |

Papyrus columns (after H. Koepf): a+b papyrus clustered column with closed and open capital,
c+d lotus column with closed and open capital,
e palm column

Egypt

The cult of the dead

The cult of the dead, resting as it did on the belief in a life after death, had a decisive influence on the development of Egyptian architecture. In addition to the burial chamber where his embalmed corpse was laid, the deceased was given a room for offering sacrifices and as many as thirty other additional rooms, according to his wealth and importance. He thus had at his disposal an extensive 'dwelling-house' decorated with statues, reliefs and paintings depicting his life and that of his household, and by this means his continued existence was assured. Such tombs continued to be carved out of the rocky ridges of the Nile Valley right up to the end of the Egyptian Empire. Among the most magnificent sites of this type are the rock temples of Rameses II, dating from the Nineteenth Dynasty (1314–1197 B.C.).

Tombs

Apart from rock tombs, another type of tomb, which was partially above ground, was also used from the very earliest times. This was the mastaba, built of sun-dried brick and elongated in shape, with a flat top and sloping walls *(fig. page 9)*. The largest collections of them have been discovered in the Giza and Saqqara necropoles of Lower Egypt. The mastaba is assumed to have been the forerunner of the pyramid. The *Step Pyramid of King Zoser, Saqqara* (Third Dynasty, 2780–2680) in fact consists of six graduated mastabas placed one on top of the other *(ill. 1)*. The ground plan has become almost square, and the pyramid reaches a height of 59 m. It contains only the small sealed burial chamber, placed in such a position as to be undetectable from outside. Even these precautions, however, did not protect them from being robbed. The dead man's dwelling-house is situated away from the pyramid in the temple area. The rectangular site is not axially oriented as was to be the practice later, but the arrangement of the various parts is extremely regular. The enclosing wall is articulated with projections and recesses, which resemble those used at the same time and even earlier in Mesopotamia. The east façade of the North Palace is decorated with papyrus half-columns; fluted and clustered columns are used in other parts of the site. Papyrus columns were originally made from the plant itself, though subsequently wood was used and, by the Third Dynasty, limestone. The way the limestone is worked demonstrates that the Egyptians had achieved complete mastery of the material by this period; indeed, without this accomplishment, the imposing decoration of their tomb and temple complexes would not have been possible.

Domestic houses

The use of limestone and granite was confined to tombs and temples. Houses and other utilitarian structures, even royal residences, continued to be built almost exclusively of sun-dried brick and wood. As a result almost no domestic architecture has survived. Reproductions in reliefs and frescoes give some idea of what such buildings looked like, but it was only the houses of the rich that were reproduced in this case. The common people lived in extremely primitive huts, probably very much like those of present-day Egypt. The plan of a rich man's house was as follows: an entrance court led by way of an adjoining vestibule with a row of columns into a wide hypostyle entrance hall, which in turn led to the main hypostyle hall which was either square or rectangular. All these rooms were planned symmetrically on an axis. The bedrooms, servants' quarters, kitchen, storage rooms, etc. were laid out on either side and were all contained within a large rectangle. Many houses probably had a second storey as well, consisting of further rooms, as well as open loggias and terraces. The whole house was whitewashed inside and outside. The interior was decorated with paintings on walls and ceilings, and coloured floors.

1   Giza, Chephren Pyramid, plan of the temple site

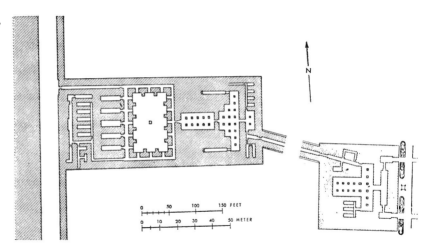

The Pyramids

A glance at the temple site of the *Pyramid of Chephren, Giza (fig. 1)*, which dates from the Fourth Dynasty (2680–2565), reveals that the basic plan of the rich dwelling-house was used for the funerary temples at the Pyramids. The valley temple in the eastern part of the site has a vestibule, a wide hypostyle hall and a second elongated hypostyle hall, all in exact axial symmetry. A walled causeway 450 m long connects the valley temple with the larger funerary temple, introducing a pronounced shift in the axis. The funerary temple has a similar but richer symmetrical balance than the valley temple. The pyramid itself *(ill. 2, centre)*, which stands between the rather smaller and more recent Mycerinus Pyramid and the older and larger Cheops Pyramid, measures 215 m square at the base, and is 143 m high. It still preserves some traces of the casing of carefully smoothed stone slabs with which all the pyramids were originally covered. Apart from the huge Fourth Dynasty burial grounds at Giza, there are other sites at Saqqara and Abusir, dating from the Fifth Dynasty (2565–2420), and south of Saqqara, dating from the Sixth Dynasty (2420–2258).

The Middle Kingdom

Much less has been preserved from the period of the Middle Kingdom, although we do know that several large temples were built, mostly in Upper Egypt, following the ground plan that had been established at the beginning. The funerary temple of Mentuhotep at Deir el-Bahari opposite Thebes, which dates from the Eleventh Dynasty (2134–1991), is remarkable for its novel use of terraces and for its magnificent compactness.

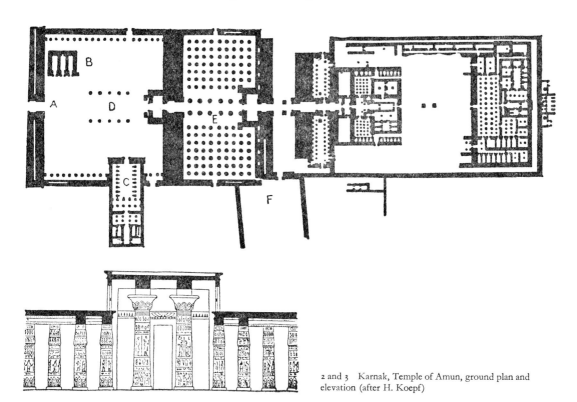

2 and 3   Karnak, Temple of Amun, ground plan and elevation (after H. Koepf)

Temples of the New Kingdom

An understanding of the ground plan is most clearly obtained by a view of the large temples built during the New Kingdom (1570–1085), and particularly the *Temple of Amun, Karnak (ill. 3* and *figs. 2* and *3)*, which was built by several Eighteenth Dynasty (1570–1314) and Nineteenth Dynasty (1314–1197) rulers, including Tuthmosis I and III, Hatshepsut, Sethos I, and Rameses I, II and III. The illustration shows a view of the whole site (118 × 260 m), with the First Pylon (A) in the background and Hatshepsut's Fifth Pylon on the left. The Fifth Pylon belongs to a line of pylons leading towards the temple from the south (F). The site lies on an easterly axis, and its symmetry is disturbed only by the inclusion of two smaller temples (B and C) in the first forecourt (D). The processional path leads from the Second Pylon through a large hypostyle hall (52 × 103 m) supported by 134 papyrus columns. The two middle rows bear a raised portion of the roof (24 m); the columns of the fourteen aisles are 14 m high. – *Queen Hatshepsut's Funerary Temple, Deir el-Bahari*, which stands next to the older temple of

Mentuhotep II, is laid out in terraces which are obviously influenced by it *(ill. 6)*. Ramps lead from the forecourt to the middle court, and from there to the highest sanctuary, which is a smaller court surrounded by colonnades. This site is distinguished by the unusual generosity of its proportions.

The Temple of Amun, Luxor (ill. 4 and *fig. 4)* also dates from the Eighteenth and Nineteenth Dynasties. Amenhotep III built the colonnades, courts and hypostyle halls (B and C) that lead in completely regular succession to the Holy of Holies (55 × 260 m). The axis of the site was altered by the court, laid out in front by Rameses II, which was surrounded by a double row of seventy-four papyrus columns (A). This shift was made so as to preserve an older temple built by Tuthmosis III. The illustration shows the vestibule of the Holy of Holies, with its thirty-four clustered papyrus columns. Clearly, in the design of the interior the impression of space was of only secondary importance; what mattered was the solid, monumental effect created by the forest of columns. The column represented majesty and eternity, as did the vast enclosing walls of pylons. – We should mention here, among other temples of the New Kingdom, the Ramesseum or Funerary Temple of Rameses II at Thebes (57 × 180 m), and the Funerary Temple of Rameses III at Medinet Habu (*c.* 50 × 150 m).

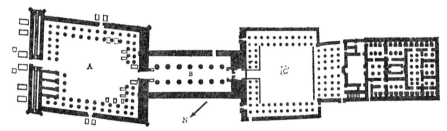

4 Luxor, Temple of Amun, plan of the temple site (after N. de Garis Davies)

The late Ptolemaic and Roman periods

The tradition of building such monuments extends into the late Ptolemaic and Roman periods. The *Temple of Horus, Edfu* (237–212), with its extremely regular arrangement incorporating every element which had been developed over several millennia, is a supreme example of Egyptian architecture *(ill. 5* and *fig. 5)*. The various sections are laid out with almost textbook clarity. But at the same time, the aridity of its elements bears witness to the by now decadent rigidity of an architectural style that had reached its peak of development during the New Kingdom.

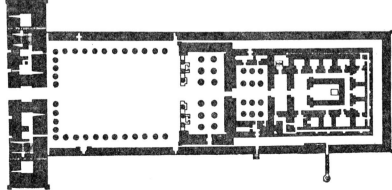

5 Edfu, Temple of Horus, plan of the temple

The Sumerians

The architecture of the ancient civilizations of the Near East, which began to develop even before that of Egypt, presents a very different picture. The urban civilization of the Sumerians in southern Mesopotamia (Ur, Warka, Eridu and Lagash), dating from as early as the fourth millennium B. C., differed from the Nile Valley civilization both in its architectural requirements and in its geographical conditions. There was no cult of the dead, and consequently there was no development of monumental tombs with funerary temples and temples of the dead arranged in orderly succession along a sacred path, as in Egypt. Temples were built solely for the worship of the gods. Again, the plan of the dwelling-house had a decisive influence on temple architecture. In contrast to the axially symmetrical layout of the Egyptian house, the Sumerian house consisted of a number of rooms grouped round a rectangular inner courtyard. The Sumerians also built vast palaces which were far more imposing in their form and construction than their usually fairly simple Egyptian counterparts. They were built almost exclusively of sun-dried clay tiles, as neither stone nor wood was available. Later on, fired tiles with colourful glazes were used in conjunction with or instead of the sun-dried tiles. From the very first, colour and sculpture formed an integral part of Sumerian architecture.

Warka (Uruk)

From the small, primitive temples of the early Sumerian period, between 3500 and 3000 B.C., a regular form gradually emerged which was distinguished from other buildings by the addition of buttresses inside and out, numerous small recesses, and decorative mosaics composed of coloured terracotta cones embedded in the thick plaster of the walls. The excavation of the *White Temple, Warka* (Uruk) has revealed not only the complete ground plan *(fig. 6)*, but also large sections of mosaic wall. Of significance was the fact that this temple was built on an artificial mound 12 m high, thereby establishing the basic form of the ziggurat or high temple which remained unchanged until the end of the Sumerian civilization (the seventh-century 'Tower of Babel'). The White Temple contained all the elements which were to determine the style of later colossal buildings. In the flat country of Mesopotamia, the artificial mound took on great meaning; not only was the house of the god thus made visible for miles around, but it was also brought closer to heaven.

The City States of Isin, Larsa and Babylon (third and second millennia)

The *Temple of Ishtar-Kititum, Ishchali* (c. 2000–1900) dates from the post-Sumerian period of the city states of Isin, Larsa and Babylon (2025–1594). A reconstruction of the temple *(fig. 7)* shows the extent of the development of colossal architecture in the intervening period. A long rectangle containing four inner courtyards stood on a raised platform. The outer and inner surfaces of the enclosing wall were topped by wide offsets between slightly extended masonry members. The irregularly distributed portals were flanked by projecting towers, square in section, their faces indented with tall narrow rectangular niches, giving the temple the appearance of a citadel or fortress. Arches and vaults were known at the time but did not play any

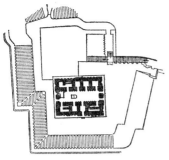

6 Warka (Uruk), ground plan of the White Temple (after H. Frankfort)

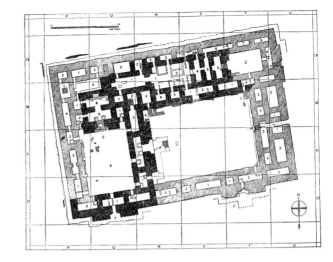

7 Ishchali, plan of the Temple of Ishtar-Kititum

significant part in construction. The architecture of this period was characterized, like that of Egypt, by smooth surfaces and vertical and horizontal lines. – Genuine architectural sculptures appeared for the first time on the small Inanna Temple of King Karaindash at Warka, built *c.* 1440 during the Kassite dynasty (*c.* 1600–1100). The sculptures were constructed of the same tile as the walls, and were placed in the hollows in the façade *(ill. 7* and *fig. page 9)*. This type of architectural sculpture was used in a far more imposing way in Babylonian temples almost a thousand years later. The temple was based on a regular plan, with the entrance on the axis, and with the corners accentuated by a kind of bulwark.

Assyria

The best known building of the later Assyrian period (*c.* 1000–612) is the *Palace of Sargon II* (742–705) at Khorsabad. The palace (300 × 400 m) was situated on the north side of the city, which was rectangular in shape and covered almost a square mile, and jutted out beyond the city wall *(ill. 8)*. The temples were decorated with colourful reliefs of glazed tile, and enormous sculptures of winged bulls with human heads watched over the throne room and the gates *(fig. 8)*. Of the ziggurat which stood within the palace grounds, three and a half steps have been preserved. Each one was painted a different colour, and there were probably seven in all, reaching a height of about 45 m, i.e. corresponding to the length of the base.

8 Khorsabad, Palace of Sargon II, reconstruction of the gates to throne hall VII, drawing of a section

15

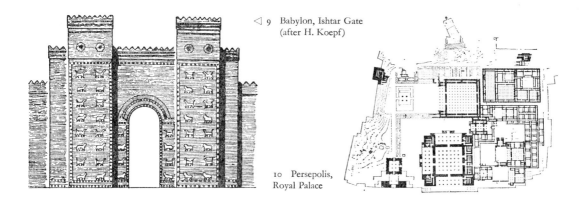

9 Babylon, Ishtar Gate
(after H. Koepf)

10 Persepolis,
Royal Palace

The Neo-Babylonian period

The *Ishtar Gate* from Babylon (*c.* 575), which has been reconstructed complete with its co-loured tiles and reliefs in the Berlin State Museum *(fig. 9)*, belongs to the final era of ancient oriental art, the Neo-Babylonian period (*c.* 612–539). It stood at the junction of the processional way which, flanked by lion reliefs, led into the city from the festival arena outside the walls. It is not possible to give an exact description of the biblical 'Tower of Babel', although it very probably reached a height of 90 m and was surmounted by a temple. We do know that it was a stepped structure with a ramp rising from step to step around the outside.

Persia

In 539, Babylon was captured by the Persians under Cyrus, and in 525 Cambyses conquered Egypt. The *Palace of Persepolis* was begun in 518 under Darius I (522–486), and was not completed until 460 *(ill. 9* and *fig. 10)*. It was a near-megalomanic syncretism of ancient oriental and Egyptian ideas. The exaggerated use of columns in the enormous halls can only have been derived from Egyptian temple sites, though the columns themselves are considerably thinner than their Egyptian counterparts, and are made either of stone or wood covered with a thick layer of plaster and subsequently painted. Ionic capitals were introduced by Greek workmen from western Asia Minor, but their use in Persepolis in no way displays the logical clarity of Greek architecture. The same applies to the way in which the stone was worked and assembled. Instead of using regular blocks, blocks of widely differing sizes were cut. Stone door frames, for example, instead of being built in four parts (doorstep, posts and lintel), were often in one piece, or in two or three sections. The entire palace complex seems to have been put together on similar lines.

Troy

We need only concern ourselves with two more Near-Eastern civilizations of the third and second millennia B.C.: Troy and the Hittites. Troy deserves mention because as early as the third millennium we find there, as we do on Lesbos, a type of house which may be regarded as an early form of the megaron described by Homer one thousand years later. It consists of two or three rooms laid out one behind the other forming a small rectangle, with the side-walls extended at one or both ends in a way that anticipates the plan of the Greek temple.

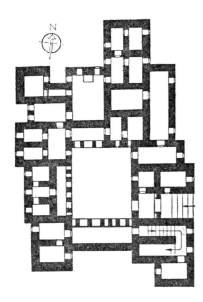

11 Boghazköy,
Temple III
and Lion Gate

The Hittites

Hittite migration into Asia Minor reached a peak in the eighteenth century B.C., and the Hittite Empire was at its most powerful and extensive between 1400 and 1200. The capital city of Hattusas (Boghazköy) was heavily fortified and contained several temples. The walls and gates were built of huge blocks of stone (known as cyclopean masonry), and were occasionally decorated with sculpture, like the *Lion Gate*, built *c.* 1250 *(fig. 11)*. The temple entrances were similarly decorated. The foundations of larger buildings and the lower part of the walls were of stone, the rest of the walls consisting of tiles reinforced with wooden beams. The layout of the Hittite temple was extremely irregular. The only clearly laid out section of *Temple III, Boghazköy (fig. 11)* was the large colonnaded inner court. A remarkable feature of this building was the large number of windows. Both the cyclopean masonry and the Lion Gate show certain similarities to the contemporary Mycenaean architecture of the Greek mainland, and may possibly have influenced it.

Crete and Mycenae

Crete

The other early civilization with which we are concerned is the Creto-Minoan civilization, which began to develop shortly after 2000. At first it was closely linked with the civilizations of Egypt and Mesopotamia, but it soon assumed a character of its own. A typical feature were unfortified palaces with richly painted decoration. There were no temples. Burial monuments were of little importance, but round stone burial mounds existed as early as the third millennium. The walls of these tombs inclined inwards, and we may assume the existence of a curvature, probably constructed of clay tiles. The plan of the Cretan palace also recalls the architecture of the third millennium. It was based on the houses of that period, which were totally asymmetrical and had very small rooms.

Knossos

The great period of Cretan palace-building was between 1650 and 1400 B.C. This was the period of Knossos, Phaestos, Mallia and the large villa at Ayia Triada. The plan of the *Palace of Minos, Knossos (fig. 12)* demonstrates clearly how the legend of the labyrinth of Minos arose. An ernormous number of small, rectangular rooms were grouped asymmetrically round a large central courtyard. The layout of the rooms was extremely intricate; there was frequently no access from room to room, except by way of a long narrow passage which wound backwards and forwards between them. This confusion was continued through several storeys, which necessitated the incorporation of lightshafts and staircases *(ill. 10)*. It was the first time in the history of architecture that these features had been exploited in an artistic way; they did not reappear in this way again until the Renaissance, three thousand years later. Reinforcement was by means of rectangular pillars (the knowledge of their use had been brought from Egypt and Syria), and wooden columns which tapered towards the base and stood on hollowed-out stone slabs. The walls were constructed of quarry stone, clay mortar, clay tile and wooden reinforcement, and were plastered throughout. It has proved difficult to reconstruct the arrangement of the upper storeys. A certain number of the parition walls, which formed many tiny rooms on the ground floor, may in fact have been supporting walls, enabling larger halls and terraces to be built on the upper floors. The massed rows of storage rooms, at any rate, were not repeated above. From the outside, the palace probably very much resembled a rich Egyptian dwelling-house or palace, though it lacked the internal order of the latter completely. Cretan architecture can certainly not be described as monumental. It is endowed with an air of geniality; the whole Cretan civilization was sensual, elegant and refined.

Cretan towns

An accurate impression of a Cretan town may be obtained from the excavations at Gournia: a vast number of tiny living-units crowded around 'streets' just wide enough to let a man or a

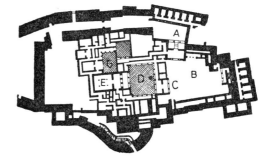

◁ 12   Knossos, Palace of Minos A = hypostyle hall; B = central courtyard; C = throne hall; D = storage rooms; E = the Queen's chamber; F = Hall of the Double Axes (After H. Koepf)

13   Tiryns, citadel complex A = greater Propylaeum; B = main courtyard; C = lesser Propylaeum; D = altar court; E = megaron (see fig. 14); F = second court with megaron (after H. Koepf)

donkey pass through. We do not know for certain whether the Cretan civilization was suddenly destroyed around 1400, or whether it slowly disintegrated over the period 1400–1200. In either event, the Mycenaeans from the Greek mainland undoubtedly played a part in its downfall, for they seem to have become masters of Crete and absorbed the island's culture some time before this period. The only way in which their culture differed markedly from that of Crete was in its architecture.

Mycenaean citadels

The large citadel complexes of *Tiryns (fig 13)* and Mycenae were modelled on those of Troy, and made use of the cyclopean masonry of the Hittites. Even the great *Lion Gate at Mycenae* (*c.* 1350–1300) may have been influenced by Hittite town gates, although the two lions on either side of the downward-tapering Cretan column demonstrate a greater measure of architectural discipline *(ill. 11)*.

The megaron

Nearly all the palace building at Tiryns and Mycenae date from the late fourteenth and thirteenth centuries. The asymmetrical layout recalls the Cretan palaces. The individual units, however, are completely regular, being in fact fully-formed megarons. Each megaron consisted of an open entrance room supported by two columns, a wide rectangular vestibule and a main room with a hearth at the centre. Four wooden columns stood in a rectangle around the

14   Ground plan of a Mycenaean megaron

hearth, and supported the raised flue *(fig. 14)*. The hearth room of the largest megaron at Tiryns measures 9.80 m × 11.80 m. The method of construction is the same as that employed in Crete, the walls consisting of a base of quarry stone surmounted by tiles with wooden reinforcement, the whole being smoothly plastered over and decorated with frescoes. The eighth-century Homeric epics, passing in silence over the dark years between, give detailed descriptions of Mycenaean life during the thirteenth and twelfth centuries.

Mycenaean round tombs

Apart from the citadel complexes, the most remarkable feature of Mycenaean architecture in the round tomb, or tholos, which first appeared shortly after 1500. Three main groups of tholoi have survived: the first group was built between 1510 and 1460, the second between 1460 and 1400, and the third between 1400 and 1300. The largest of these tombs, the *Treasury of Atreus* (*c.* 1330–1300, *fig. 15*), belongs to the third group. The beehive-like interior was achieved by making each stone course project further than the one below, creating a pseudo-vault (diameter 14.5 m, height 13.20 m). The walls were plastered and decorated. A small door

 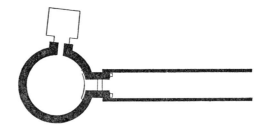

15   Mycenae, the Treasury of Atreus, elevation and ground plan

leads through to the burial chamber. The approach to the main room is through a walled passage 30 m long and 6 m wide, and a door (height 5.4 m) which was originally flanked by half-columns. Above the huge monolithic lintel, which extends far into the rounded walls, there is a triangular relieving opening. This space, now empty, was originally filled in and decorated, and was framed by two small columns. These columns were themselves decorated with zig zag bands and undulating lines.

The Mycenaean civilization was destroyed *c.* 1100 by fresh invasions from the North, and several centuries were to pass before a new civilization emerged in Greece to develop the segacy of the ancient civilizations.

2 Greece

Characteristics: The most characteristic feature of Greek architecture is the structure consisting of vertical supports (columns), bearing horizontal members (the entablature). Vaulting was not used. Size and proportions varied, but were limited by the method of construction and the materials available. Interiors were unimportant. The two main orders of building were the Doric and the Ionic. The Doric column had no base, and its capital consisted of a cushion-like disc (the echinus) surmounted by a square slab (the abacus). The Ionic column stood on a base, and its capital consisted of an ornamented cushion between two snail-shaped volutes. The Corinthian order resembled the Ionic, except that its capital took the form of a wreath of acanthus leaves with rising volutes. All proportions were derived from the human body. (See *fig.* this page.)

Materials: Marble, dressed stone and wood.

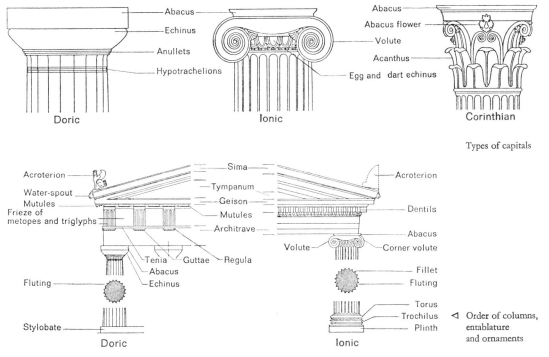

Types of capitals

◁ Order of columns, entablature and ornaments

21

Between 1210 and 1100 B.C., the Dorians from the north conquered the Peloponnesus and south-west Asia Minor, and the Ionians settled in Attica and the Aegean islands. The palace culture of Mycenae came to an abrupt end, and civilization sank back into barbarism. The architectural traditions of almost two thousand years were preserved in simple dwelling-huts. From the eighth century onwards, the wealth and influence of the Greek peoples gradually increased and the foundations of a new culture and religion were laid. During the eighth and seventh centuries, the Ionians and Aeolians systematically settled the coast of Asia Minor, and between the eighth and sixth centuries, towns were founded in Sicily, southern Italy, the south of France and on the Black Sea coast.

The beginnings of temple building
The initial focus of architectural expression was the temple, which developed from the dwelling-house or megaron. Palaces and funerary buildings were unimportant, and it was not until later that other public buildings began to evolve. We do not know exactly when Greek architecture began, but we can assume it was some time during the ninth century. Dates before 600 B.C. are difficult to assess accurately since, because of the nature of building methods before that time, nothing has survived. In the early temples, the walls of the cella consisted of a base of quarry stone covered with clay plaster, with sun-dried clay tiles above, which were also plastered. Wood was used for the columns, entablature and roof. Dressed stone first appeared as a building material towards the end of the seventh century, at the same time as the first stone sculptures. The invention of roof tiles led to the development of gabled roofs on stone buildings. Wood and tile temples gave way during the sixth century to stone temples. The principles of carpentry were simply applied to stone instead, so that the new temples had all the same structural and functional members as the old. Two orders emerged: the Doric on the mainland and in the west, and the Ionic in Asia Minor, the islands, and also to some extent in Athens.

Temple forms
The basic form of the Greek temple was that in which the walls of the cella were extended eastwards, terminating in pilasters or antae, and two columns were introduced to form a vestibule or pronaos. Occasionally another vestibule, the opisthodomos, was added at the west end. It was characteristic of the Greeks that even this simple shape was the product not of practical considerations, but of a purely aesthetic passion for symmetry. The addition of four columns,

forming a portico before the antae, was termed a prostylos, and a similar addition at the west end an amphiprostylos. The most common type of temple became the peripteros, in which the whole building was surrounded by columns. A double row of columns was called a dipteros. The cella, which contained the image of the god and to which the faithful were not admitted, was divided down the centre by columns supporting the ceiling and the roof. Usually there were two rows of columns arranged in two storeys. The temple always stood on a platform or stylobate, usually of three steps. The altar stood outside in front of the temple. Decoration consisted of sculptures on the gables, reliefs on the metopes and friezes, terracotta ornaments on the cornices and gables, and paintings. Since the interior played only an ideal and not a practical role, the important view of the temple was that of the exterior. It was essentially a plastic monument. It is difficult to know exactly what these temples looked like, since none of them have survived in their original form.

Proportions

Although there were many different ways in which the columns could be arranged, the basic form of the temple always remained the same. Only the proportions were modified, but even there limits were set by the materials and the method of construction. However, an astonishing variety of effects was created by adjustments of proportion so minute as to be undetectable by the human eye. The fact that each of the Greek temples has a distinct charakter of its own is due not only to accidents of preservation, but equally to the thoroughness with which their proportions were calculated. The height of the capitals in relation to the length of the columns, the distance between the columns themselves (the intercolumniation) and between the columns and the cella wall, the height of the entablature in relation to the length of the columns, the depth of the architrave, frieze and cornice in relation to the height of the entablature, the slight swelling of the columns in the centre (the entasis) and the degree to which they

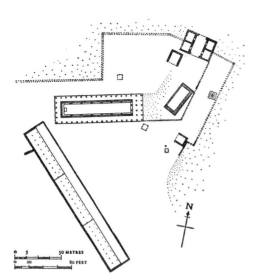

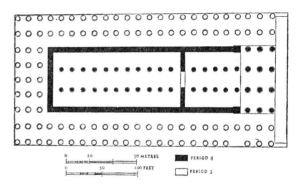

16 Samos, Sanctuary and Temple of Hera IV.

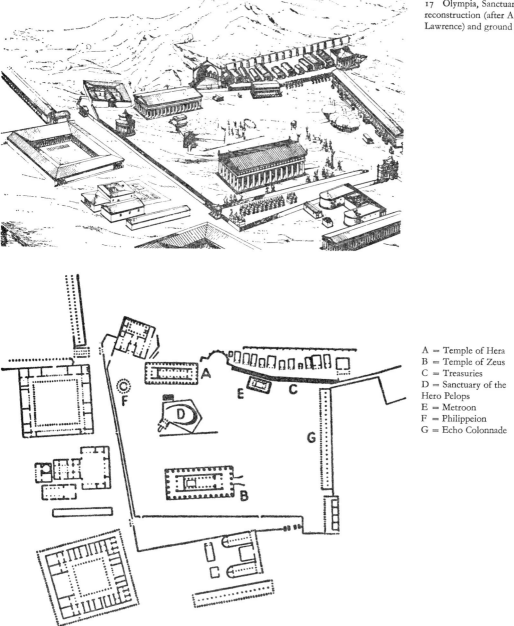

17 Olympia, Sanctuary, reconstruction (after A.W. Lawrence) and ground plan

A = Temple of Hera
B = Temple of Zeus
C = Treasuries
D = Sanctuary of the Hero Pelops
E = Metroon
F = Philippeion
G = Echo Colonnade

tapered at the top, the slightly concave curvature of the stylobate and the entablature, the angle at which the columns leant inwards, the corner-work of the entablature, etc. – all these measurements were minutely calculated according to a particular scale of proportions. In this way, the undisguised relationship of horizontal load and vertical support basic to Greek temple building was invested with a sense of life that has never been equalled in architecture either before or since. In the space of a few generations, between 600 and 400, reaching a peak between 450 and 400, the Greek spirit created something quite unique in the history of art. The temple architecture of the next three centuries, before the Greek tradition was taken over by the Romans, was often more magnificent and richer in decoration, but it never matched the classical grandeur of the fifth century.

Sanctuaries

The general classification and nomenclature of the Doric and Ionic orders are given in the two diagrams on page 21. Exceptions will be mentioned as and when they arise. Our first example, the fourth *Heraion* at the sanctuary of Samos *(fig. 16)*, is in fact already something of an exception. The first temple of Hera was probably built *c.* 800. Its proportions were unusually poor, and over the years it was gradually altered and rebuilt until it attained the typical Ionic form. The fourth and final building, a dipteros begun *c.* 530 after a fire had damaged the third temple, was never completed. Measuring 112.2 × 55.2 m, it was the largest Greek temple ever planned. A particularly interesting feature of the *Heraion* was the way in which the sanctuary evolved. It was surrounded by a wall, and a colossal entrance gate or propylon was built not on the axis of the temple, but at an angle of 45° to it, facing slightly north-east. The approaching pilgrim thus saw the temple from an angle which set it off to its best possible advantage as a sculptured monument. The other two important elements of the site – the massive altar and the stoa – were situated with similar irregularity in relation to the temple. The long stoa, dating from the middle of the sixth century, had an inner row of columns supporting a roof between the rear wall and the open colonnade, an arrangement which afforded pilgrims a protected recreation and sleeping area. The stoa probably originated at sanctuaries like the *Heraion*, which received a great many pilgrims. Later it was adopted in the market places or agora of towns. The apparently wilful irregularity with which these buildings were arranged was typical of Greek sanctuaries, and stands in strong contrast to the geometrical layout of Egyptian temple sites.

The same is true of *Olympia*, a site which contained two important sanctuaries, the temples of Hera and of Zeus *(fig. 17)*. The *Temple of Hera* was rebuilt *c.* 600 in the form of a peripteros,

18 Corfu, Temple of Artemis, reconstruction of the west façade (after Rodenwaldt)

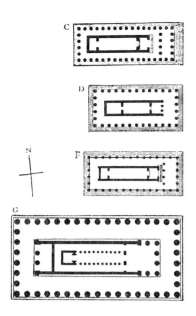

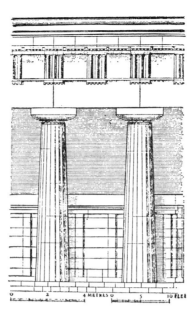

19 Selinunte, Sicily, ground plans of various temples and elevation of Temple F (after A.W. Lawrence)

six columns wide and sixteen columns long (width 18.75 m, length 50 m). The cella walls were of sun-dried brick above a limestone base; the columns, entablature and roof were made of wood. There were two rows of columns inside the cella. Stone columns gradually replaced wooden columns between the sixth century and the beginning of the Christian era.

Sixth century Doric temples: Corfu and Corinth

The first Doric peripteros to be built entirely of stone was probably the *Temple of Artemis, Corfu, c. 580*. The pediment was decorated with a relief depicting a huge Gorgon and other figures; the cornices were sheathed with coloured terracotta, and the stone members were painted with patterns or simply tinted. The reconstruction in *fig. 18* adequately conveys what the temple looked like. On the mainland, the only sixth-century Doric peripteros to have been partially preserved is the *Temple of Apollo, Corinth, c. 540 (ill. 12, 21.5 × 53.8 m)*. The monolithic columns (height 7.2 m) were strongly tapered, and the capitals were carved from separate blocks. This is the earliest instance of a stylobate with a convex curvature.

Sicily

Probably the first peripteral temple to be built in Sicily was the temple of Apollo at Syracuse. During the course of construction, the monolithic columns (height 7.8 m) were placed closer and closer together, and built to a greater thickness to ensure their stability, with the result that the building gives an unusually foreshortened and massive impression. It is six columns wide and seventeen columns long. This temple and *Temples C and F* at Selinunte, which date from the sixth century, all have a second inner row of columns behind the front colonnade *(fig. 19)*. Stone walls were erected between the columns of Temple F, a feature which was probably copied from Egyptian architecture. One of the largest of all Greek buildings was *Temple G*, begun in the late sixth century and still incomplete when Selinunte was sacked by the Carthaginians in 409. A peripteros eight columns wide and seventeen columns long (height 16.2 m), it measured 50.07 × 110.12 m. Here, too, the columns grew progressively thicker as building developed; the strongest have a diameter of 3.4 m at the base, and weight 100 tons each.

Temples at Paestum

The oldest temple at Paestum, the so-called *Basilica (ill. 14)*, dates from the middle of the sixth century. It measures 24.51 × 54.27 m, and has columns in the usual ratio of nine to eighteen, which makes the intercolumniation at the ends extremely narrow. The columns taper to about two-thirds of their base diameter, and have a particularly pronounced entasis. The Temple of Ceres, also at Paestum, was begun *c.* 530–520. It was a Doric peripteros six columns wide and thirteen columns long (14.5 × 32.9 m), and contained a very unusual pronaos. The temples built during the sixth century in southern Italy were generally distinguished from those of Sicily and Greece by their somewhat greater originality and freedom of form, coupled with a certain crudeness of execution. The study of proportion, however, which was perfected in Greece during the fifth century, put an end to such regional variations.

Fifth-century Doric temples

The third *Temple of Aphaia*, built at Aegina at the beginning of the fifth century, is unusually well preserved. Apart from the wooden ceiling and the roof, it is possible to reconstruct the building fairly exactly *(ill. 13, fig. 20)*. The peripteros consists of six columns in width and twelve columns in length, height 5.27 m, almost all of them monolithic, and measures 13.77 × 28.82 m. Traces of colour on the sculptures and on various parts of the building show a clear predominance of black and red, colours which must have contrasted strongly with the cream-coloured base, and effectively emphasized the different structural elements. – The *Temple of Zeus Olympius* at Agrigentum, in Sicily, the largest of all the Doric temples (52.74 × 110.09 m) was begun *c.* 500, and was left unfinished when the town was sacked in 406. It is remarkable in that the stylobate consisted of five steps instead of the usual three, on top of a platform which was nowhere less than fifteen feet in height. It was a pseudo-peripteros with seven by fourteen half-columns on the stuccoed outer walls, backed by corresponding rectangular pilasters within. A further very surprising feature were the nude male Atlas figures, 7.75 m in height, which supported some of the weight of the architrave on their heads and upraised arms. The building was constructed of relatively small blocks of stone faced with stucco, a factor which must have lowered transport costs considerably.

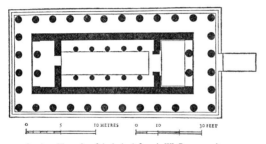

20 Aegina, Temple of Aphaia (after A. W. Lawrence)

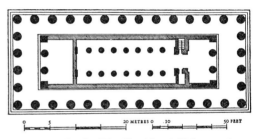

21 Paestum, Temple of Poseidon (after A. W. Lawrence)

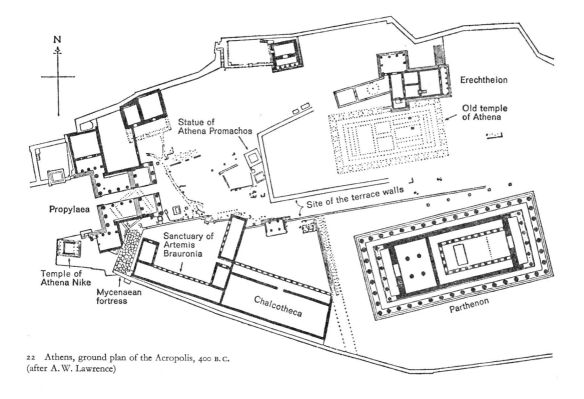

N

Erechtheion

Old temple of Athena

Statue of Athena Promachos

Propylaea

Site of the terrace walls

Temple of Athena Nike

Mycenaean fortress

Sanctuary of Artemis Brauronia

Chalcotheca

Parthenon

22 Athens, ground plan of the Acropolis, 400 B.C.
(after A. W. Lawrence)

Paestum and Olympia

The best preserved of all the Greek temples is the *Temple of Poseidon, Paestum*, which was begun shortly after 480 *(ill. 14* and *fig. 21)*. It is a peripteros six columns wide and fourteen columns long (height 8.88 m), and measures 24.26 × 59.98 m. The cella is divided into a wide main aisle and two narrower side aisles by a double row of two-storeyed columns. The outside columns are exceptionally sturdy for the period. – On the Greek mainland, dating from about the same period, *c.* 470–450, is the *Temple of Zeus, Olympia*, built by a local architect named Libon of Elis (see *fig. 17)*. A peripteros of stuccoed limestone (six columns wide and thirteen columns long, 10.4 m in height), it measures 27.68 × 64.12 m. In this temple, the Doric order reached the summit of academic perfection. Using a foot-unit of 32.6 cm, Libon made the length measure 200, the height of the columns 32, the normal intercolumniation 16, the width of the abacus 8, the distance between the triglyph centres 8, the distance between the mutules and the lions'-head waterspouts 4, and the tiles 2 units.

Athens: The Acropolis

The ultimate degree of refinement in form and proportion was achieved in the *Acropolis* at Athens, begun under Pericles in 447, and it was made possible by the use of marble *(fig. 22)*. The first all-marble building, the Treasury of the Athenians at Delphi, had been erected some time before, between 500 and 485, but that had been in the form of a simple antae temple with the relatively small dimensions of 6.68 × 9.75 m.

The Parthenon

The temple of Athena on the Acropolis, known as the *Parthenon*, was begun in 447 by the architect Ictinus – possibly together with Callicrates – and was consecrated in 438 *(ill. 15)*. Phidias' sculptures were completed in 432. The peripteros has a width of eight columns and a length of seventeen columns (height 10.4 m), and measures 30.88 × 69.5 m. All its measurements are based on a proportion ratio of 4 : 9. The cella was approached from the east and was divided by two-tiered columns; a second smaller room, reached from the opisthodomos at the other end, was supported by four columns, probably Ionic. A further Ionic element is the 159.4 m long sculptured frieze around the cella depicting the Panathenaic procession. In the Parthenon, every possible effort was made to correct the effects of optical illusion, but with such masterly discretion as to be hardly noticeable. The stylobate has a convex curvature, the columns lean inwards and their entasis and tapering further contribute to a total avoidance of geometrical rigidity. It would only be a slight exaggeration to say that there is not a single straight line, horizontal or vertical, in the entire building.

The Propylaea

A similar intention lies behind the apparently arbitrary positioning of the temple in relation to the entrance gate of the Acropolis, the *Propylaea*. As at the sanctuary on Samos, the approaching pilgrim obtained his first glimpse of the temple from its most flattering angle. The Propylaea was begun by Mnesicles in 437, but it was abandoned after five years and never completed *(ill. 16)*. In planning it, he had to allow for the unevenness of the ground and the irregularity of the old walls, which meant that the building could not be quite symmetrical. Doric columns were used on the outside, and six slender Ionic columns inside the porch. The north wing contained a pinacotheca or picture gallery. This was perhaps the first time a room had been specifically designed for exhibiting pictures, although the slightly earlier hall of the Lesche of the Cnidians at Delphi may have been used for a similar purpose. Because of the lie of the land, the south wing could not be built to match the north wing either in width or in depth. They were made to resemble each other, however, by the addition of an otherwise useless pillar to the south wing, and the illusion was completed by the addition in 425 of the *Temple of Athena Nike*, a delicate Ionic building erected by Callicrates on the bastion that juts out on the south side.

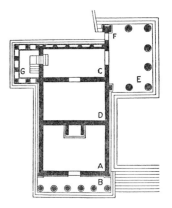

23 Athens, Erechtheion A = main room; B = eastern portico; C–D = western shrines;
E = northern portico; F = door to the sacred precincts; G = southern or Caryatid portico

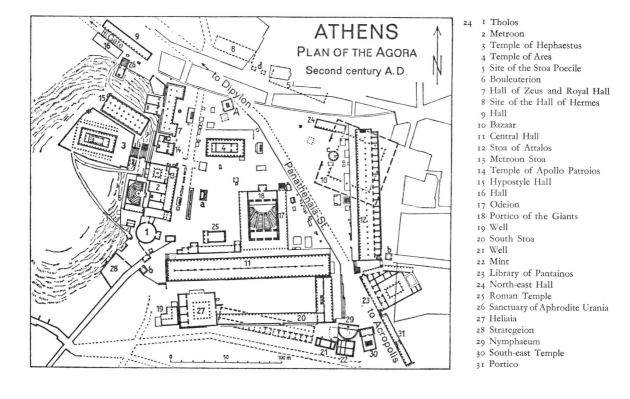

The Erechtheion

Soon afterwards, between 421 and 406, the *Erechtheion* was added, an Ionic temple probably designed by Mnesicles *(ill. 17* and *fig. 23)*. Once again the unevenness of the ground, as well as the need to preserve older centres of worship, led to the erection of an asymmetrical building. The roof of the smaller south porch is supported not by columns but by six caryatids, figures of women in heavy drapery. A similar feature had been used almost a century before in the *Siphnian Treasury* at Delphi, *c.* 525 *(ill. 18)*.

The Theseion

Work was begun on the *Temple of Hephaestus*, the 'Theseion', which stands on the western side of the agora in Athens *(ill. 19* and *fig. 24)* probably two years before the building of the Parthenon. It may have been the first temple to be built entirely of marble, and it is the best preserved of all the temples in Greece. It is six columns in width and thirteen columns in length (height 5.8 m), and it measures 13.708 × 31.77 m. Differences in construction between the pronaos and the opisthodomos, and the presence of rich decoration on the east end indicate that the temple was designed to be viewed from the agora below. – The Temple of Apollo at Bassae in Arcadia, which was built by Ictinus, dates from the same period as the Theseion and the Parthenon. It is a limestone peripteros six columns wide and fifteen columns long, measuring 14.48 × 38.24 m, and it contains the first known example of a Corinthian capital. The Corinthian did not constitute a third order, but grew within the Ionic order.

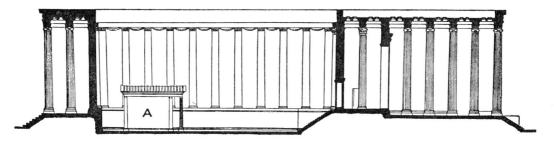

25　Temple of Apollo Didymaeus, near Miletus A = small temple containing the Sacred image of Apollo (after H. Koepf)

Sounion

A few years later, *c.* 440, the marble *Temple of Poseidon at Sounion (ill. 21)* was begun, a peripteros six culumns wide and thirteen columns long, 6.1 m in height, measuring 13.1 × 30.2 m. The unusual size and slimness of the columns were governed by the fact that the building stood on a promontory, and was designed to be viewed from the sea, since one of the busiest shipping-lanes of Greece passed close to the shore at this point. – Dating from the end of the fifth century is the unfinished Doric temple at Segesta in Sicily, a peripteros six columns wide and fourteen columns long, measuring 23.12 × 58.04 m. The cella was never begun and the columns were left unfluted. Fluting was always effectuated after the columns had been erected; prior working of the drums individually in the workshop would have presented problems of coordination subsequently.

Hellenistic temples

Among fourth-century temples, only three need be mentioned: the Doric Temple of Apollo at Delphi, built some time after 373, the Temple of Athena Polias build by Pythius at Priene *c.* 350–334, the finest of all the Ionic temples, and the fifth Temple of Artemis at Ephesus, which was built some time after the fourth temple dating from the fifth century had been destroyed by Herostratus in 356. – The conquests of Alexander, who extended the Greek Empire to include Persia, Mesopotamia, Syria and Egypt, ushered in the Hellenistic period, and from that period dates the powerful *Temples of Apollo Didymaeus*, near Miletus, which was begun towards the end of the fourth century, and took over three hundred years to complete *(fig. 25)*. It is a dipteros measuring 51.13 × 109.34 m, resting on a stylobate of seven huge

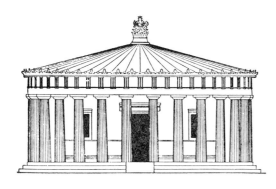

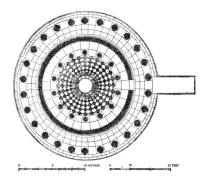

26　Epidaurus, Tholos, elevation and ground plan

steps. Its 112 Ionic columns were the tallest (19.7 m) and slimmest of any Greek temple. – Third-century temple sites are extremely rare, but in the second century the Temple of Zeus Olympius in Athens was built from a donation by Antiochus IV of Syria. It was begun in 174, on a stylobate dating from *c.* 500, and was completed 300 years later by the Emperor Hadrian. It was a dipteros eight Corinthian columns wide and twenty columns long (height 17.2 m), and it measured 41.1 × 107.89 m. The last temple building of any size to be built before the beginning of the Christian era was the Ionic temple of Artemis Leukophryene at Magnesia, begun in 130 by Hermogenes.

Round buildings

Forms of building other than the normal rectangular temple are more rarely found in Greek architecture. The first genuinely circular building or tholos appears to have been built *c.* 550 in the sanctuary at Delphi, but it has not been preserved. A tholos with a conical roof was built *c.* 470 in the agora in Athens, and served as a dining-room for citizens engaged in the city's administration. In Delphi, a marble tholos of *c.* 390, with a diameter of 13.5 m, has been partially preserved. Twenty Doric columns formed the peripteros, and twenty Corinthian columns stood around the inside of the cella wall. It served as the model for the limestone and marble *Tholos* built *c.* 360–320 by Polycleitus the Younger in the sanctuary at *Epidaurus (fig. 26)*. This had a diameter of 21.82 m, with a peripteros of twenty-six Doric columns, and fourteen Corinthian columns inside the cella. The *Choragic Monument of Lysicrates in Athens*, consecrated in 334 to commemorate a choral singing victory during the festival of Dionysus *(ill. 20)*, is another circular building of importance. Standing on a square limestone base 4 m in height is a marble drum 6.5 m in height, decorated with six Corinthian columns, which supports the victory tripod.

Theatres

Every sanctuary had its hippodrome, stadium and theatre, although the hippodrome and stadium were never given architectural form. Theatre building only began to develop from the mid-fifth century onwards, when it was felt necessary to have a scenic background to the

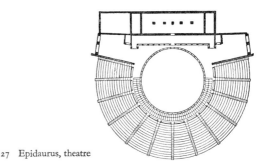

27 Epidaurus, theatre

stage, and a circular area for the audience in front of it. The stage itself was originally made of wood, and initially there were no regular rows of seats. It was only towards the end of the fifth century, with the building of the Theatre of Dionysus in Athens, that a new type of scene building made of stone and rows of seats was first devised. The fact that the rows of seats were prolonged beyond a semicircle had many disadvantages for the spectators sitting at the sides, but this arrangement was maintained by the naturally conservative Greeks until the Romans developed a more practical design. One of the most perfect theatre buildings is that at the sanctuary of *Epidaurus (ill. 22 and fig. 27)*, begun *c.* 350 by Polycleitus the Younger, and there are other examples at Priene and Ephesus.

Urban architecture

Greek urban architecture, both public and private, is a far-reaching subject, but one which does not greatly concern us here. It possessed none of the architectural value of the sanctuaries and temples, and in any case it was not designed to last. Dwelling-houses were simple constructions of clay tile with a wooden framework on a low base of quarry stone. The walls were plastered, and contained almost no windows, since the houses were designed around a central court. In two-storeyed houses, the court also contained a veranda. Towns were usually very small and very irregularly laid out. It was not until *c.* 470–460 that Hippodamus of Miletus introduced the first regular town plan based on the rectangular grid system. He divided *Miletus* into a northern sector and a southern sector, separated by an agora containing wide stoas, a Council House and other public buildings *(fig. 28*, left). The Council House, built *c.* 170 by Antiochus IV, was situated at the end of a colonnaded court, entered through a large propylon *(fig. 28*, right). It was a spacious building (24.28 × 34.84 m), with semicircular benches seating more than twelve hundred people. A slightly earlier meeting hall was the Ecclesiasterion at Priene, built *c.* 200. It measured 20.25 × 21.06 m and had ascending rows of benches on three sides, meeting at right-angles and providing seating for between six and seven hundred people.

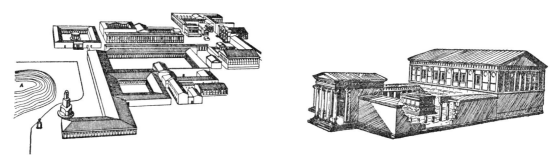

28   Miletus, reconstruction of the town and Council House (after H. Koepf)

The stoa

Mention has already been made of the stoa, which originated in the recreation and sleeping rooms provided for pilgrims at the sanctuaries. The double-aisled version, which made its first appearance during the sixth century at Samos, was adopted for the larger stoas built in towns. During the fifth century, shops and offices began to appear along the inner wall. Later they were even constructed on two storeys. The stoa built by Attalus II of Pergamon along the east side of the agora in Athens is a fine example. It has been reconstructed by American archeologists and is now a museum. This ample building dates from immediately before the Roman conquest in 136. After that date, building virtually ceased in Greece until the time of Augustus.

Building techniques

Our last example of Greek architecture, the third-century *Fortress of Aegosthena* at the eastern end of the Gulf of Corinth, demonstrates the sophistication of Greek building techniques, particularly in stone-masonry *(ill. 25)*. The walls and towers of this fortress were erected entirely without mortar, which was made possible only by a high degree of accuracy in the cutting and joining of the blocks of stone. In the case of temples, bronze and iron dowel pins held the blocks of stone together, but at Aegosthena even those were not used. The spirit of Greek architecture is most fully revealed in this precision. Their architecture was never very bold or very imaginative; rather more, it blended logic and sensitivity in a beautiful, harmonious tranquillity that is without parallel in history.

3 Roman Architecture

Characteristics: Roman architecture was on a far more colossal scale than Greek architecture. This was made possible by the use of strong walls, arches and various types of vaults (domes, tunnel vaults and groin vaults). The Greek orders were preserved, but for decorative rather than constructional purposes (see *fig.* page 21).

New materials and methods of construction made possible the erection of very large buildings with vast, open interiors – such as had never existed in older civilizations – as well as brilliant engineering structures like aqueducts and bridges.

Materials: Freestone, brick, cast masonry resembling concrete (made with a base of mortar and rubble), and marble (usually for facing).

Composite capital

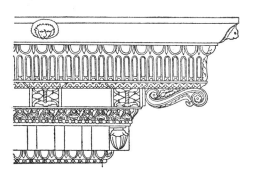

Roman temple, bracket cornice

Example of
Roman arch

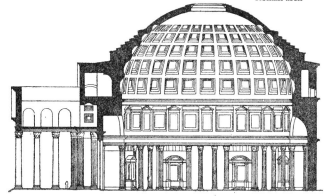

Rome, the Pantheon

The Etruscans

At the beginning of the first millennium B.C., shortly after the Dorian invasion of Greece, the Etruscans invaded northern and central Italy. Their culture was strongly influenced by Greece and blossomed from the eighth century onwards, about the same time as the foundation of the Greek city states in Sicily and southern Italy, until the fourth century. Certain branches of it even survived until the first century. From the frescoes and stucco reliefs which decorated their underground burial chambers, we are able to reconstruct the basic form of the Etruscan house. Unlike the megaron, it had an open atrium with an impluvium or rainwater basin at the centre *(ill. 24)*, and it was taken as the model for the Roman house. It was built of quarry stone, mortar, clay tile and wood. The walls were plastered and the wooden elements sheathed with terracotta. Dressed stone was used for the walls and gates of towns, and in the construction of the latter, genuine tunnel-vaulting was employed (e.g. in the *Porta Augusta, Perugia,* second century B.C., *fig. 29)*. Basket-vaulting, as used in Creto-Mycenaean burial chambers, is found in Etruscan graves from the seventh century onwards. Proper arch and vault constructions appeared towards the end of the fourth century, and these were further developed and perfected by the Romans, using their newly-invented cast masonry (opus caementicium) between wooden moulds or brick or freestone walls.

29 Perugia, Porta Augusta (after H. Koepf)

The Etrusco-Roman temple

From a description by Vitruvius and from foundations which have survived, it is clear that the Etruscan temple was the forerunner of the Roman. Set on a high podium approached on the entrance side by a wide flight of steps, it consisted of a portico with several rows of columns and a short cella with either one room or three parallel chambers. Free standing columns or engaged half-columns surrounded the walls. The chief difference between this temple and the Greek temple was in the unmistakably axial layout. The *Maison Carrée* at Nîmes, completed in 16 B.C., is the best example *(ill. 23)*. Its Greek presentation does nothing to alter the basic Etruscan form.

Roman architecture

Roman architecture proper, which began to develop during the last century B.C., was decisively influenced by Greek and Etruscan forms. The Romans acquired their knowledge of Greek art from the southern Italian towns which they conquered during the third century, and even more through the conquest of Greece itself and the hellenized East during the second century. The Etrusco-Italian basis, however, prevented a mere imitation of Greek styles. The distinctly individual character of Roman architecture can best be demonstrated by a comparison of the Pantheon in Rome and the Parthenon in Athens.

The Pantheon

The *Pantheon (fig. 30* and *fig. page 35)* was begun by Agrippa in 27 B.C., and rebuilt under Hadrian *c.* A.D. 117–125 after a fire. Its preservation until today is due not only to the technical perfection of its construction – this would not have sufficed in the case of determined destruction – but also to the fact that it has been used since 609 as the church of S. Maria ad Martyres, now known as S. Maria Rotonda. The diameter of the cylindrical substructure is the same as the height above ground of the 9 m wide opening at the crown of the hemispherical dome –

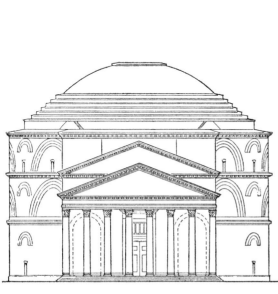

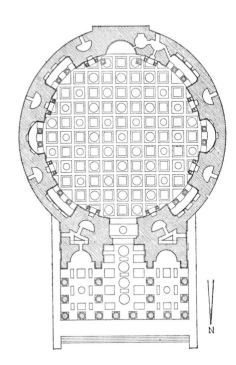

30   Rome, Pantheon, elevation and ground plan

43.3 m. The coffers inside the dome decrease in size towards the apex, creating an illusion of greater height. The height of the walls is the same as the radius of the dome. The walls are 6.2 m thick, and consist of a core of concrete faced with brick and tile. The inner surface of the wall is hollowed out by the entrance, and by seven alternately rectangular and semicircular recesses screened by two columns. The wall-facing above the recesses dates from the seventeenth century. A rectangular structure with two side niches forms an entrance façade, and to this a columned portico was added somewhat later. The unbroken outer wall was finished with marble slabs below and stucco above. A third storey was added, beginning at the level of the base of the dome and serving both as an abutment to the cast shell of the dome, and as a load on the drum below. The dome was further strengthened by the addition of stepped rings above the level of the surrounding wall. As a result the exterior view of the dome, instead of presenting a free-rising hemisphere, appears rather flattened. A very high degree of architectural mastery is revealed by the use of hollow spaces and reinforcing arches within the cylindrical wall to strengthen the construction. The Pantheon achieved something which no earlier culture had ever achieved or even envisaged – the creation of a vast interior experienced as a spatial entity.

The arrangement of space and mass

The regular arrangement of internal space was followed by the organization of the exterior. The portico of the Pantheon stands at the narrow end of a large colonnaded entrance court, with a gate at the opposite end. The axial symmetry of this progression recalls that of Egyptian temple sites, though it differed completely from the latter in the number and arrangement of the spatial units. The layout of the Etruscan dwelling-house was adopted, and it continued to determine the style of the Roman house. Even when the Romans added a peristyle in the Greek manner, as was done in the case of particularly imposing houses, it was laid down on the axis of the atrium house. The plan of the *House of Pansa at Pompeii (fig. 31)* and the exterior of the first-century B.C. *House of Neptune and Amphitrite at Herculaneum*, seen through the atrium *(ill. 26)*, are two good examples of Roman domestic architecture.

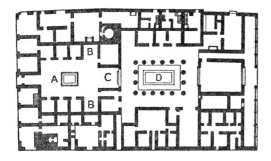

31   Pompeii, House of Pansa
ground plan   A = atrium with impluvium
                      B = recesses (alae)
                      C = main room
                      D = peristyle court
and elevation (after H. Koepf)

The Forum at Pompeii

This relationship of space and mass, far more rigorously adhered to than in the Hellenistic prototypes, can be observed most clearly in the *Forum* at Pompeii which can be precisely reconstructed *(fig. 32)*. The principal buildings dated from the period of Samnite ascendancy

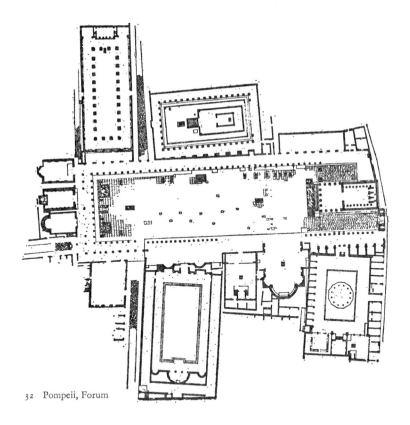

32 Pompeii, Forum

between the fourth and second centuries B.C. The town did not become a Roman colony until 80 B.C. The forum was a regular elongated rectangle, measuring 38 × 142 m, surrounded by colonnades. At the northern end, situated exactly on the axis, stood the majestic Temple of Zeus. Other important buildings were gradually grouped around the forum.

The Basilica at Pompeii

The most significant of these was the basilica in the south-west corner of the forum. It dates from the end oft he second century B.C., and originally resembled the forum itself in a smaller replica – an open rectangular court surrounded by colonnades, which may have had galleries, and with the tribunal at the west end. This court represented a concentration and systematization of the stoas which the Greeks had deliberately placed around their agora. It served as a meeting-place, as a centre for the transaction of business, and for the public execution of law. Some time during the first century B.C., the basilica was roofed in, creating a vast enclosed space with surrounding colonnades and galleries. Similar basilicas, often with a raised central aisle with a clerestory to admit light, were erected on the fora of all the principal Roman towns, including of course Rome. The *Forum Romanum*, at the foot of the Capitol and Palatine hills, never had a regular plan, and over the centuries it became crowded with temples, monuments, basilicas and all kinds of public buildings *(fig. 33)*.

The Forum of Trajan in Rome

Perfect order, however, was achieved in the imperial fora which were created between the Quirinal hill and the north-east side of the old forum *(fig. 34)*. The most splendid of them was the *Forum of Trajan*, built by Apollodorus of Damascus *c*. A.D. 113–17. The entrance gate led into a large rectangular court surrounded by colonnades, which contained the equestrian statue of the Emperor. In the centre of the side walls were two semicircular exedrae, and beyond the eastern exedra a multi-storeyed bazaar was built, containing internal streets and innumerable shops. Next to the court, but positioned laterally across the axis, was the Basilica Ulpia with its five aisles, two storeys and two exedrae corresponding to those in the side walls of the court. Trajan's column, flanked by two libraries, rose behind the basilica, and beyond that the Temple of Trajan completed the site. The whole complex measured 195 × 275 m. The forum was essentially a place for strolling, and the Forum of Trajan, with its monumental arrangement of internal and external spaces, is one of the finest expressions of this idea. To a certain extent the imperial fora were sanctuaries. They had, at any rate, something of the same solemnity of conception.

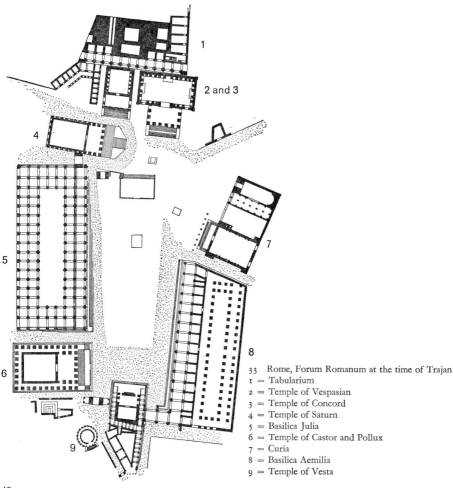

33   Rome, Forum Romanum at the time of Trajan
1 = Tabularium
2 = Temple of Vespasian
3 = Temple of Concord
4 = Temple of Saturn
5 = Basilica Julia
6 = Temple of Castor and Pollux
7 = Curia
8 = Basilica Aemilia
9 = Temple of Vesta

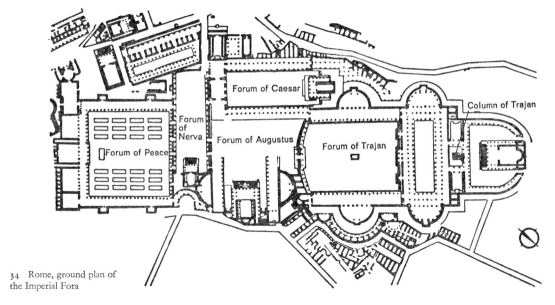

34 Rome, ground plan of
the Imperial Fora

Palestrina: The Sanctuary of Fortuna Primigenia
The first really large building to have this kind of regular arrangement dates back to the Republican period and the beginning of the first century B.C. The *Sanctuary of Fortuna Primigenia at Palestrina* (Praeneste), which was built on several terraces and made extensive use of arches and vaulting *(ill. 28)*, took up again and developed several ideas which had made their first appearance in the Sanctuary of Asclepius on Cos shortly before 150 B.C. Mention must also be made of *Leptis Magna* in Libya, which dates from the beginning of the third century A.D. and is remarkable for the splendour of its street plan and the unusual basilica with its double apses *(fig. 35)*.

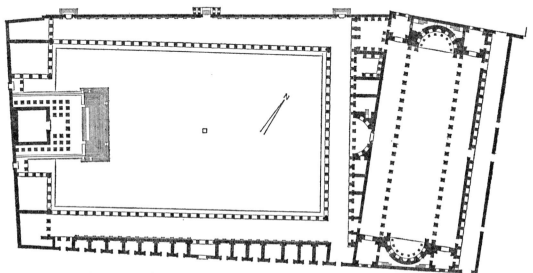

35 Leptis Magna, Libya, Forum, *c.* A.D. 203

41

Imperial palaces: The Flavian Palace on the Palatine Hill

The palaces of the emperors were also built on this model. The most famous was the *Flavian Palace* on the Palatine Hill in Rome *(fig. 36)*, begun by Augustus and altered and rebuilt under Domitian A.D. 81–96. It was of decisive importance to the evolutionary process which transformed rich dwelling-houses into buildings with cultural and ceremonial significance. The important elements were those adjoining the forum. They stood on an elevated substructure, and were surrounded by colonnades. In the centre was the throne room (C), with the house chapel (A) on the left and the basilica (B) on the right. Beyond was a court, 54 m long and surrounded by colonnades (D), and beyond that, still on exactly the same axis, were the imperial apartments with the dining hall (E) in the centre. Affairs of court were conducted in the basilica, with the emperor presiding from his throne in the raised apse. The narrow side aisles were separated from the main aisle by two-storeyed columns. They probably contained galleries. The layout is similar to that of the cella of many Greek temples, except that the 'forbidden' room has now become a room of inportance, used for the business of goverment. This domestic basilica differed from public basilicas in being very much smaller, and particularly by the fact that there was an uninterrupted line from entrance to apse. This was the form that was to be used later for the basilicas of the Christian church, and was indeed already being used for certain mystery cults (e. g. the underground basilica near the Porta Maggiore in Rome).

Hadrian's Villa near Tivoli

The most beautiful of the imperial palaces, *Hadrian's Villa near Tivoli*, built by the Emperor between 125 and 135, shows how rapidly such buildings became more lavish in design and decoration. The whole palace complex covered some 800,000 square metres, but we need only consider two sections of it here: the east palace or palace of the Piazza d'Oro with its domed

36 Rome, the Flavian Palace,
elevation and ground plan (after H. Koepf)

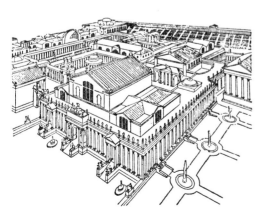

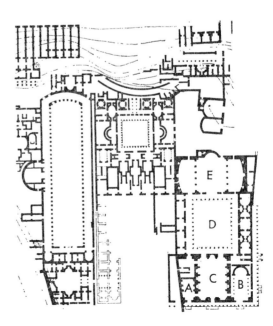

main room 17.5 m in diameter, and the circular Casino, an intricate little building surrounded by a canal *(ill. 27)*. The lively and completely original form of these buildings was very different from the usual rigid arrangement of space and mass. The fluid line of columns formed a clear if ornamental plan, but left the spatial relationships of the rooms far less determinate; the central room and the curiously shaped side rooms seem to flow into and out of each other, creating an effect of interlocking volumes reminiscent of the Baroque architecture of the seventeenth century. The vaulting has been almost wholly destroyed, and it is impossible to reconstruct it with any degree of accuracy. The technical problem of vaulting such complex rooms was solved by casting, for the mould could be designed to exactly the shape required.

The growth of creativity in architecture up to the third century A.D.
The growth of creative ideas that characterized Roman architecture is particularly evident if we compare the *Temple of Sibylla at Tivoli* and the Temple of Venus at Baalbeck. The former, dating from the beginning of the first century B.C., is basically a Greek tholos, except that it stands on a podium *(ill. 29)*. A circle of eighteen Corinthian columns surrounds the drum,

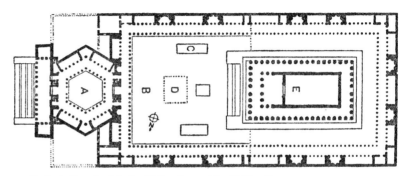

37 Baalbeck, Temple of Jupiter Heliopolitanus (after H. Koepf)

which was formed of cast masonry between stone walls. It was a form that recurred over and over again, and it seemed to be incapable of variation. However, we suddenly find it utterly transformed in the *Temple of Venus at Baalbeck (ill. 30)*. Not only was the entablature radically altered, but the drum was hollowed out with deep niches. – Such a degree of freedom was not possible in the case of the rectangular temple, but considerable variation was nevertheless achieved, as may be seen from the inner wall of the cella in the second-century *Temple of Bacchus at Baalbeck (ill. 31)*. Such treatment would have been inconceivable in the case of a Greek temple. At the top of the half-columns, we can still see traces of the springers of the reinforcing arches that carried the tunnel vault. The Greek concern for proportion has clearly no longer played any part in the design of these buildings. The larger *Temple of Jupiter Heliopolitanus at Baalbeck*, which dates from the first and second centuries A.D., again displays an axially symmetrical layout *(fig. 37)*. A flight of steps 43 m wide gives access to the vestibule (A), which leads into the altar court (B) containing two cleansing bowls (C) and a sacrificial altar (D). The colonnades surrounding the altar court also enclose the main sanctuary (E).

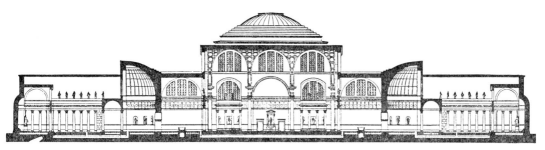

38 Rome, Baths of Caracalla, elevation and ground plan of the central portion (after H. Koepf)

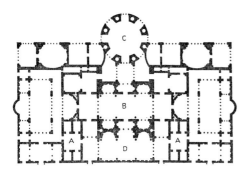

39 Rome, Temple of ▷
Minerva Medica

Thermae

The Romans' mastery of construction, particularly in the erection of huge domes and groin vaults, is nowhere more apparent than in the thermae or baths which were built throughout the Empire. They too, like the fora and the sanctuaries, served as centres of public life, though in a different way, grouping together playing fields, recreation rooms, libraries, aulae, picture galleries, etc. The largest thermae date from the time of the later emperors, and cover an area of up to 100,000 sq.m. The *Baths of Caracalla in Rome* measured 330 sq.m. overall, with the central group of buildings covering an area 114 × 220 m. The progression of the rooms was designed with the utmost meticulousness *(fig. 38)*. The three main rooms of the bathing area lay on the central axis. These were the frigidarium (D) measuring 17 × 51 m, the tepidarium (B) with its three groin vaults (height 33 m, span 25 m) and the domed caldarium (C), with a diameter of 35 m and a height of 49 m. On either side, placed symmetrically, were changing rooms (A), cleansing basins, sweat rooms, massage rooms, anointing rooms, etc. The Thermae of Diocletian in Rome, built at the beginning of the fourth century, measured 316 × 356 m overall, and the principal rooms were even larger than those of the Baths of Caracalla. The tepidarium was later converted by Michelangelo into the church of S. Maria degli Angeli; the Piazza dell'Esedra in front of the church follows the line of the original exedrae, and the round buildings which stood at the south and west corners of the original site have now vanished among the streets, houses and courtyards in front of the main station of the city in the present day. – Another important early fourth-century building is the *Temple of Minerva Medica in Rome*, a decagonal centralized structure 24 m in diameter with nine apses with conches *(fig. 39)*. It was part of a palace, possibly the throne room, and from the early fifteenth-century Renaissance onwards, it was one of the most extensively studied and influential of all classical models.

Late Roman imperial palaces

Regular in form, but rather different from earlier palaces was the *Palace of Diocletian at Split* (Spalato), *c.* 300. It was rectangular in shape, measuring 175 × 214 m, and was divided by cardo and decumanus on the model of a legionary camp *(fig. 40)*. The imperial apartments (A) were fronted by a colonnade on the seaward side, and the palace was fortified on the other three sides by strong walls and towers (B, C, D). To the right of the magnificent vestibule (E) of the imperial apartments stood the temple (F), and to the left the mausoleum (G). This was an octagonal building 13 m in internal diameter and 21 m in height, surmounted by a dome; its interior walls were enlivened by two-tiered columns and niches *(ill. 32)*. – Some time later, Constantine built a palace at Trier of which only the basilica or audience hall remains. The two storeys, both fenestrated, are linked by blind arcades, these being the only articulation or decoration in the entire building. The Greek decorative style is abandoned, revealing the clear, massive lines of the building unadorned. Previously this had only been acceptable for purely functional buildings and all sacred, imperial or public buildings had to have their Greek ornamentation. Now an absence of decoration became acceptable for the latter as well. It was an important step towards the creation of the Christian basilica, which was to follow immediately.

The Basilica of Constantine

It was in fact at about the same time, in 313, that Constantine completed the basilica in Rome that had been begun by Maxentius in 307 *(ill. 33* and *fig. 41)*. It measures 76 × 100 m and is, in contrast to earlier forum basilicas, very symmetrically laid out. The apse at the side is a later addition. Also, following the model of the principal rooms of the thermae, this was the first basilica to be roofed with a vault. The central nave had three groin vaults, 25 m wide and 35 m high, supported by three laterally positioned tunnel vaults 24.5 m high. The only Greek

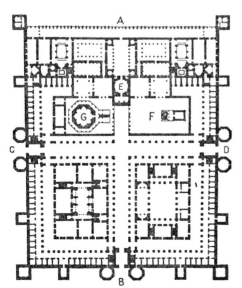

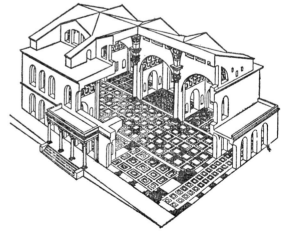

41   Rome, Basilica of Constantine, drawing of reconstruction (after Huelsen)

◁ 40   Split, Palace of Diocletian (after H. Koepf)

45

decoration that remained were the eight monolithic columns within, which appeared to carry the groin vaults but did not in fact do so and the stucco-work on the outside which was made to look like dressed stone.

Theatres

The subject of Greek decoration has been mentioned several times. Its characteristics will become clear if we examine the subject of theatres and amphitheatres. Unlike the Greeks who arranged the seating of the theatre around a depression in the ground so that only the stage itself needed to be constructed, the Romans erected a theatre on flat ground. They kept the semicircle of ascending rows of seats, however, which meant they were obliged to build an outer wall several storeys high. This wall was pierced by arch openings formed by the groin and tunnel vaulted passageways which supported and gave access to the rows of seats. To lend importance to the outer face of the wall, columns following the Greek orders were applied. These had lost all their functional meaning in terms of load and support, and were reduced to a purely decorative role. One of the earliest examples, dating from the end of the first century B. C., is the *Theatre of Marcellus in Rome*. The Doric order of the ground floor and the Ionic order of the first floor have been preserved *(fig. 42)*. The second floor had Corinthian columns. The theatre was designed to seat 20,500 spectators. Similar buildings have been preserved elsewhere throughout the Roman Empire (e. g. Pompeii, Arles, Orange, Ephesus, Timgad and others). The form of the Roman stage building was based on Hellenistic models in Asia Minor. No stage wall has been preserved in its entirety, so a related example must serve as an illustration: the *Market Gate of Miletus*, now reconstructed in Berlin, which was built by the Romans *c.* A. D. 160 *(ill. 36)*. The two-storeyed gate, 29 m wide, with its pairs of columns, projections and indentations in the entablature and niches containing statues of the gods, is in fact exactly like a stage wall. Particularly noticeable is the split gable in the centre; this was to play an important part in Baroque architecture.

Amphitheatres

The amphitheatres, a Roman invention, represents as it were an extension of the semicircular theatre to form an ellipse. Some seventy amphitheatres are extant, all more or less identical in their construction, which corresponds to that of the theatres. This can be seen most clearly in the *Colosseum* in Rome, built A. D. 72–80 *(ill. 34* and *fig. 43)*. The arena, which was used for gladiatorial contests, fights with wild animals, crocodile hunts and mock sea-battles is 17 m wide and 46 m long, and rests on a substructure containing numerous chambers. The three tiers are honeycombed with circular and radial passages and staircases, which allowed the tens of thousands of spectators to enter and leave the building very quickly. The outer wall is 48 m high, 527 m in circumference, and has a diameter of 156 × 185 m. The three storeys were decorated with the three orders of columns, and contained 240 arch openings. At the very top was a wall decorated with pilasters, to which masts were attached to support the velarium. The Colosseum was the last of the very large Roman buildings to be built of freestone and brick without the use of casting.

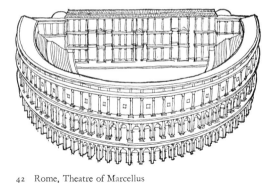

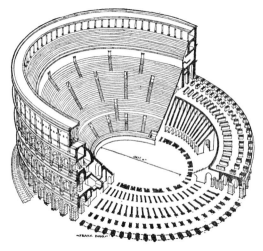

42 Rome, Theatre of Marcellus

43 Rome, the Colosseum

Tombs

The tombs of the emperors, even if they were not actual architectural structures, were monumental in their proportions. That of Augustus, for example, consisted of a drum 89 m in diameter. Hadrian's mausoleum (now the Castel S. Angelo) in Rome, completed in A.D. 139, consisted of a substructure 84 m square, supporting a drum 64 m in diameter, which was crowned by a sort of tholos built on steps. The tomb of Caecilia Metella in Rome should also be mentioned. Built at about the time of the birth of Christ, it consisted of a drum, 20 m in diameter, on top of a square substructure. The *Mausoleum of the Julii* at Saint-Rémy *(ill. 35)* was erected early in the first century A.D., and consists of a tholos dominating a square pedestal decorated with reliefs and pierced by four arches. The 23 m high funeral monument of the Secundini family (the Igel monument) near Trier was built about 200 years later, and consisted of a curved pyramidal superstructure on top of a square pedestal.

Triumphal arches

Just as Roman funerary monuments were based on Hellenic models (e.g. the mausoleum of Halicarnossos), their triumphal arches were modelled on Hellenic town gates. The Romans, however, were the first to conceive of the arch as free-standing. During the Imperial period, many such arches were erected, and today a hundred are extant. The earliest examples of the single-arch type date from the end of the first century B.C. (e.g. Rimini, Aosta, Susa), but the finest example is the *Arch of Titus* in the Forum Romanum, erected in A.D. 70 after the capture of Jerusalem *(fig. 44)*. The two faces of the arch are framed by columns with composite capitals standing on high pedestals. The spandrels were decorated with reliefs of victories. The entablature and the high attic storey have corner mouldings, and originally bore the emperor's quadriga. Besides the single-arch type, structures with triple openings (e.g. Orange) were erected as early as the end of the first century B.C. The last example was the magnificent *Arch of Constantine in Rome*, erected after the defeat of Maxentius and constructed of numerous

47

44 Rome, Arch of Titus

45 Trier, Porta Nigra

fragments of older arches *(ill. 37)*. This type of arch influenced Renaissance architects from the fifteenth century onwards. – There were also triumphal arches which had four openings, and were square in plan (e.g. the Arch of Caracalla at Tebessa and the Arch of Galerius at Salonica).

Engineering structures
This survey would be incomplete if the purely functional structures which were among the Romans' greatest feats of engineering were omitted. We shall look at two examples, one from the beginning of the Roman period and one from the end. The *Pont du Gard near Nîmes*, erected at the beginning of the first century B.C., served as both a viaduct and an aqueduct, spanning the river valley with three rows of arches *(ill. 38)*. The top row carried the water pipe, and the central row carried the roadway. No decoration was needed, and from the beginning the function of the structure and its technical supremacy were clearly apparent. These two technical feats, the building of aqueducts and of roads, both of which had been mastered completely by the Romans, were responsible more than anything else for the successful administration and coordination of their vast empire over such a long period. – Four hundred years later, at the beginning of the fourth century A.D., the *Porta Nigra*, a fortified town gate, was built at *Trier (fig. 45)*. In view of the sacred significance of town gates, the orders were not entirely omitted, but the building's function was so strongly stressed that the decoration receded into the background.

It was Roman architecture, as displayed by the thousands of buildings that the Romans erected throughout their empire, and not Greek architecture, that laid the foundations of the many developments that were to take place in the centuries to come. Its influence remained strong right up to the eighteenth century.

4 Early Christian and Byzantine Architecture

Characteristics: The Roman emphasis on space was developed, but the massive character of Roman buildings gave way to a new lightness. Walls and vaults were in fact lightened to such an extent that even the largest structures of this period give an impression of weightlessness.

Columns, straight entablatures and arches remained by and large within the tradition inherited from Greece and Rome, although capitals underwent continuous modification.

Materials: Mostly brick, with freestone, marble and wood.

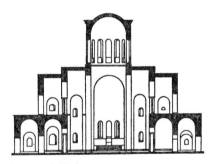

Ravenna, S. Vitale

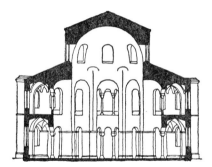

Kiev, Cathedral of S. Sophia

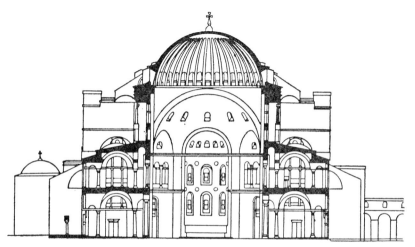

Constantinople, Hagia Sophia

Strictly speaking, the Early Christian architecture of the fourth to the sixth centuries in the eastern and western parts of the Roman Empire does not merit a chapter of its own, since it was not an individual style but was derived rather from what we call the Classical style. It is only by virtue of their functionalism that Early Christian churches deserve to be considered separately. The architecture of the Eastern Empire during the sixth century is generally referred to as 'Byzantine', although Byzantine architecture properly speaking did not begin until later. For practical reasons, it is included in this chapter.

Christianity was recognized by the Edict of Milan in 313, and it became necessary to build churches for the new official religion. In accordance with the attitude of Constantine himself, and with the architectural ideas current in the early fourth century, they were inevitably monumental buildings. Both models and the requisite technical means were available, and there is no evidence of any diminution of architectural skill. There were many examples of both rectangular and centralized buildings to choose from as models. The classical temple was, of course, out of the question; temples were execrated by the Christians as places of idolatry, and in any case they did not possess adequate interior space to accommodate the faithful. The basilica in its various forms was the natural starting-point for the congregational houses of the new Christian community.

I Basilican Churches of the Eastern and Western Empires, Fourth to Sixth Centuries

The basilican churches of Constantine in Rome

The architecture of the Roman Empire during the fourth century presents a very varied picture, but of foremost importance are the large basilican churches of the city of Rome – S. Giovanni in Laterano, founded by Constantine himself in the very year of the Edict of Milan, Old St. Peter's, planned 324–30 and begun in 333, and S. Paolo fuori le Mura, built 385–400 (and reconstructed in the nineteenth century after a fire). Like the old heathen basilicas, with the exception of the Basilica of Constantine, these buildings had five aisles and were unvaulted.

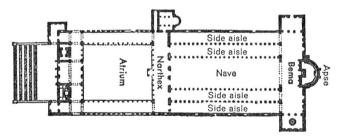

46   Rome, Old St. Peter's

St.Peter's (fig. 46) and S.Giovanni, which was the episcopal church of Rome, both had an apse at the west end. Orientation was not at first obligatory, and indeed it was sometimes ignored even in later churches. St.Peter's also had a large transept between the apse and the nave, a most unusual feature for the time, and one which did not come into general use until the Carolingian period. S.Paolo was also built with a transept, but the transept in S.Giovanni was added during the Middle Ages. The grave of St.Peter was at the west end of the church, so that the transept and apse together constitute the martyrium, with the nave and side aisles as a sort of covered graveyard. The nave had a straight entablature, though the other churches had arches. Ample lighting was provided by a clerestory with large windows. Decoration (which consisted of gilded roof-beams, mosaics, murals, facings of coloured marble on the columns, and the church furnishings) was restricted to the interior. The exterior, in accordance with the tradition that had evolved during the Late Roman period, was left plain. Basically the church consisted of a colonnaded atrium with a porch in front and a wide flight of steps, providing a monumental approach in the tradition of the imperial basilicas.

The Church of the Nativity, Bethlehem

The principle of axial symmetry was continued in the *Church of the Nativity at Bethlehem*, begun at about the same time as St.Peter's *(fig. 47)*. It consisted of a colonnaded atrium, a basilica with five aisles but no transept, and at the east end an octagonal shrine on the site of the stable where Christ was born. One is reminded of the similar conjunction of an octagonal structure and a temple in the sanctuary of Jupiter at Baalbeck (see *fig. 37*).

47   Bethlehem, Church of the Nativity (after Krautheimer)

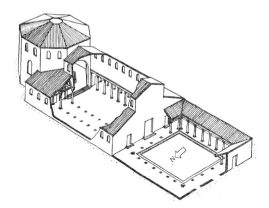

The Episcopal Church at Trier

A further example will serve to illustrate the wide variety of forms which Christian churches took during the fourth century. The first *Episcopal Church at Trier (fig. 48)*, built *c.* 326–48, consisted of a square atrium placed before a three-aisled basilica, which was already as wide as the later Romanesque cathedral eventually became. It had a spacious sanctuary at the east end, probably with a straight end-wall. Under Gratianus (375–83), the eastern part of the church was replaced by a new building which is still contained within the present cathedral, and explains why it is of a different form to any other medieval church. Four tall columns supported a tower-like superstructure above a smaller polygonal structure, also consisting of columns. The whole construction was mounted on steps to make it more visible from the

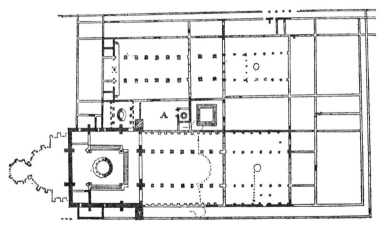

48 Trier, Episcopal church

congregational part of the church. At the same time, galleries were added to the side aisles. The curious structure at the east end may have been a shrine of some kind, like those in the Church of the Nativity at Bethlehem or in another Constantinian galleried church, the Church of the Holy Sepulchre at Jerusalem. Or it may have been a sort of throne hall or royal mausoleum, or a martyrium. Whatever its purpose, the superstructure with its tower-like crown and possibly four towers at the corners had a palatial quality, and represented a transference of secular forms to a Christian sanctuary that constituted not a profanation of the latter, but a glorification of the former. – A second church, consisting of an atrium, a vestibule with three bays, and a three-aisled basilica measuring 32×48 m with a straight chancel-end, was built to the south of the main church and parallel to it. Remains of this site were used for services

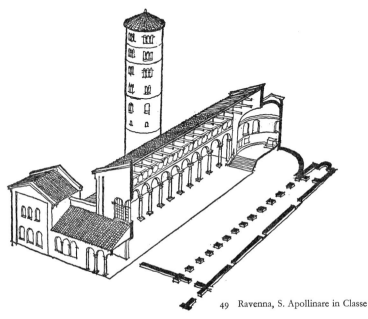

49 Ravenna, S. Apollinare in Classe

until the Gothic Liebfrauenkirche was built in the thirteenth century. The vestibule also served the baptistery which was built between the two churches. Several other similar double churches with baptisteries were built during the fourth century, particularly in northern Italy and Dalmatia.

Fifth-century basilican churches in Rome

A well preserved and excellently reconstructed example of the normal type of basilica, with three aisles and no transepts, is *S. Sabina in Rome*, built 422–32 *(ill. 39)*. The building is of considerable size (24.8 × 54.5 m). Above the columns, the wall rises smoothly, and its relative narrowness can be gauged from the clerestory arches. The wall is decorated with colourful mosaics, with patterns covering the part between the arches and immediately above, and a wide pictorial frieze extending from there to the clerestory windows. These windows are large, matching the arches below, so that the church is filled with evenly distributed light. The low, flat-roofed side aisles were originally unfenestrated. The nave had an open roof framework. The interior of the church, which is strongly focused on the apse, has a sort of soothing clarity. – The next basilican church to be built in Rome was *S. Maria Maggiore*, 432–40, which also had three aisles and no transepts *(ill. 40)*. The interior, however, looks very different from that of S. Sabina. Quite apart from the coffered ceiling, which dates from the Renaissance, S. Maria Maggiore has a straight entablature, giving the interior a more solid, compact, hall-like appearance which was closer to the classical Roman spirit.

Sixth-century basilican churches in Ravenna

Another three-aisled basilican church without transept that seems to have an even slighter connection with the Roman tradition is *S. Apollinare Nuovo in Ravenna*, built by Theodoric, king of the Ostrogoths, next to his palace *(ill. 41)*. Basically it has the same design as S. Sabina but here everything has become much finer, lighter and more transparent. The spirit of Imperial Rome is not entirely absent even here, however; the coloured marble columns alone convey all the solemn dignity of a long and sacred heritage. – The basilican church of *S. Apollinare in Classe, Ravenna (fig. 49)*, built *c.* 530–49, also followed the same form. The campanile that stands beside the church dates from the tenth century.

Fifth-century basilican churches in the Eastern Empire

We mentioned the addition of galleries to the Episcopal Church at Trier towards the end of the fourth century. Galleries originated in the eastern part of the Empire, and the model was probably Constantine's Church of the Holy Sepulchre at Jerusalem. A good example of a very elaborate galleried basilican church of the fifth century is *S. Demetrios, Salonica (fig. 50)*. It measures over 55 m in length, and has five aisles and low transepts. The interior is characterized by alternating columns and massive piers in the sequence 4 : 5 : 4. – Galleries first appeared in Rome during the sixth century. Between 579 and 590, three wings with galleries were added to the east end of the Church of S. Lorenzo fuori le Mura around the tomb of the saint. They adjoined the Constantinian basilica, the chancel of which had originally been at the west end. Another fourth-century Roman burial and graveyard church, S. Agnese fuori le Mura, had galleries added in 625–38.

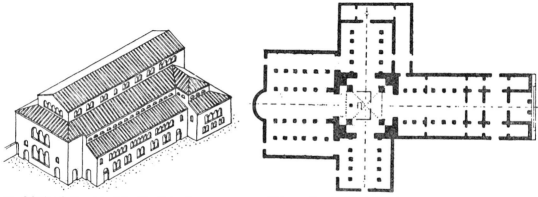

50 Salonica, S. Demetrios (after Krautheimer)   51 Ephesus, Church of St. John (after Krautheimer)

The great variety of forms used by the Early Christian builders, particularly in the Eastern Empire, is well illustrated by the vast *Church of St. John, Ephesus*, which dates from the early fifth century *(fig. 51)*. From the tomb or martyrium in the centre, four basilica-like arms radiate out in the shape of a cross. The western arm is slightly longer than the others, and the eastern arm, which was probably reserved for the use of the clergy, is wider than the others and has five aisles. It was probably modelled on the Church of the Apostles in Constantinople, which was founded by Constantine, rebuilt by Justinian in 536, and pulled down in 1469 to make room for the Fatih Mosque.

Fifth-century basilican churches in Syria
The *Martyrium of Kalat Siman* in northern Syria, *c.* 470 *(fig. 52)*, is one of the finest examples of Early Christian architecture. It, too, is in the shape of a cross, consisting of four three-aisled basilicas radiating out from an octagonal central building, the martyrium itself. The latter originally had a wooden roof, and contained the pillar of S. Simeon Stylites. Apart from the roofs, the whole building was built of large blocks of limestone, which gave it a quite different external appearance from the brick buildings which predominated in the Eastern Empire. The martyrium certainly recalls the Graeco-Roman architecture of the first to the third centuries, but also foreshadows in a curious way the Romanesque architecture of the eleventh and twelfth centuries. The *Turmanîn* (Dêr Termanîn) in the hinterland of Antioch (Syria), dating from the second half of the fifth century, has an extremely simple plan, comprising a three-aisled basilica without transepts, with the two rooms flanking the apse matched by two rooms

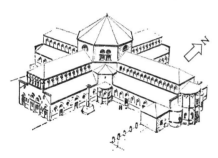

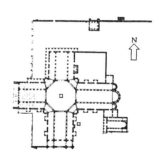

52 Kalat Siman, Syria, Martyrium, reconstruction and ground plan (after Krautheimer)

at the other end flanking the entrance vestibule *(ill. 42* and *fig. 53)*, but the plan gives no indication of the considerable development that had taken place in the elevation. At the end of the basilica stood a façade with two towers flanking the nave-end, and forming a richly satisfying unity. A flight of steps led up from ground level to the top of the platform on which the whole building was erected, meeting the wide entrance arch and its two beautifully outlined windows. The side aisle and clerestory fenestration was of similar distinction. Every detail blended into the whole to form a highly expressive composition. Its powerful exterior, in particular, was in marked contrast to the usual Early Christian basilican church. Similar basilican churches were erected somewhat later at Qalb Louzeh, Ruweha and R'safah.

II Centralized Structures

The uninterrupted continuation of Roman architectural ideas is also evident in the centralized structures built during this period. The circular *S. Costanza* in Rome, for example, which was built *c.* 350 as a mausoleum for one of Constantine's daughters, is hardly distinguishable from a pagan building *(ill. 43* and *fig. 54)*. Radially-positioned pairs of columns with fragmentary architraves support the arches and the drum. This is pierced by large windows placed close together, rising almost to the base of the dome vault. The circular ambulatory is roofed with a tunnel vault, and its strong outer wall is hollowed out with niches that are alternately rectangular and semicircular in section. The wide vestibule has semicircular ends and two rectangular niches flank the entrance. A row of columns built around the outside was never completed. The interior was completely covered with marble incrustations and mosaics. – A considerably larger circular building, *S. Stefano Rotondo*, was erected in Rome more than a century later, 468–83 *(ill. 44)*. The diameter of the entire building was 64 m. The drum was supported by a circle of columns bearing an architrave, and there were two ambulatories, the outer consisting of four chapels arranged in the shape of a cross and joined by open courts. The building was originally probably a martyrium, and it has been very largely preserved.

Even within the context of the centralized structure, a wide variety of shapes proved possible. The original church of *St. Gereon, Cologne (fig. 55)*, which was preserved as the core of the present church, rebuilt in 1219–27, was oval in shape, measuring 23.53 × 18.65 m. It

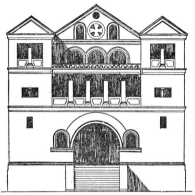

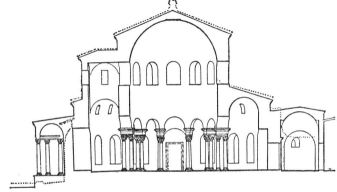

53 Antioch, Syria, the Turmanin   54 Rome, S. Costanza, section

can be safely attributed to the last quarter of the fourth century. The side walls each contained four niches with windows, and a pair of columns stood against the wall between each niche. The apse at the east end was wider and deeper than the niches. The interior was richly decorated with mosaic floors, marble incrustations on the walls, and probably also mosaics above the windows. The church was entered through a vestibule with apsidal ends like that of S. Costanza, measuring 7.5 × 11.8 m.

Baptisteries

The fact that the centralized structure became the norm for baptisteries was due to a theological association with burial buildings. For baptism, which was by complete immersion in water, was at first only administered to adults, and signified the death of the old Adam. It was also the precondition of resurrection after death. The association with bathing naturally led the early Christians to imitate the thermae, of which the principal rooms were centralized. In fact, the first known baptistery, that of *S. Giovanni in Laterano, Rome*, was probably erected on a thermae site. The original building (*c.* 315), as altered and perfected under Sixtus III (432–40), is still recognizable in the present church. A high octagonal structure stood like a canopy over the font, with an octagonal, tunnel-vaulted ambulatory around it with a vestibule leading off *(fig. 56)*. – The *Orthodox Baptistery, Ravenna* dates from the first half of the fifth century, and has been preserved in its entirety. It is an octagonal domed building richly decorated with marble incrustations, mosaics and stucco-work *(ill. 45)*. At ground-floor level, shallow flat niches beneath blind arches alternate with deep, semicircular niches or apses which protrude outside. The fenestration storey, too, is decorated with blind arcades. The exterior, on the other hand, is virtually unadorned. The brickwork was left unplastered, and the only decoration used on the outside walls were blind arches of the type already used in the imperial basilica at Trier. These blind arches became a recognizable feature of the architecture of Ravenna, and it was probably from there that they were taken up by Romanesque architects hundreds of years later.

55 Cologne, St. Gereon, reconstruction

56 Rome, S. Giovanni in Laterano

Burial buildings

The cruciform *Mausoleum of Galla Placidia, Ravenna (ill. 46)*, built *c.* 425, comprises four tunnel-vaulted arms about a taller square structure with a cupola. Here again the magnificent decoration of the interior contrasts sharply with the ascetic simplicity of the exterior. – *Theodoric,* king of the Ostrogoths, built himself a *tomb* at Ravenna some time after 500 *(fig. 57)*. He died in 526. A decagonal substructure with niches outside and a cruciform passage inside supports a circular structure, also with niches, which was originally encircled by columns. An enormous monolith in the shape of a flattened dome rests on the summit. The stones are cut and joined with a very high degree of technical mastery. The fact that this Germanic king built his tomb of stone rather than the brick he had used for his residence revealed an ironic loyalty to the traditions of Imperial Rome.

S. Lorenzo Maggiore, Milan

The use of centralized structures, however, was not confined to baptisteries, burial churches and martyriums, which were mostly quite small. The magnificent church of *S. Lorenzo Maggiore* in Milan is another example *(ill. 47* and *fig. 58)*. The evidence seems to indicate that this was built between 355 and 372, and served originally as a church for Arian Christians. The original ground plan is preserved almost intact in the present church, despite much restoration and alteration between the eleventh and seventeenth centuries. If we include the three chapels added during the fourth and fifth centuries, the building more or less constitutes a showcase of the various forms of centralized structures used during the period. The main building has a square ground plan with a tower at each corner. Between the towers, two-storeyed exedrae project, forming a sort of galleried ambulatory within. Originally, the central area was roofed with a groin vault, with the four vault heads in the shape of blown-out sails. To the west stood an atrium of quite imperial proportions, so much so that the part which is preserved, the large colonnade on the entrance side, was for a long time thought to belong to a third-century imperial thermae site. Bramante and Leonardo derived many of their ideas about centralized structures from this church.

57 Ravenna, Tomb of Theodoric

58 Milan, S. Lorenzo Maggiore (after Calverini)

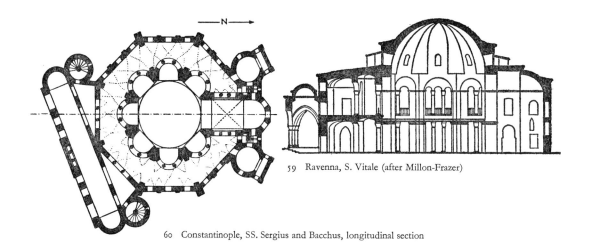

60   Constantinople, SS. Sergius and Bacchus, longitudinal section

S. Vitale, Ravenna

Even during the sixth century, the architecture of the Eastern Empire did not represent a break with the classical tradition but rather a continuation and development of it, though with certain amendments. There is no better way of illustrating both the continuity and the modification than by comparing S. Lorenzo Maggiore in Milan with *S. Vitale, Ravenna*, which dates from the first half of the sixth century *(ill. 48*, and *fig. 59* and *page 49)*. The square ground plan of the former is replaced by an octagon. With the exception of the chancel, which is open up to its full height, all the other sides have two-storeyed exedrae, forming an ambulatory below and a gallery above, interrupted by the chancel. A fenestrated octagonal drum supports the hemispherical dome, which is constructed of earthenware pots to reduce the weight. Every element is far slighter than in the Milan church, and there is more emphasis on the vertical, so that a sort of courtly elegance is introduced whose refinement also signifies spirituality, and the house of God becomes as incorporeal as it is possible for a building to appear. The external surfaces are plain and unadorned; only the chancel and narthex are slightly more elaborate. – We find what seems to have been the model for this church in Constantinople, the church of *SS. Sergius and Bacchus (ill. 49* and *fig. 60)*. It too is a centralized structure, giving the impression from the outside that it is a square enclosing an octagon. But it only displays protruding exedrae on the diagonals, and moreover a straight entablature on the ground floor, so that despite similarities with S. Vitale, the overall impression is quite different. Both buildings were begun *c.* 525.

Hagia Sophia, Constantinople

A few years later, 532–7, the Emperor Justinian built *Hagia Sophia in Constantinople*, close to the imperial palace and the hippodrome, probably to replace a wooden-roofed basilican church with five aisles which had burnt down in January 532 *(ill. 50, figs. 61* and *page 49)*. The architects were Isodorus of Miletus and Anthemius of Tralles, who was a famous engineer and mathematician. The dome was raised by 7 m after collapsing in 558, and at the end of the thirteenth century and even later during the Turkish period, the building was strengthened with buttresses. When it became a mosque in 1453, the building was not altered in any way. At the centre of the church is a square with 24.3 m high piers at the corners, supporting arches 31.3 m wide and 15.65 m high. Pendentives develop from the square to the hemispherical dome, which is 13.8 m high and 33 m in diameter. The overall height of this central space is 55.6 m. A row of forty windows encircles the bottom of the dome, robbing it of a firm base and making it appear to float above the drum. The pressure of the dome is diverted into half-cupolas to east and west, and again from there into smaller half-cupolas above two-storeyed exedrae which resemble those of S. Vitale in the positioning of their columns. Strong interior buttresses also counter the pressure of the dome from the sides. These buttresses are pierced by wide openings forming continuous side aisles, separated from the nave by columns at ground-floor and gallery level. In this way, the architects achieved a fusion between a basilica and a centralized domed structure. The whole building is 80.9 m long, and 69.7 m wide and is built of brick throughout, with the exception of the four piers of the crossing which are made of limestone blocks. The walls are finished with slabs of multi-coloured marble, and the vaults with mosaics. Despite its enormous size, Hagia Sophia lacks any form of heaviness. The transformation from the massiveness of Roman buildings to a more spiritual form of architecture is complete.

The Church of Hagia Sophia had no successor. The Church of the Apostles in Constantinople, which was built at the same time by the Empress Theodora, had a far greater influence on future developments. This was a pure centralized structure in the shape of a Greek cross, with a large central dome and four smaller domes on the arms of the cross. It has not been preserved, but its influence can be traced in later Byzantine and Russian architecture. In the West, two buildings that followed the same plan were St. Mark's in Venice and St. Front in Périgueux. – For a long time, it was assumed that Justinian architecture in Constantinople and the architecture of Ravenna represented the beginning of Byzantine architecture, but today this view has largely become unacceptable. It is probably more correct to regard these huge edifices of the first half of the sixth century as representing the final flowering of the art of Imperial Rome, springing as they do from the plethora of forms that developed in the eastern and western parts of the Empire during the final centuries of Roman rule, and as it were drawing them all together.

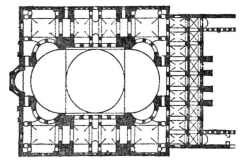

61   Constantinople, Hagia Sophia, longitudinal section (after Gurlitt) and ground plan (after von Sybel)

Byzantine churches

The genuine Byzantine architecture of the following centuries certainly grew out of the sixth-century architecture of the Eastern Empire, but differed radically from it in the paucity of its architectural ideas, its usually very modest proportions and its extremely weak lighting. Virtually the only form used was the domed cruciform church. One of the largest sites, though small in comparison with Early Christian buildings, is the group of churches in the monastery of Hosios Loukas, Phocis, in Greece, dating from the first half of the eleventh century *(ill. 53)*. The larger church, S. Lukas of Stiris, has a shallow drum and cupola above the crossing, and a smaller cupola above the east transept arm, whereas the Church of S. Maria has only a high vaulted drum. The interior is characterized by tall rectangular piers, and rather obscure vistas into tiny corner rooms. The exterior is a rather erratic and picturesque affair, with its freestone walls, brick arches and numerous narrow arched windows divided by columns. The value of these buildings lies in the rich mosaics and frescoes of the interiors.

Byzantine Churches in Russia

A single example will, of course, not do justice to Byzantine architecture, nor can justice be done to Russian architecture, even by quoting several examples. Russian architecture, which developed essentially out of Byzantine architecture, originated during the eleventh century in the towns of Kiev and Novgorod. The first major building was the *Cathedral of S. Sophia in Kiev*, built 1018–37 *(ill. 51, figs. 62* and *page 49)*. This was followed in 1056–62 by the somewhat simpler *Cathedral of S. Sophia in Novgorod (fig. 63)*. The Greek cruciform shape is combined with five aisles. A characteristic feature are the tall, narrow spatial units; the largest unit, the central crossing, measures barely 6 m square. This way of dividing up space, which made the interior extremely dark, corresponded exactly to the Byzantine style and was in the greatest possible contrast to the spaciousness of Early Christian architecture up to the sixth century, and of contemporary Romanesque architecture in the West. It prevailed in Russian architecture right up to the end of its development in the eighteenth century. Russian

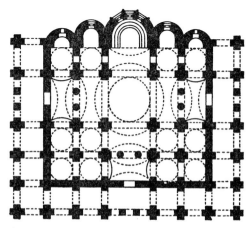

62 Kiev, Cathedral of S. Sophia

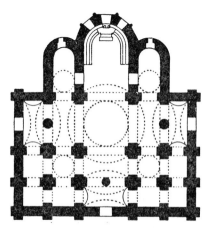

63 Novgorod, Cathedral of S. Sophia

architecture diverged from Byzantine architecture in that the three apses grouped at the east end were extended upwards to the height of the body of the building, and more markedly by the addition of high tower-like drums below the cupolas, and from the twelfth century onwards, by the substitution of onion-shaped domes. This, with several fanciful elaborations, is basically the form of the *Pokrov Cathedral* in Moscow, built by Postnik and Barma in 1555–60 *(fig. 64)*.

Turkish mosques

Justinian's Hagia Sophia did find a strange successor, not in Byzantine, Russian or Western architecture, but in fifteenth-century Turkey, with the *Suleiman Mosque in Istanbul*, built 1550–7 *(fig. 65)*.

64 Moscow, Pokrov Cathedral

65 Istanbul, Suleiman Mosque

5 Carolingian and Ottonian Architecture

Characteristics: More traditionally, these styles are known as Early or Pre-Romanesque. They are characterized by usually fairly heavy, plain, smooth walls. Arches were widely used, vaulting only very rarely. Supporting members (rectangular piers or round columns) lost their classical proportions, and became either squat or overextended. The various parts of buildings – and buildings became more and more complex as time went on – did not form a cohesive unity but remained as separate units. Gradually, a clearly defined crossing appeared in the body of the church, and this square was used to determine the proportions of the rest of the building. The chief impression given by these buildings is of a collection of blocks of space and mass enlivened with towers.

Materials: Freestone, brick (rare) and wood.

Corvey, Abbey Church

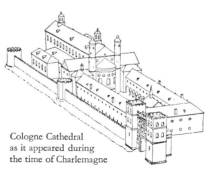

Cologne Cathedral
as it appeared during
the time of Charlemagne

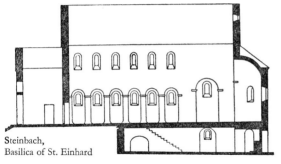

Steinbach,
Basilica of St. Einhard

Essen Cathedral, westwork as it
appeared during the Ottonian period

The gestation of western architecture from the soil of the old Western Empire was a long and slow process. The centuries following the Teutonic invasions saw tremendous variety in building. The new masters of Germany, Gaul and Iberia, and finally of Italy itself, had no tradition of building in stone or brick. They built in wood, and their architecture was confined to simple huts and halls, so that at first the palaces and churches of the conquered lands were completely alien to them. And, although it became necessary for them to adopt such buildings once they had taken over the political and spiritual legacy of the Roman Empire, this was no easy matter. The adoption represented a deliberate effort rather than any particular desire for expression, and as a result, it was indiscriminate; the existing culture was primitivized and reduced to its simplest form. Everything from the simplest basilica to the most intricate centralized structure, whether from Rome, North Africa, Syria or Asia Minor, was seized upon as a model and modified in this way. Archeologists are continually uncovering a bewildering variety of types of buildings, and it is impossible to define clear lines of development. The impression given by sixth- to eighth-century sources, which hinted at church buildings comparable in size to those of Early Christian architecture, has continually been qualified by discoveries which show that what was actually built was on an extremely modest scale. What grandeur these buildings did possess lay probably in their decoration, for we know that the Teutons and Celts were great lovers of precious jewellery.

I Carolingian Architecture

Imperial buildings at Lorsch and Aachen

It was only during the Carolingian period that architects attempted to match the grandeur and importance of Late Roman and Early Christian buildings. Charlemagne deliberately adopted the mantle of Rome in order to make his Frankish 'world empire' the equal of the Eastern Holy Roman Empire. A good illustration of this process is the *Gate-hall of the Monastery of Lorsch, 767–74 (ill. 52)*. Its three tunnel-vaulted passages are framed by Corinthian half-columns. Above the frieze-band is a row of Ionic pilasters, supporting small triangular gables. The wall surfaces are dressed with tiles of various colours. The application of the Roman orders indicates that the building was perhaps modelled on a Roman triumphal arch, or more probably on the entrance building of Old St. Peter's. The gate-hall stood in the centre of the outer court of the monastery and was evidently built for the Emperor's own use. The monastery church itself consisted of a narthex, a westwork and a pillared basilica with three aisles.

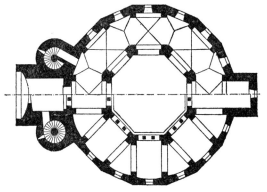

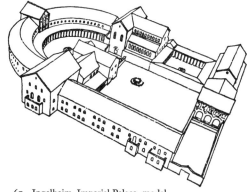

66 Aachen, Palace Chapel of Charlemagne   67 Ingelheim, Imperial Palace, model

When Charlemagne built his palace at Aachen at the end of the eighth century, he added a *Royal chapel*. The basic structure was completed in 798, and in 805 it was consecrated by Leo III *(ill. 54* and *fig. 66)*. Charlemagne himself was buried in it in 814. The architect, Odo of Metz, modelled the building on S. Vitale in Ravenna, though it differs considerably from the original. The central octagon is 14.4 m in diameter, and the sixteen-sided polygon that surrounds it is 29.5 m in diameter. The octagon has no columns on the ground floor, but two storeys of columns form a gallery above. The piers and arches are made of very precisely cut freestone. The walls are of quarry stone embedded in mortar, and are 1.6 m thick. The architect had obviously made a close study of Roman techniques. The alternating square and triangular segments of the ambulatory are roofed with groin arches, and the gallery with high tunnel vaults. Above the gallery rises a freestanding octagonal fenestration storey, 5.8 m in height, surmounted by an octagonal hipped cupola. The crown of the cupola is 31.6 m above the floor. The interior is heavier and has a more solid appearance than S. Vitale. The piers and arches round the ground floor of the central octagon are very weighty and powerful. The contrasting Late Gothic choir which was added in 1355–1414 even heightens their solemnity. – On the west side is a two-storeyed vaulted hall flanked by staircase towers, with a large niche at its centre overlooking the atrium. Such enormous niches were a traditional motif in palace architecture and in public buildings associated with the ruler. Through this monumental apse-like opening, the Emperor could emerge from his gallery within to face the people congregated in the atrium.

A different type of centralized structure from the same period is Theodulf's oratory at Germigny-des-Près, consecrated in 806. The ground plan, a Greek cross within a square, is typically Byzantine, but the horseshoe-shaped apses were inspired by the Visigothic architecture of Spain.

Imperial palaces

Just as they drew upon Early Christian tradition for their palace chapels, so the emperors drew upon classical tradition for their palaces. None of these palaces has survived, but some of them can be reconstructed. Our reconstruction of the *Palace of Ingelheim* (after 788–819, *fig. 67)*, though it may not be accurate in every respect, does convey the generosity of scale by

64

which its architects sought to compete with the imperial palaces of Rome and more particularly with the imperial palace at Constantinople. An almost perfect square was extended to the east by a semicircle of two storeys, with a colonnaded ambulatory and a gatehouse. To the west an outer court led to the Emperor's hall, a long three-aisled basilica with an enormous throne apse. The position of the throne apse indicates that, contrary to the Germanic tradition of broad, shallow halls, this hall was laid out lengthwise, though it was still positioned laterally in relation to the colonnaded atrium which led to the palace chapel. This was a columnar basilica with several aisles, a transept and a semicircular apse. It is not clear whether the transept was continuous, or whether it was divided into three cells.

Hall of the Germanic Kings

One such hall has been preserved, possibly the first example of the transition from wood to stone. This is *S. Maria de Naranco in Asturias (ill. 57)*. Asturias was the only part of the Visigothic Empire to survive the Arab conquest of the Iberian peninsula, which began in 711. The building is ascribed to several kings from 750 onwards. The thermae in the basement and the lateral position both indicate that it was a secular building forming part of a royal palace. It was consecrated as a church, however, as early as 848, under Ramiro I. Entrance was made in the middle of the north side, from a raised platform with a flight of steps leading up to it. The tunnel-vaulted hall opens at both ends onto loggias, each with three arcades. The throne was probably situated opposite the entrance before a second platform, which was only accessible from the hall. This feature was to appear again in eleventh-century German imperial palaces.

The Plan of the Monastery of St. Gallen

While travelling about the Empire, the Emperor occasionally stayed not in palaces but in monasteries, over which he had certain rights. Apart from the diocesan administration of the bishops, which perpetuated the administrative framework of the Roman Empire and thus provided the nucleus for a new secular administration, the only stable organization was the Benedictine order of monasticism, which was founded in 529. It was through this order that many of the traditions of the classical period were preserved. After the collapse of the Roman network of towns and of the architectural impetus of which it had been the source, the chief impetus, apart from imperial palaces and episcopal seats, was provided by the monasteries, who demanded some architectural expression of their communal life, thus raising architecture once more above the level of simple dwelling-houses and giving it artistic significance. Monastery planning crystallized at an early stage in the Carolingian period, as can be seen from the remarkable parchment plan of the *Monastery of St. Gallen (fig. 68)*, which probably arrived in St. Gallen *c.* 820. The layout was extremely orderly. To the west were the secular buildings such as workshops, etc. To the east was the church, with the monastery proper lying round a cloister court to the south of the church. The south wing contained the refectory, the kitchen was in the south-west corner and the west wing consisted of store rooms. The east wing, which was closest to the sanctuary and the monks' choir, was reserved for the dormitory, with the calefactorium or heating-room below it. East of the church, in the quietest part of the site, were the graveyard, the school for novices and the infirmary, with a small double church serving both the novices and the sick.

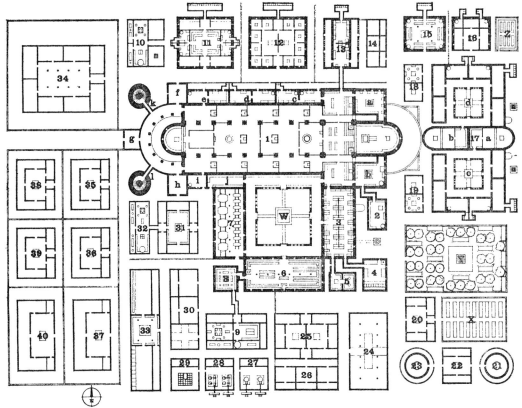

68 St. Gallen, Plan of the monastery (← N)

1 Church a Scriptorium on the ground floor, library on first floor b Sacristy on ground floor, room for storage of vestments on first floor c Apartment for visiting monks d Apartment for Principal of outer school e Gatekeeper's rooms f Entrance hall to the house for distinguished guests and to outer school g Reception for visitors h Passage to pilgrim and poor house and to administrative quarter i Room of Principal of pilgrim and poor house j Monks' discussion-room k St. Michael's Tower l Gabriel's Tower 2 Room for the preparation of the Holy Bread and Oil 3 Monks' dormitory on first floor, heated room on ground floor 4 Monks' lavatory 5 Monks' wash-room & bath 6 Monks' refectory on ground floor, dressing room on first floor 7 Wine and beer cellar on ground floor, storeroom on first floor 8 Monks' Kitchen 9 Monks' bakery and brewery 10 Guests' kitchen, bakery, and brewery 11 House for distinguished guests 12 Outer school 13 Abbot's house 14 Abbot's kitchen, cellar and bathroom 15 Bleeding house 16 Doctor's house 17 Noviciate and infirmary 18 Kitchen and bath of infirmary 19 Kitchen and bath of Noviciate 20 Gardener's house 21 Poultry-house 22 Poultry-keepers' house 23 Poultry-house 24 Barn 25 Craftman's House 26 Annexe to craftman's house 27 Grinding-mill 28 Crushing-mill 29 Kiln 30 Coopery. turners' shop, grain-storage for brewery 31 Pilgrims' house 32 Kitchen 33 Horses Stables Oxen 34 Coach-house 35 Sheep 36 Goats 37 Cows 38 Servants' house 39 Pigs 40 Stud stables

Churches with two chancels

There are several peculiarities about the plan of the church of which the most conspicuous is the fact that it has double chancels. Furthermore, the intersection tower above the crossing of the nave and transept presupposes the existence of a choir bay in front of the apse. Double chancels were to figure prominently in German architecture right up to the thirteenth century, but their origin remains somewhat obscure. They were known in North Africa as early as the fourth century, but it is extremely unlikely that they influenced the Carolingian plan. We may assume that they arose out of the fact that there were two principal patron saints, and thus two high altars were needed. The east apse of the St. Gallen church was dedicated to St. Paul and the west apse to St. Peter, and in this connection it is interesting to note that Old St. Peter's in Rome had the apse at the west end. Another remarkable feature are the two round towers at the west end, dedicated to the archangels Michael and Gabriel. The veneration of archangels played an important part in Benedictine liturgy, particularly in the north. It centred on the archangel Michael, the leader of the hosts of Heaven whose task it was to defend the heavenly Jerusalem from the powers of evil. These powers always arose from the west, which is why the fortress-like towers stood at the west end of the church. The church was built according to the smaller of the two sets of measurements indicated on the plan. – The larger plan was, however, followed closely by another building of the Carolingian period, the first cathedral at *Cologne* (817–70, *fig. page 62*). It was 40 m long, with two chancels, a transept at the east end and a square bay before each apse. The transept was divided into three cells, which meant that there was no distinct crossing. Another transept was added to the west chancel and two towers were also added at the west end. The east chancel was dedicated to Our Lady and the west chancel to St. Peter. At the time Cologne Cathedral was regarded as one of the most beautiful churches in Christendom.

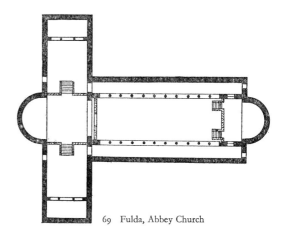

69 Fulda, Abbey Church

The westerly orientation of Old St. Peter's served as a model for other churches too, but the eastern apse was never abandoned, as we see in the case of the *Abbey Church of S. Salvator at Fulda*. This church is an excellent example of how the cross-fertilization of ideas produced new architectural forms. The present cathedral, built 1704–12 by Johann Dientzenhofer *(fig. 69)*, is the same size as the Carolingian church (length *c*. 100 m, width of nave 14.5 m), which was built 791–819 on the site of an earlier (744) basilican church with an eastern apse but no transept. The east end of the new building followed the old plan, but a broad transept with a semicircular apse was added at the west end. The west altar was dedicated to St. Boniface who was buried there. As the 'Apostle to the German peoples', he was granted a status equal to that of St. Peter, and it was on the model of St. Peter's in Rome that the west transept was added. A further novel feature of the Fulda church was the addition some years later of spacious three-aisled crypts beneath both chancels for the worship of relics, which meant that the chancel floors had to be raised.

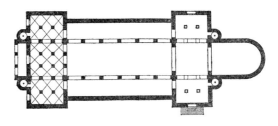

70 St. Riquier (Centula), Abbey Church, sketch and ground plan

Churches with westworks

The Abbey Church of *St. Riquier (Centula) near Amiens (fig. 70)* was one of the most extra-ordinary inventions of the Carolingian period. Abbot Angilbert III (790–814), a close confidant of Charlemagne, was made responsible for the rebuilding of the seventh-century monastery, and the work was heavily subsidized by the Emperor. A quite accurate reconstruction of the church is made possible by remains in the present church and from contemporary illustrations. It included a fully-fledged westwork, a three-aisled basilica, an east transept, a choir bay and an apse. From the outside the west and east ends are almost identical, but from inside the westwork looks like a separate centralized structure. The ground floor is divided by columns, with a central square measuring 10 m surrounded on three sides by galleries. The fourth side probably opened out through arcades into the nave. It seems likely that Charlemagne used this part of the church as a sort of palace chapel. A similar westwork probably existed at Lorsch, and possibly also in the Abbey Church of St. Denis. The latter was consecrated in

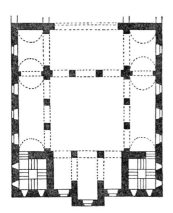

71 Corvey, Abbey Church of St. Michael, ground plan and section through west work

775, but it had maintained a strong royal connection since Merovingian times. – The earliest westwork still standing today is that of the *Abbey Church of St. Michael, Corvey* (873–85) on the Weser, which was founded by the West Frankish monastery of Corbie in north-east France *(ill. 55, figs. 71 and page 62)*. It is a centralized structure, with staircase towers and surrounding galleries above a square vaulted hall on the ground floor.

II Ottonian Architecture

The Carolingian heritage
The buildings that had been erected during the Carolingian period, 750–850, became after a century of darkness and unrest the starting-point for the full flowering of European architecture which began in the second half of the tenth century. Its development followed different rhythms in Germany, France, England, Spain and Italy, with certain common features and certain dissimilarities. Fresh adaptations from Early Christian and Byzantine architecture as well as influences from the Islamic world led to a general enrichment of style, giving rise to such a diversity of solutions that it is difficult to trace a common denominator. Stylistic divisions become somewhat problematical at this point. Should this new style, for example, already be considered Romanesque? If not, where are we to draw the line? The term 'Ottonian architecture' has come into general use because it was in the region of East Francia, ruled by the Saxon imperial house of the Ottonians (919–1024), that the new richness of architectural techniques first appeared, largely as a result of a strong link with Carolingian architecture. It was not until the first quarter of the eleventh century that France and Italy began to play an important part in the development of the new architecture, with the large, vaulted buildings that can properly be termed Romanesque.

The two-chancel Church of St. Michael at Hildesheim
Although the structure of society was undoubtedly changing by the Ottonian period, its architectural needs still remained the same as before. Churches and monastic buildings were undoubtedly the most important, with palaces taking second place. At first, there were no significant developments in the construction of houses for princes or knights, and even less in those for the urban bourgeois. However, there was a great deal of building during this period, and if we take as our first example the *Church of St. Michael at Hildesheim*, it is because it was the most perfectly homogeneous structure erected around the turn of the millennium, revealing at the same time most clearly its Carolingian ancestry *(ill. 56 and fig. 72)*. The foundation stone of the west crypt was laid by Bishop Bernward in 1010, and the crypt was consecrated in 1015. The whole church was consecrated in 1033. It is 69 m long, the width of the nave is 8.6 m and the height 16 m. The decks, except over the crypt and apse, are flat. The clearly defined ground plan, based on the square of the crossing (this is the first example of a genuinely separate crossing), is also distinguishable from the exterior. As at Centula, two identical structures with towers stood at either end of the basilica, the only difference being that at Hildesheim there was a raised chancel above the crypt instead of a westwork. The conception of a crypt with an ambulatory, which became the tomb of the bishop, came from the Church of St. Martin at Tours. At the ends of the transepts were two-storeyed galleries, creating a

richly satisfying subdivision of space, which also found expression in the three square bays of the nave. These were divided by piers with columns between. The cubiform capitals were a sort of symbol of the way the whole building was conceived, linking the supports and the walls in an exemplary composition.

Westworks

That the concept of the westwork also enhanced the west chancel is illustrated by the example of *Essen Cathedral*, built *c*. 1000 *(ill. 58* and *fig. page 62)*. By taking as a model the palace chapel at Aachen, with its ambulatory and galleries, but only using half of it, one of the most original solutions to be found in Ottonian architecture was evolved. It also retained the popular exterior formation of a central tower flanked by two staircase towers. – A genuine westwork, like that at Corvey, survives in the Benedictine Abbey Church of St. Pantaleon at Cologne (966–80). The *Liebfrauenkirche at Maastricht (ill. 59)* was given one of the most powerful west-works of the late tenth century. Another centralized structure modelled on the palace chapel at Aachen was the Ritterstiftskirche (Knight's Collegiate church) at Wimpfen im Tal, built 979–98, of which only the western part is preserved.

Basilican churches with and without galleries

The earliest preserved Ottonian basilican church is the *Convent Church of St. Cyriakus* at Gern-rode, which was begun in 961 *(ill. 61* and *fig. 73)*. It has three aisles with alternating columns and piers, and a gallery which also surrounded the original transept-like westwork that was later transformed into a chancel. The clearly defined crossing of the east transept was also a later addition. The east chancel stands above a crypt, and has two small apses on the transept arms. *Ste. Gertrude at Nivelles*, 1000–46, was one of the largest pillared basilicas built during this period *(ill. 60* and *fig. 74)*. It has two choirs and two transepts, and an extremely elaborate and complex westwork. Contemporary with Nivelles was St. Rémy at Reims, built 1005–49, a galleried basilica with clustered piers. The original plan comprised five aisles, which would have made it the largest church building in France. Modelled as it was on the Early Christian basilica, with its orderly arrangement and the absence of any exterior articulation, particularly at the west end, it stands outside the German tradition.

 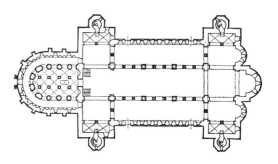

72 Hildesheim, St. Michael, model and ground plan

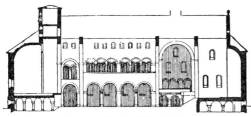

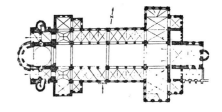

73 Gernrode, Convent Church of St. Cyriakus

74 Nivelles, Ste. Gertrude (after Millon-Frazer)

Departures from the current style

Trier Cathedral, built towards the end of this period (1017–47), is a more particular example since it retained the Early Christian structure and therefore departed from the normal basilican scheme *(ill. 63* and *fig. 48)*. But it too had two chancels. The west façade, with its offsets and blind and open arcades, marks the beginning of the fully-developed articulation of exterior walls. – Another unusual building was the Wiperti crypt at Quedlinburg from the mid-tenth century, a small three-aisled hall with longitudinal tunnel-vaulting. The side aisles were prolonged in a semicircle around the apse. Whether there was any connection between this and the choir ambulatory that appeared in France at about the same time is not clear. The building originally was very simple; it was only when a superstructure was added at a later date that it became a crypt. A much more perfect example of a columnar hall is the *Chapel of St. Bartholomew at Paderborn*. Erected by Greek workmen in 1017, it has three aisles of four bays vaulted with domes on pendentives. Pillars and niches alternate along the walls. Just as in Early Christian architecture, the simple exterior conveys nothing of the elegance of the interior *(ill. 62)*.

III French Architecture around 1000

The choir ambulatory with radial chapels

Although France could not compare with Germany in the wealth of buildings erected during this period, it was the scene of certain experiments and discoveries which were to point the way for the future. The most important of these was the choir ambulatory with radial chapels, as seen in the extremely complex *Church of St. Philibert at Tournus (c.* 950–1120, *ill. 64* and *fig. 75)*. This ambulatory, with its three rectangular chapels, was first built around the crypt, which was consecrated in 979, and was then repeated in the chancel erected above the crypt and consecrated in 1019. Another interesting feature of this church, and one which marked it out from other eleventh-century churches, was its system of vaulting, illustrating as it did the problems which particularly preoccupied French architects of the period.

Tunnel vaults

One of the most surprising buildings of the period was *St. Bénigne at Dijon*, built in 1001–18 by Wilhelm von Volpiano *(fig. 76)*. It is approximately 100 m long, comprising a five-aisled pillared basilica roofed with tunnel vaults and surrounded by a gallery, an east transept and a richly developed chancel. Adjoining it was a centralized structure which is now only partially preserved. It was modelled on the Early Christian Church of the Holy Sepulchre at Jerusalem.

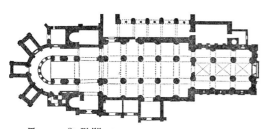

75 Tournus, St. Philibert

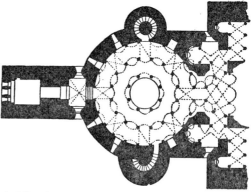

76 Dijon, St. Bénigne (after Dehio and Bezold)

The Cluniac reforms

Cluny was the most important Benedictine monastic establishment north of the Alps, and the principal aims of its reforming efforts were to deepen Christian thought and to strengthen the authority of the Papacy, which meant combating the designs of the German emperors. In the second Abbey Church at Cluny, consecrated in 981, all the altars were gathered at the east end in the graduated chancel, and the church was clearly oriented on a west-east axis. The layout of this church was to have far-reaching effects. The arrangement of the interior space closely follows the example of the Early Christian basilicas, rejecting the later tradition of the west-work and west chancel. The immediate successors of the Cluny church followed the same form, as for example the *Abbey Church of Bernay* (1017–40), which was the first large building undertaken during the course of the reformation of the Norman monasteries under Duke Richard II *(ill. 65* and *fig. 77)*. It was in fact larger than Cluny. Built originally with a flat ceiling, this basilica had a broad transept, and contained a particularly clear example of the new graduated chancel.

Spain and Italy

This concentration of the altars at the east end occurred at the same period, though in a slightly different way, in Spain with the monastic church of *S. Maria at Ripoll (c.* 1020–32, *ill*

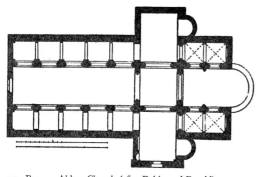

77 Bernay, Abbey Church (after Dehio and Bezold)

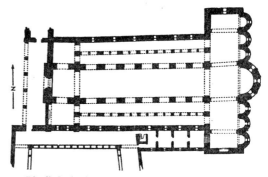

78 Ripoll, Spain, S. Maria (after Millon-Frazer)

66 and *fig. 78*). This was a five-aisled basilican church with a large transept and seven contiguous apses. With the exception of the large number of apses and the tunnel vaulting, it is obviously modelled on Old St. Peter's. – Before 1000, Italy played almost no part in the architectural developments which were taking place north of the Alps, but in the early eleventh century a number of large buildings were erected in Italy which attempted in their own way to realize the grand ideas of the new European architecture. We may conclude this survey, which has already led us into the Romanesque period, with the little-known Church of S. Maria di Portonovo near Ancona, completed in 1034.

England

What little has survived of English architecture of the pre-Norman period shows almost no connection with developments on the Continent during the tenth and early eleventh centuries. The west tower of the church at *Earls Barton, Northamptonshire, c.* 1000, is decorated with long thin slabs of stone forming small arches, and small triangular gables somewhat reminiscent of the decoration on the Carolingian gate-hall at Lorsch *(ill. 67)*.

6 Romanesque Architecture

Characteristics: A striking feature of Romanesque architecture were its powerful walls and vaults. Internal and external walls were articulated to an increasing degree by means of projections, blind arcades, niches, etc. There was considerable experimentation with vaulting; domical vaults, round and pointed tunnel vaults and square and rectangular groin vaults were all used.

Interiors were generally based on the square formed by the crossing. Supporting members, often consisting of alternating piers and half-columns, lost the rigorous proportions of their Classical antecedents. Only the round arch was used, except in Burgundy. Wall-surfaces were frequently enlivened with sculptures.

Materials: Mostly freestone, with marble (in Italy), brick and wood.

Caen, St. Etienne, articulation of wall

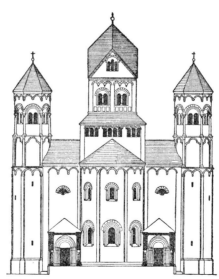

Maria Laach, Benedictine Abbey Church,
a three-aisled groin-vaulted basilica

The pace of building began to increase steadily from the second quarter of the eleventh century onwards, though it was still largely confined to churches and monasteries, but no really systematic form of classification, whether chronological, regional or according to types, is possible. We shall begin therefore by examining ten major buildings which illustrate the wealth of architectural ideas which were then current.

I Ten Key Buildings of the Eleventh and Twelfth Centuries

Speyer: groin-vaulting

The earliest of our examples is *Speyer Cathedral (ill. 68* and *fig. 79)*, begun by Conrad II between 1024 and 1033. The original plan was for a flat-ceilinged, pillared basilican church with a vestibule at the west end and a transept with apse at the east end. The eastern part of the building had to be raised 3.4 m above the level of the nave to accommodate the large groin-vaulted crypt below. However, the plan was altered as building progressed. The side aisles were given groin vaults, supported on half-columns engaged with the piers, and the corresponding members in the nave were continued upwards to form arches above the clerestory windows, giving a rhythmic articulation to the nave walls. The cathedral measured 31.7 × 133 m and was consecrated in 1061. Despite the fact that it had neither a westwork nor a west chancel, the customary group of three towers was retained at both ends of the building. Under Henry IV (1056–1106), groin vaults were added to the nave and transept as well, which

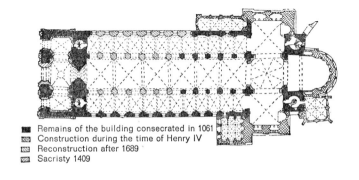

▨ Remains of the building consecrated in 1061
▩ Construction during the time of Henry IV
▨ Reconstruction after 1689
▨ Sacristy 1409

79   Speyer Cathedral, view of exterior (after H. Koepf) and ground plan

necessitated an alteration to the nave walls. A pilaster strip with half-column was added to every second pier to support the reinforcing and arcaded arches of the vaults, giving an even more pronounced articulation to the walls. The external walls were also enlivened. It was the architecture of Ravenna and the Lombardy region that provided the model for the blind arcading and the dwarf gallery, which were added first to the apse and later continued around the entire building. – Speyer Cathedral is a classic, both technically and aesthetically, and it represents the perfection of the Carolingian-Ottonian tradition.

Como

In Lombardy and the neighbouring regions, creative energy was directed more towards detail than towards overall composition. *S. Abbondio, Como* (1027–95), was built at the same time as Speyer Cathedral. It is an unvaulted columnar basilica with five aisles and no transepts. The aisles are relatively high in proportion to their width; such tall, slim spatial forms are most unusual for the period. They are separated by powerful arcades of round piers reminiscent of St. Philibert, Tournus. The most richly articulated section of the exterior is the east end with its two square towers rising above the apses of the inner side aisles *(ill. 69)*. The wall surfaces are treated artistically with a number of details derived originally from Ravenna, but which had been developed and perfected in Lombardy during the last three centuries, notably offsets with engaged columns, friezes of round arches and decorated window surrounds.

Cologne

Our third example, *S. Maria im Kapitol, Cologne*, built *c.* 1030–65 *(ill. 70* and *fig. 80)*, shows that it was still in the North that the most imaginative architecture was being produced. This was the first large church to include a triconchal structure – a development of the pure centralized structure – in conjunction with a basilican nave. The side aisles were extended to form a continuous ambulatory around the three arms and the square crossing. The aisles and ambulatory were groin-vaulted, the rest of the church was flat-ceilinged. The suspended cupola above the crossing, and the tunnel-vaulting above the side arms were added *c.* 1200, but the nave was not vaulted until 1240. The large crypt at the east end was built in such a way that it was not necessary to raise the floor of the crossing and chancel. This gave the interior of the church an ample spaciousness reminiscent of Early Christian buildings like S. Lorenzo, Milan, and S. Vitale, Ravenna, but quite unique in the eleventh century.

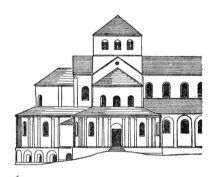
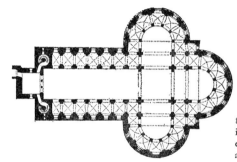

80 Cologne, St. Maria im Kapitol, view of exterior (after H. Koepf) and ground plan

Venice: cupolas

A number of large churches – some vaulted throughout and some not – built during the third quarter of the eleventh century in various localities demonstrate the same desire for grandeur of expression that moved the architects of Speyer Cathedral. The rebuilding of *St. Mark's, Venice*, was probably begun around the middle of the century, and according to an old inscription, it was completed in 1071, but the dates more usually assigned to the third church are 1063 to 1085 or even 1094. During the twelfth century, the façade was advanced and the building was developed to its present extent *(ill. 71* and *fig. 81)*. The bulk of the decoration, which consists of marble facing, mosaics and sculptures, was added at various times up to the fifteenth century. The eleventh-century church, a brick building richly articulated with niches, offsets and blind fenestration, would have presented a much less cluttered appearance. It was in the shape of a Greek cross surmounted by a series of cupolas, and it was modelled on Justinian's Church of the Apostles in Constantinople. The side aisles, which are roofed with tunnel vaults matching those between the cupolas, have no galleries but open directly on to the nave above the arcades. It is these massive arches and their supporting piers which give the interior of St. Mark's its power and solidity and place the building, despite its Early Christian ground plan, firmly within the Western Romanesque style of the eleventh century.

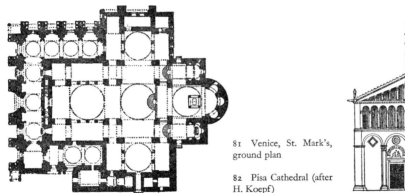

81 Venice, St. Mark's, ground plan

82 Pisa Cathedral (after H. Koepf)

Pisa

After Venice, the next largest maritime and commercial city in Italy was Pisa, which reached the height of its power during the eleventh century. The buildings erected to give expression to this prosperity were not placed in the centre of the city as in Venice, but in an isolated position on the outskirts, thereby emphasizing their monumental character. The architectural group comprising the Cathedral, the Campanile, the Baptistery and the Campo Santo *(ill. 72)* was built over a period of several centuries, yet in spite of this, a profound coherence exists, which was achieved by the use of the same material throughout – white and coloured marble – and by the repetition of certain architectural motifs. – The *Cathedral* was founded in 1063 *(fig. 82)*. The present plan is almost exactly that envisaged by the architect, Busketos; only the three bays at the west end of the nave have been subsequently added. The west façade was completed during the thirteenth century and the whole building was finally finished during the fourteenth century. In plan it comprises a five-aisled gallery basilica and two three-aisled transept arms, also with galleries and terminating in apses. The intersection of what are virtually three basilicas is emphasized by an elliptical dome. All the side aisles are groin-vaulted; the nave and galleries have open roofs. The transept arms are lower than the nave and chancel and consequently join the intersection tower at a different level. Compared to the sort of methodical composition which characterized contemporary German architecture and to the systematic logic of contemporary French architecture, this solution might appear somewhat clumsy, but not to the Italians. In their view, there was no discrepancy in thus illustrating the fact that two basically self-contained basilicas met at the crossing and were linked with the third and principal basilica merely by side aisles and galleries. This highly imaginative building owed a great deal to the Early Christian architecture of the Eastern Empire – Kalat Siman, S. Demetrios, Salonica, and S. Irene, Constantinople, are referred to as possible influences – but it also has a number of distinctively Western features, notably the neatness and firmness of the overall composition, the precision of the individual members and their strictly rhythmic succession, and the lively articulation of the exterior by means of blind arcades and open galleries.

Santiago de Compostela: tunnel-vaulting

The systematic logic which characterized French architecture during this period received one of its finest expressions in the great *Pilgrimage church at Santiago de Compostela* in Spain *(ill. 73 and fig. 83)*, a good example of a type of pilgrim church that had been developed in France. The fact that the Apostle James was buried there had made Santiago de Compostela one of the most important pilgrimages in Christendom. The first church had been destroyed in 997 and work on the new church was begun *c.* 1075, under the direction of an architect from the Auvergne. Completed in 1128, it consists of a three-aisled longitudinal basilica crossed by a three-aised lateral basilica forming a large transept. All the side aisles have galleries, and these are continued around the transept ends and the end of the chancel. Chapels clustered on the transept arms and around the chancel ambulatory, in obedience to the Clunaic demand that all altars should be at the east end, draw attention strongly towards the Holy of Holies. The west façade with its two towers forms a triumphal entrance. The only tower at the east end is above the crossing. It had become customary by this time, everywhere with the exception of Italy, for all large buildings to be vaulted throughout. This was due in part to the purely practical necessity of reducing the risk of fire, but the desire to give the sanctuary in particular a greater and more representative degree of monumental perfection which only vaulting could achieve was even more decisive. It gave rise to some difficult technical problems, for architects did not as yet have a great deal of experience in this field. Tunnel-vaulting was chosen for Santiago de Compostela, as a result of experience gained in France, with groin-vaulting for the side aisles and ambulatory. A tunnel vault of such proportion required a great deal of lateral rein-forcement, which accounts for the presence of galleries when there was no liturgical reason for them or need for the extra space. These galleries are vaulted with quarter-tunnels and serve as buttresses to the central tunnel vault, the load and thrust of which could not have been countered in any other way. An unfortunate consequence was that there could be no clerestory fenestration, which made the interior rather dark. The wall-surfaces were split up and treated sculpturally, a practice that was by now universal. The almost imperceptible alternation of columns and piers reveals that the plan of the church was based on the square of the crossing.

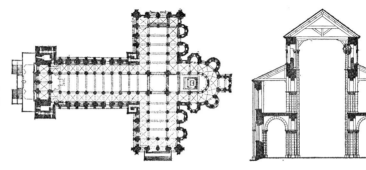

83 Santiago de Compostela, Pilgrimage Church

84 Caen, St. Etienne, reconstruction before addition of vaulting (after H. Koepf)

S. Savin-sur-Gartempe: a hall-church

Another solution to the problem of vaulting was discovered by the Poitou School. The chancel, ambulatory and radial chapels of the Church of *St. Savin-sur-Gartempe* were built *c.* 1060–75 and a few years later, *c.* 1095–1115, a nave and two side aisles were added. The nave is roofed with a continuous tunnel vault resting on arcades of tall columns *(ill. 74)*. The pressure is countered by the groin vaults of the side aisles which are raised up to the level of the springers of the tunnel vault. This type of basilican church with side aisles and nave of the same height was later to achieve great prominence as the 'hall-church' of the German Gothic.

Fontevrault: series of domes, the Aquitaine School

The problem of vaulting was tackled in yet another different way in south-west France, particularly in Aquitaine. The nave of the *Abbey Church of Fontevrault, c.* 1100–19, was vaulted with a series of four domes *(ill. 75)*. In consequence no side aisles were included. Half-columns on three sides of each of the massive rectangular piers carry the reinforcing arches. Between the piers, the lower part of the walls consists of a blind arcade, while the upper part is fenestrated. The total effect is extremely heavy and solemn. This particular development, which was influenced by the Early Christian architecture of the Eastern Empire, was not taken further.

Caen: Norman rib-vaulting

A far greater influence upon future developments was exercised by the Norman school. *St. Etienne, Caen*, was begun between 1063 and 1066 and consecrated some time after 1077 *(ill. 76)*. The chancel was replaced in 1200 by a Gothic structure. The original church was a three-aisled gallery basilica with groin vaults above the side aisles, and flat ceilings or open roofs above the galleries and nave *(fig. 84)*. The galleries, however, indicate that vaulting was contemplated by the architect but that he did not at first attempt to introduce it since a fenestrated clerestory had been retained which had been split into two layers- an outer layer containing the windows and an inner arcade. This division is in fact an artistic continuation of the articulation of the wall-surface which begins at ground-floor level. The piers supporting the wide arches of the arcades on the ground floor and along the gallery are modelled with angular projections and half-columns in such a way that no smooth, unbroken surfaces remain, and the engaged columns on the inner face of the wall rise right up to include the gallery in a series of vertical units. A tunnel vault would have been unthinkable here for both technical and aesthetic

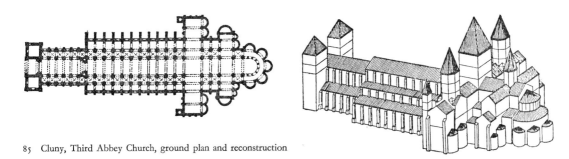

85 Cluny, Third Abbey Church, ground plan and reconstruction

reasons. The only solution that would harmonize with the articulation of the walls was groin-vaulting, which would allow the line of the engaged columns on the walls to be continued upwards over the reinforcing arches and along the groins. The sexpartite rib vaults erected probably around 1100 or shortly afterwards do exactly this. Each vaulting compartment comprises two bays, forming a square, and quarter tunnel vaults above the galleries counteract the thrust. – An even clearer example of how such 'false' rib vaults came about is the contemporary church of La Trinité, also at Caen. Here it is obvious that ordinary groin vaults were first erected, and that at a later stage diagonal ribs were added along the groins together with transverse ribs of the same shape. The aesthetic perfection of this form of vaulting ensured its retention by later architects, and a few decades later, in the Early Gothic period, its immense technical and constructional possibilities were discovered. – Another feature of St. Etienne which was to be very influential was its striking west façade flanked by two towers. This was the result of a long process of evolution which ultimately went back to the Carolingian period.

Burgundy: pointed tunnel-vaulting
Another signpost for the future was the principal building of the Burgundy school, the third *Abbey Church of Cluny*, begun in 1088 under Abbot Hugh and almost entirely destroyed in 1807 *(fig. 85)*. This was an even more developed expression of the Cluniac practice of assembling all the altars at the east end of the church. The church comprised a nave of eleven bays with double side aisles, a broad transept containing four chapels, a second, shorter transept further to the east, also containing four chapels, and a chancel with ambulatory and five radial chapels. The easterly concentration was echoed on the exterior by six towers at the east end. The nave and transepts were roofed with pointed tunnel vaults above reinforcing arches. The advantages of this new method of vaulting lay in its lighter construction and its better distribution of thrust, which meant that galleries were no longer necessary as abutments to the vaulting, and the fenestrated clerestory could be retained. The lack of galleries was compensated by higher side aisles. Yet despite all these precautions the vaults collapsed in 1125, and had to be re-erected. A good impression of the church's appearance from within can be gained from *St. Lazare, Autun (ill. 77)*. This church was built in 1116–32 and although somewhat smaller, it is very similar to Cluny III in elevation. The arcades with their pointed arches correspond to the latter's pointed tunnel vault. The wall-surface is articulated with fluted pilasters, obviously suggested by the Roman town-gate at Autun, and with a triforium running along above the side aisle arcades and below the clerestory fenestration, as if a gallery had been projected onto the surface of the wall. At Cluny III, there was still a passageway behind the triforium.

These ten examples obviously give no more than an initial impression of the vast flowering of architecture which took place during the Romanesque period, and the wealth and variety of the architectural solutions in use by the end of the eleventh century. A further, smaller selection from among the many hundreds of churches which have been preserved from this period will complete the picture to some extent. And if we return once more first to Germany, it is not because Germany was the scene of any particular architectural advances (it was not), but on the contrary because it displayed great conservatism. In many places in Germany, the Carolingian-Ottonian tradition continued well into the thirteenth century.

The Cluniac Reformation: the rejection of vaults

The *Abbey Church, Limburg an der Hardt*, built 1025–42, provides a good initial example. Today it lies in ruins, but even so its simple grandeur is immediately apparent. It was a three-aisled columnar basilica with a flat ceiling, a transept with two semicircular apses, a rectangular chancel end and a western vestibule with an atrium or paradise *(fig. 86)*. The simple plan and the absence of towers accorded with the reforming demands of Cluny II, but the size and power of the building show a close affinity to the spirit of imperial architecture as exemplified by Speyer Cathedral. The same applies to the ruins of the *Abbey Church of Hersfeld*, built in 1037 *(ill. 78)*. – A similar spirit is evident outside Germany in another mid-century building – the Norman *Abbey Church of Notre Dame, Jumièges* (1037–66, *ill. 79*), an unvaulted gallery basilica with three aisles and a chancel ambulatory. In the degree of articulation and build-up of the walls, however, it went far beyond anything built in Germany at the time and pointed the way towards St. Etienne, Caen. The Cluniac reformation did not achieve its full effect in Germany until quite late. It was the church of SS. Peter and Paul, Hirsau (1082–91), now destroyed, which provided the decisive impulse. In contrast to the richness of Cluny III, with which it was contemporary, it retained older, simpler forms and in particular the flat ceiling. The ascetic strength of this type of architecture can be seen clearly in the ruins of the *Abbey Church of Paulinzella in Thuringia, c.* 1112–32 *(ill. 80)*. This three-aisled basilica was of the utmost simplicity and had flat ceilings throughout. Sculpture and painting were omitted, and instead of the richly formed capitals used shortly afterwards at Speyer, the old-fashioned cubiform capital was retained. The extreme precision of the masonry, however, gives an impression of flawless dignity, even grandeur. Two other German churches stylistically related to Paulinzella are those at Alpirsbach in the Black Forest, built in the early twelfth century, and Talbürgel in Thuringia, dating from the second half of the twelfth century.

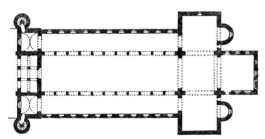

86 Limburg an der Hardt, Abbey Church, ground plan and elevation (after H. Koepf)

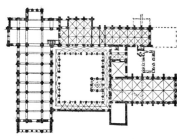
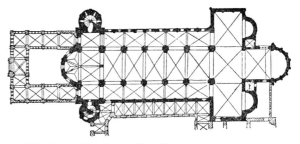

87 Fontenay, Cistercian Church   88   Maria Laach, Benedictine Abbey Church

Brick buildings
The first brick building to be erected east of the Elbe after 1150 was the Premonstratensian Abbey Church at Jerichow, a three-aisled columnar basilica with a flat ceiling and a transept. The three aisles of the chancel were vaulted with pointed tunnels.

The Cistercians
The inspiration for the Jerichow church came from Burgundy, though not from Cluny. The elaborateness of Cluny III had given rise to a revulsion of feeling and a fresh desire for reformation, and in 1098 the monastery of Cîteaux was founded, giving its name to the new Cistercian Order. The Cistercian reformation began to get properly under way from 1112–14 onwards under Bernard of Clairvaux, who founded the Abbey of Clairvaux in 1115 as a model for the strict monastic life, and shortly afterwards founded Fontenay on the same plan. *Fontenay* was built *c.* 1139–47 and still remains today *(ill. 81* and *fig. 87)*. A pointed tunnel on lateral reinforcing arches vaults the nave right up to the rectangular chancel, which is vaulted with a lower pointed tunnel. Lateral pointed tunnels vault the side aisles and the transept arms, forming bays. There is no fenestration in the nave; light enters through the side aisles and through dense groups of windows in the entrance wall, the chancel walls and the end walls of the transept. The interior was plastered and white paint – the only colour permitted – was applied to the joints. Apart from that there was no decoration, neither sculpture nor painting, in the entire building. This simple austerity proved to be extraordinarily popular. The Cistercian Order spread throughout Europe in a remarkably short time. It was important not only from the viewpoint of religious influence, but also because it gave a wide distribution to the Gothic forms to which Fontenay had given birth.

Maria Laach and Vézelay: groin-vaulting over oblong compartments
The *Benedictine Abbey Church of Maria Laach* (1093 to *c.* 1177, *ill. 82* and *fig. 88)* stands in the greatest possible contrast to the Cistercians' efforts at reform, returning to the double-chancel plan with rich groups of towers at both east and west ends. The groin-vaulting, which dates from *c.* 1150 and was modelled on that of Speyer Cathedral, was erected over oblong compartments, but this attempt to break out of a system based on the square was not at first taken any further in Germany. – The only other example of oblong groin vaults over a nave is the Abbey Church of *Ste. Madeleine, Vézelay*, which dates from 1120 *(ill. 83)*. Although here the division

into bays embraces all three aisles, the result is the same. The chief difficulty of this system lay in the form of the arches: either the wall arches had to be steeply stilted or the reinforcing arches had to be exaggeratedly depressed, and in either case distortion was the result. Quite apart from their very different exteriors, these two churches are surprisingly dissimilar in view of the fact that they follow basically the same construction. The extremely austere and almost gloomy severity of the interior of Maria Laach is in complete contrast to the wealth of colour and decoration in Ste. Madeleine.

Vaulted buildings in Lombardy

A further example of a groin-vaulted basilica is *S. Ambrogio, Milan (ill. 84)*, a three-aisled gallery basilica with no transept or clerestory and with a ground plan based on the square of the crossing. The vaulting compartments each comprise two bays under one domed groin vault *(fig. 89)*. The groins are lined with heavy ribs, rectangular in section, which have the effect of diagonal reinforcing arches. This type of vault has no relation to the genuine Gothic rib vault, although it was at the source of the argument in connection with the invention of the latter. The nave of S. Ambrogio was probably not built until *c.* 1100–28 so in any case it could not have had any influence on the Norman and English rib vaults of *c.* 1100 and the development of rib-vaulting in the Ile-de-France immediately afterwards. However, S. Ambrogio did have considerable influence in the region around Milan and even as far north as Zürich and Basle. One of the churches inspired by it was *S. Michele, Pavia*, built between 1117 and 1155. This has neither towers nor a transept and the only monumental element on the exterior is the enormous façade *(ill. 85)*. Four clusters of pilasters and engaged columns divide this vast wall into three sections corresponding to the three aisles. At the top a dwarf gallery follows the slope of the gable. Sculptured bands grow along the whole width of the surface rather like wall plants. At the same period in France, from Aquitaine and Burgundy right up to the Ile-de-

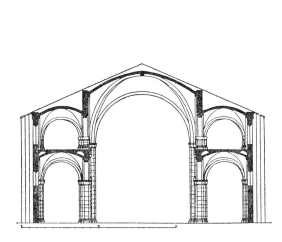

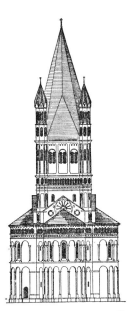

89 Milan, S. Ambrogio
(after H. Koepf)

90 Cologne, Great St. Martin
(after H. Koepf)

France, the most perfect and coherent system of monumental sculpture in the whole history of architecture was beginning to develop. – Other related buildings in northern Italy are the cathedrals of Modena, Parma and Piacenza.

Triconchal structures on the Rhine
German architects still had a predilection for some of the less usual architectural forms in the late twelfth century, as we see from a number of triconchal churches built along the Rhine during that period. The *Church of the Apostles, Cologne (ill. 86)*, was given a triconchal choir *c*. 1200, making it one of the most beautiful compositions of the Romanesque period. The triconchal choir of *Great St. Martin, Cologne*, with its powerful central tower *(fig. 90)*, was built about the same time. The Church of Our Lady at Roermond in Holland is slightly later, and the Church of St. Quirin, Neuss, even dates from after 1209. – The double chapel at Schwarzrheindorf near Bonn, built 1151–73, deserves mention for its aesthetic perfection. A castle- and burial-chapel, it was built with two storeys on the model of the Palace Chapel at Aachen.

Westworks
The Carolingian westwork was another form that found a number of worthy successors during the twelfth century. Four splendid examples are the Cathedral of St. Patroclus, Soest, the seminary church at Freckenhorst and the monastery churches of Münstereifel and *Maursmün-ster (Lower Alsace)*, and of these the last-named is particularly remarkable for its balanced symmetry *(ill. 87)*.

Double chancels
Lastly, the imperial cathedrals of Mainz and Worms need further mention. These were begun during the Ottonian period but the main fabric of the present buildings dates from the twelfth

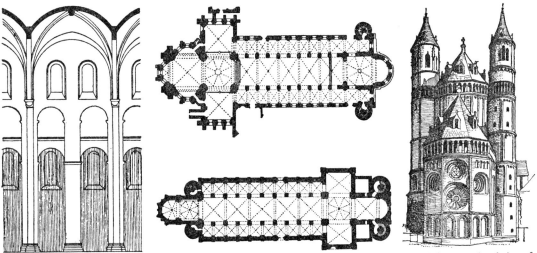

91 Mainz Cathedral, elevation (left) and ground plan (above centre)

92 Worms Cathedral, ground plan (below centre) and view of exterior

and thirteenth centuries. Both have double chancels with intricate tower complexes at the east and west ends, and they are vaulted on the square system. The nave of *Mainz Cathedral* was built during the period 1118–37 and the west end was added *c.* 1200–39 *(ill. 88* and *fig. 91)*. The west chancel is triconchal, as may have been the original building of 975–1009. The eastern part of Worms Cathedral dates from 1181, the nave from 1200 and the west end from the early thirteenth century *(fig. 92)*. The polygonal west end is strongly articulated and represents one of the finest achievements of the Late Romanesque Hohenstaufen style.

III Italy

Like German architecture, Italian architecture of the twelfth and thirteenth centuries did not have a uniform or systematic development. S. Zeno, Verona, built principally between 1125 and 1178, is a flat-ceilinged basilica with three aisles and a raised choir. Beneath the choir, the crypt opens out along its full width into the nave. The alternating columns and piers indicate a connection with Germany, but the tripartite monumental façade is typically Italian. The west façade of *S. Michele, Lucca (ill. 89)*, with its four storeys of colonnaded galleries, was built *c.* 1239 and belongs to the Late Romanesque style. The side walls are also articulated with blind arches and colonnades. Similar features are to be found on other buildings at Lucca, Pisa, Arezzo and Massa Maritima. Some of them were given an even more florid appearance by the use of variously coloured marble.

The Florentine Pre-Renaissance
Another type of marble decoration for interiors and façades was developed in Florence, involving the use of incrustations of coloured marble based on Early Christian and even Late Classical models. The most beautiful example is the small three-aisled basilican church of *S. Miniato al Monte, Florence*, built 1060/70–1207. It has an open roof and no transept *(ill. 90* and *fig. 93)*. The simple interior, which is more like an Early Christian than a Romanesque basilica, is

93   Florence, S. Miniato al Monte

94   Florence, Baptistery of S. Giovanni (after H. Koepf)

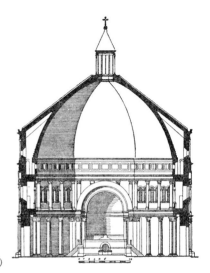

characterized by a raised chancel above an open crypt, and by alternating columns and piers with half-columns supporting arches spanning the nave. Because it provides a link between the Classical period and the early fifteenth-century Renaissance, eleventh- and twelfth-century Florentine architecture has been styled 'Pre-Renaissance'. Contemporary with S. Miniato is the *Baptistery of S. Giovanni, Florence*, a two-storeyed octagonal centralized structure roofed with a domical vault which is decorated with mosaics *(ill. 91* and *fig. 94)*. The practice of building separate, self-contained baptisteries had already been abandoned in other countries, and its retention in Italy further illustrates the affinity with Late Classical and Early Christian traditions. The baptisteries at Pisa, Cremona and Parma are of even later construction.

The Normans in Sicily

Twelfth-century Sicilian architecture occupies rather a special position because it represents a mixture of Norman, Byzantine and Arabic elements. This is illustrated particularly well by the chancel end of *Monreale Cathedral near Palermo*, a three-aisled flat-ceilinged basilica begun in 1174 *(ill. 92)*. The exterior view of the east end of Cefalù Cathedral, begun in 1131, presents a strong contrast to Monreale, being markedly northern Romanesque in character. The finest example of this hybrid architecture is the Cappella Palatina (1132–40) in the Norman royal palace at Palermo.

IV France

Tunnel-vaulted churches with galleries

The French schools of architecture were extremely active during this period, but only a few examples of their work can be mentioned here. *St. Sernin, Toulouse*, a three-aisled gallery basilica built 1095–1135, is of particular relevance as being a sister-building to Santiago de Compostela *(ill. 93* and *fig. 95)*. In plan, it corresponded to the gallery churches usually native to the Auvergne of which the best example is *St. Etienne, Nevers (ill. 95)*. Begun in 1063, it was one of the earliest large buildings in the West to be vaulted throughout. One of the most beautiful churches in Poitou in central France is St. Benoît-sur-Loire (1071–1131), a three-aisled basilica with an imposing square entrance building reminiscent of the German westwork, and a tunnel-vaulted chancel with ambulatory lined with chapels.

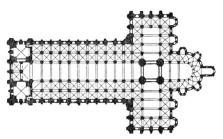

95   Toulouse, St. Sernin

96   Périgueux, St. Front (after H. Koepf)

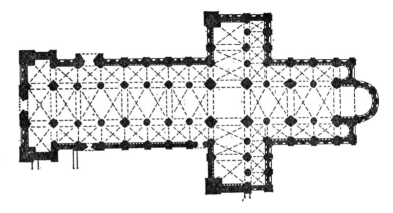

97 Durham Cathedral

Hall-churches

Notre Dame la Grande, Poitiers, is a typical example of Poitevin architecture in the first half of the twelfth century. It is a hall-church with tunnel-vaulted nave and narrow groin-vaulted side aisles. Its most impressive feature by far is the façade *(ill. 96)*. The central portal is flanked by two deep blind arches in a simulated version of the three-portal façade which was developed in the contemporary Abbey Church of St. Denis and which became a characteristic feature of Early and High Gothic architecture. Here the whole façade appears to have been made up of a mixture of elements borrowed from Roman triumphal arches and Roman town gates. The roughly contemporary façade of Angoulême Cathedral is related to it in style, although the interior follows the domed churches native to Aquitaine.

Domed churches

The most important of the domed churches of Aquitaine is *St. Front, Périgueux (ill. 94* and *fig. 96)*. It was begun *c.* 1120 and is on the plan of a Greek cross, following the pattern of St. Mark's, Venice. In both buildings the huge piers and broad tunnel arches have very much the same form, and above all give the interior the same heavy, bulky appearance. The concept of these massive walls and powerful arches is definitely Western rather than Early Christian or Byzantine.

V England

Durham: Norman rib-vaulting

Of all the French Romanesque schools, the Norman was the most capable of future development, and it was in England, after the Conquest in 1066, that the Norman school achieved its greatest successes. Among the many large churches begun soon after the Conquest, *Durham Cathedral* is one of the most impressive *(ill. 97* and *fig. 97)*. The foundation stone was laid in 1091. The cathedral was attached to a Benedictine abbey, an unknown situation on the Continent; the conjunction of cathedral and monastery was peculiarly English. It is a three-aisled gallery basilica with a double-tower façade, a nave of eight bays, a transept with an eastern side aisle and a three-aisled chancel consisting of a further three, or, including the transept side aisle, four bays. The chancel originally terminated in three semicircular apses, but these were replaced in 1242–89 with a straight-ended eastern transept known as the Chapel of the Nine Altars. The chancel aisles were vaulted *c.* 1096 and the rest of the building *c.* 1130. Rib vaults were used from the very beginning, and they are the first example of this type of vault that can be given a definite date. What we were discussing in connection with St. Etienne at Caen now becomes clear. The ribs, which constitute a plastic extension of the formative features of the walls, were erected in conjunction with the vaults themselves, and not put up previously to form a framework on which to compose the vaults *(ill. 98)*. The vaults are extremely heavy, being constructed of blocks of stone with copious mortaring, and they are markedly Romanesque in style. The thrust is taken up partly by the walls, and partly by flying buttresses situated below the gallery roof. The elevation was modelled on St. Etienne. Walls, supports and all structural elements are remarkably thick and powerful. The nave is *c.* 145 m long and only 9.96 m wide, a somewhat unusual proportion that was to become characteristic of English churches and was probably a legacy of the Anglo-Saxon period.

Ely: an unvaulted gallery basilica

The cathedrals of Winchester, Gloucester, Ely and several others were built at about the same time as Durham, and of these we shall briefly examine *Ely (ill. 99)*. It was begun in 1087 and work on the eastern part proceeded fairly rapidly until 1117. The cathedral was completed by the end of the twelfth century. In plan it roughly resembles Durham although even longer. There are thirteen bays in the nave and the two side aisles up to the three-aisled transept, and there were originally four chancel bays beyond. A further five bays were added *c.* 1240, terminating in a straight chancel end. The Norman building was unvaulted. In elevation, it consists of three storeys of almost equal height, comprising arcades, galleries and fenestration. This was the usual Norman way of treating the walls. The Ely nave offers a faster, tighter rhythm than Durham, being more rigorously articulated with a greater emphasis on the vertical. The division of the wall-surface into a clearly ordered series of boldly sculptured structural elements was taken even further than it had been at Caen. The west façade, which is formed like a transept and has central and corner towers, is a derivative of the Carolingian westwork.

VI The Range of Twelfth-Century Architecture

Tournai

The rib vaults of Durham Cathedral and the rigorous articulation of the walls of Ely together contained all the elements of the Gothic style, but the decisive step in that direction was taken neither in England nor in Normandy but in the Ile-de-France, where the first truly Gothic buildings were being erected at about this time. But we should not conclude our discussion on the Romanesque style without considering the immense variety of architectural solutions which characterized it. Another important twelfth-century building, which recalls both French and German influences, is *Tournai Cathedral (ill. 100)*, begun shortly before 1116 and virtually complete by the end of the twelfth century. It is a three-aisled gallery basilica with a three-aisled transept, also with galleries. The transept arms end in semicircular apses. The choir is a Gothic addition dating from 1242–1325. The transept was vaulted immediately, but the nave was not vaulted until 1777. This essentially horizontal elevation, comprising four storeys with no vertical interconnection at all, has been termed the 'viaduct system'. In view of the decisive part which vertical articulation played in almost every other large building of the time, its complete absence at Tournai is quite astonishing. By way of compensation, as it were, there is an extraordinarily powerful composition of five towers at the east end which makes the sanctuary appear a veritable citadel of God. This feature was influenced by the Carolingian-Ottonian tradition and appears in fact on several contemporary Early Gothic buildings.

Rome

Before proceeding to a consideration of Gothic architecture, one further example will illustrate the enormous architectural range of the twelfth century – the Church of *S. Maria in Trastevere, Rome*, which probably received its present form under Innocent II from 1138 onwards *(ill. 102)*. In the middle of the twelfth century, a complete throw-back to the Early Christian period was evolved. It is a three-aisled architrave basilica with heavy bracketed cornices, and a transept with a semicircular apse immediately ajoining it, but it does not bring into use any one of the many architectural ideas developed in the West, although by this time these ideas had reached their most perfect form almost everywhere.

7 Early and High Gothic

Characteristics: The invention of rib-vaulting signified that it was no longer necessary for vaulting compartments to be square, but it involved the exclusive use of pointed arches. Wall-surfaces were increasingly broken up to become pure articulated supporting structures, and to include large areas of window. The parts of the wall that had been suppressed reappeared on the outside in the form of buttresses and flying buttresses.

This system of construction necessitated a standardization of spatial units. Gothic architecture stood in a similar relationship to Romanesque as Early Christian and Byzantine architecture did to Roman in that it introduced a new element of weightlessness and spirituality, although with the difference that the greatly increased height of Gothic buildings did away with the last remaining vestiges of Classical proportion.

Materials: Freestone, brick, marble (in Italy) and wood.

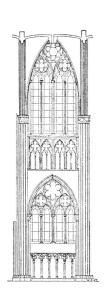

Strasbourg Cathedral, elevation

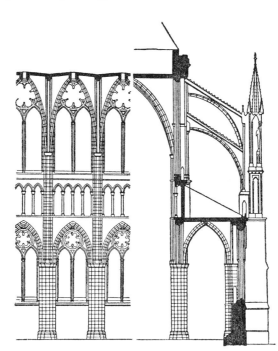

Reims Cathedral, longitudinal and cross section

I Early Gothic in Twelfth-Century France

The development of Gothic forms which began in the Ile-de-France around 1130 took place in the midst of the continuing influence of many Romanesque schools of architecture. These continued to thrive right up to the end of the century, and in many cases even into the middle of the next century. The Gothic school did not therefore immediately replace the Romanesque schools, but initially formed a part of them. It is only towards 1200, when the possibilities of the Gothic style began to crystallize that we can talk in terms of an actual Gothic style. Nevertheless we shall describe the evolution of this style within its context, from the very beginning right up to the full perfection which it achieved during the thirteenth century.

St. Denis: decorated portals and rib-vaulting
One of the key buildings of Early Gothic is the *Abbey Church of St. Denis*, near Paris *(ill. 101* and *fig. 98)*. The west front (without the tower extensions) was built by Abbot Suger in 1137–40. The twin-tower façade, modelled on that of St. Etienne, Caen, links the towers with the main building in a more organic way than does the original model. A new motif – the rose window – makes its appearance. Of particular importance are the three portals, where the concentration of sculptural decoration is more systematic than had been seen in France hitherto. These portals became a model for others, of which the first were those of the west façade of *Chartres Cathedral*, begun in 1140 and completed in the first stage when the south tower was finished in 1164 *(ill. 103)*. The next stage in the building of St. Denis was the erection of the chancel in 1140–4. The Carolingian church probably remained standing until the nave and transepts were built in the thirteenth century, when the superstructure of Suger's chancel was altered. We need only consider the lower part of the chancel in this case, which is completely original. Instead of the usual simple curved ambulatory with chapels radiating outwards from

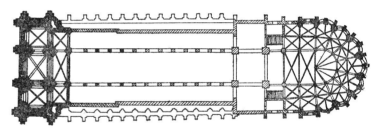

98 Paris, Abbey Church of St. Denis

it, this is a much more complex design, with a double ambulatory arising out of the double side aisles of the chancel, the outer wall consisting of a continuous, undulating succession of bays. The flowing line of this outer wall could then be completely broken up with windows. However, the multiple fragments of space thus formed could not be roofed with groin-vaulting on account of their irregular shape. By using Norman rib-vaulting, but erecting the ribs first in the manner of scaffolding, and the filling subsequently, the architects managed not only to reduce the weight and lighten the construction, but also to free themselves from the tyranny of the semicircle and the square ground plan. The pointed arches developed in Burgundy could now be used in conjunction with groins and partition and reinforcing arches. All these discoveries allowed a far freer and more flowing interplay of space than had hitherto been possible. The wall was displaced to an even greater extent, and replaced by large windows which, rather than admitting the unbroken light of day, produced a kind of multi-coloured twilight by means of stained glass. Thus the inside area viewed from within appeared enveloped in a shimmering film of gorgeous splendour.

Sens

Shortly after 1130, at about the same time as St. Denis, work was begun on *Sens Cathedral*, which was completed in 1168 *(ill. 104)*. Sens was the most important archdiocese in France, with the suffraganates of Paris and Chartres under its aegis. The cathedral comprises a nave and two side aisles, a chancel ending in a semicircle, with ambulatory, three irregularly-shaped chapels and no transepts, and its size is remarkable: length 113.5 m, width of nave 15.25 m, height 24.4 m. The width and height of the nave are related in a proportion of approximately 1 : 1.6. The extremely marked alternation of columns and pillars groups together the twelve bays in pairs under sexpartite Norman rib vaults. The elevation is in three storeys, although the triforium is not yet a genuine one but seems rather to recall a gallery arcade, which moreover does not lead into a gallery but underneath the side aisle roof. The powerful walls are articulated as far as possible with sculptured sections. The round columns, varying in strength according to whether they support reinforcing arches, diagonal ribs or partition arches, rise without interruption up to the beginning of the vault. The remaining wall-surface is sharply delineated with round and rectangular strips. The way the arrangement of masses is conceived is still Romanesque and gives an impression of quietness, solidity and power.

Churches with galleries and triforia

During the latter half of the twelfth century, new cathedrals sprang up in rapid succession all over the Ile-de-France and the neighbouring regions of Champagne and Picardy, making use of the forms that had been tried out at St. Denis and Sens without, however, at first developing them in any systematic way. The legacy of the Romanesque style is still strongly in evidence, particularly in the inclusion of galleries; these were considered necessary inasmuch as they assumed some of the weight off the main nave vault and were used in the cathedrals of Senlis, Noyon, Soissons, Laon, Paris (Notre Dame), Mantes and Châlons-sur-Marne. *Noyon Cathedral*, begun *c.* 1150, is remarkable in that for the first time a genuine triforium appears, dissolving the remaining solid wall-surface between gallery and window area by means of arcades which enclose a passage-way. The choir resembles St. Denis, reproducing the shape of the original

99 Laon Cathedral, west façade
(after Dehio Atlas, IV, plate 408)

model particularly when viewed from the outside *(ill. 105)*. The transept arms, like the
chancel, terminate in a semicircle.

The Romanesque spirit is strongly in evidence in *Laon Cathedral*, 1155/60 to *c*. 1220 *(fig.
100)*, a three-aisled gallery basilica with a three-aisled transept, also with galleries. The original
chancel comprised three bays with a semicircular end and an ambulatory, but this was replaced in the early thirteenth century by a ten-bayed chancel 45 m long with a straight end,

100 Laon
Cathedral,
elevation
and section
(after Dehio
Atlas, IV,
plate 373)

making the overall length of the cathedral 110.5 m. The nave was 12 m wide and 24 m high.
Each sexpartite rib vault embraces two bays to form a square. The four-storeyed elevation
includes a genuine triforium. The plastic articulation of the walls has here been taken even
further, although the use of round and pointed arches side by side made a systematic continuity of line impossible. Particularly Romanesque is the fact that the canopies of the vaults
and the articulation of the walls are not identical in form, although they are closely connected.
The 40 m high crossing and the long chancel show an English influence. As well as the tower
crossing there were to have been four high towers at the transept ends, like at Tournai, but
only two of them were erected. However, these two, together with the twin towers of the
façade, created a rich exterior formation not unlike that of certain German buildings *(fig. 99)*.
This fact as well as the extreme plastic articulation of the façade and towers explains why Laon
Cathedral was to have such influence on German architecture.

Notre Dame, Paris: increased height

At the same time as Laon Cathedral was being built, work was begun on the *Cathedral of
Notre Dame in Paris (ills 106 and 107)*. The foundations were probably laid in 1163 under
Bishop Maurice de Sully. By 1177, the chancel was almost finished and by 1196 virtually the
whole building was complete except for the roof. It consists of five continuous aisles, forming
a double ambulatory round the chancel end, and measures 130 m in length. The width of the
nave is 12 m and the height 35 m. The original elevation comprised four storeys. Instead of a

triforium above the galleries, there was a strip of wall containing circular openings, and above that a series of small windows developed continuously immediately beneath the vaults. During the nineteenth century, these features were restored by Viollet-le-Duc in the last bay of the nave before the crossing. The lighting, which is weak even today, was even less adequate in the original building. As at Laon, the canopies of the sexpartite vaults rest on slender engaged columns dividing the wall-surface, but here they seem to merge more closely into each other because all the members are simpler and because the increased height (the proportion is almost 1 : 3) imparts an insubstantial character to the interior.

Hall-churches in Poitou

The series of classic Gothic buildings begins with the erection of the cathedrals of Bourges and Chartres, but before turning to them we must consider a few examples of Early Gothic outside the central area of development. These are often later in date than the earliest buildings of the High Gothic style, and they demonstrate the relatively slow process of adoption of the new architectural language. – In Poitou, a unique solution was discovered which found few successors in France but which had a decisive influence on German architecture. The first genuine hall-church, *Poitiers Cathedral (ill. 108)*, developed out of the Romanesque tunnel-vaulted church with nave and side aisles of almost equal height. Planned in 1162 and begun in 1166, the cathedral was completed in 1271 with the exception of the two western bays which are later and different in style. There is no transept, and the straight chancel end contains three shallow apses. The nave and side aisles are of the same height and almost the same width. The arcades between them extend right up to the vaults, and have extremely widely spaced pillars. Eight-part domical vaults rest on lateral, longitudinal and diagonal ribs, almost as if one of the domed churches of Aquitaine had been combined with a typically Poitevin hall-church.

Hall-churches in Westphalia

Paderborn Cathedral is a good example of the hall-church as developed in Germany, possibly without any connection with Poitou. In the rebuilding which took place *c*. 1225–80, certain elements of the old structure were retained, notably the two chancels and two transepts, and the nave became a three-aisled hall with unribbed groin-vaulting *(ill. 109)*. Such features of the Early Gothic style as were adopted appear to have been re-transformed into the Romanesque.

II Cistercian Gothic

To date, with the exception of St. Denis, only cathedrals have been mentioned. This is not so much a deliberate choice as a reflection of the fact that by this period episcopal churches had assumed the greater importance, architecturally speaking. Next in importance was still the ascetic ideology of the Cistercian Order. In discussing Fontenay, the closeness of the Romanesque style of the Burgundy school to Early Gothic became evident. As a result the Cistercians had no difficulty in adopting the new architectural language in its simplest forms and even spreading it outside France.

Hall-churches in Portugal

An example of this diffusion was the monastery church of *Alcobaça*, north of Lisbon, which was originally intended to follow the plan of Clairvaux as extended in 1154–74. Begun after 1178 and completed in 1223, it did in fact follow the Clairvaux plan, but the elevation was altered to conform with the Poitou school *(ill. 110)*. It became a three-aisled hall-church of twelve bays, with transept and chancel ambulatory with nine radial chapels. The rib vaults are markedly domical in form like those in Poitiers Cathedral. Alcobaça is one of the finest examples of Cistercian Gothic architecture. Bare of any sculptural or painted decoration, its sole effect lies in the simple beauty of its form, the rhythmic succession of the bays and the perfection of its proportions. The monastery itself, which grew steadily in size right up until the eighteenth century, is also very beautiful in its simplicity and is an excellent example of highly functional organization.

Italy

It was the Cistercians too who first introduced Gothic forms to Italy, as they had done to Spain and Portugal. The three-aisled basilican monastery church of *Fossanova* (1187–1208) was built according to the strict plan of the mother churches in Burgundy. Instead of an ambulatory with radial chapels, it has a straight chancel end and the nave is still groin-vaulted *(ill. 111)*. Only the Cistercian church at Casamari (1203–17) had rib vaults throughout.

III Early Gothic and Romanesque

The Cistercians also introduced the Early Gothic style into Germany. The Romanesque pillared basilica (originally flat-ceilinged) of the monastery at *Maulbronn* was completed in 1178, and beginning in 1210 a vestibule was added to it. The springers of the vault ribs in the vestibule were set at different heights to give the arches the same radii *(ill. 112)*, a further example of a Gothic construction being given a Romanesque interpretation. The chancel of Magdeburg Cathedral, built 1209–31, has galleries vaulted in a similar manner. Magdeburg's heavy, compact articulation is typically Romanesque.

Double chancels

The pronounced solemnity of the Romanesque style also characterizes the cathedrals of Bamberg and Naumburg, which date from the first half of the thirteenth century and are famous for their sculptures. Both basilicas have double chancels, plans based on the square of the crossing and rich tower formations. The west towers were modelled on Laon, and those of *Bamberg* are particularly opulent *(fig. 101)*.

Limburg an der Lahn

The seminary church of *St. Georg, Limburg an der Lahn*, was also modelled on Laon, not in form but as far as the number of towers and the whole pattern of the interior elevation were concerned. St. Georg was begun before 1220 and consecrated in 1235 *(fig. 102)*. The building is very low (length 54.5 m, width 35.4 m), so that the seven towers are grouped close together

forming a powerfully vertical composition. The rich articulation of the four-storeyed interior, crowded as it is on to a relatively small area, hollows out and shapes the walls in a way that is eminently Late Romanesque *(ill. 113)*.

England

In many respects, a similar adaptation of French Early Gothic forms occurred in the rebuilding of *Canterbury Cathedral (ill. 114)* undertaken by William of Sens in 1175. This three-aisled basilican church with transept, galleries, chancel ambulatory and round eastern apse retained a good deal of the Late Romanesque spirit in the robust formation of all its members, the slightly unsettled crowding together of different shapes and the ponderousness of the vaulting. Between 1397 and 1400, a new nave and transept and a 71 m high crossing tower were added, and the old building became the chancel of the new cathedral, which received the elongated form typical of English cathedrals, measuring 155.5 m in length.

Assisi

The first church of the Franciscan Order of mendicant friars, *S. Francesco, Assisi*, another example of the combination of Romanesque and Early Gothic elements was begun in 1228 *(ill. 115)*. It was required to be as simple as a Cistercian church and was to be used principally for preaching, so it took the form of a single-aisled hall-like church with transept and apse (length 74.1 m, width 13.6 m). It was built on top of an older structure that was to become the tomb of St. Francis. The crossing, the transept arms and the four bays of the nave are all square, and are roofed with rib vaults resting on powerful clusters of engaged columns. The lower half of the walls presents a smooth surface and the upper, fenestrated half is set back, leaving a narrow passageway. The church was probably inspired by Angers Cathedral which was also single-aisled and of which at least the nave and one of the transept arms were completed by *c.* 1230. The engaged columns and the capitals, however, were derived from the Cistercian Early Gothic style of Burgundy.

Bourges

The transition from Early to High Gothic is represented by *Bourges Cathedral*. It was begun *c.*
1190 by Archbishop Henry de Sully, a brother of the founder of Notre Dame, Paris, and
finished towards 1300 with the completion of the five-part west façade. In plan, it is related to
Notre Dame, having no transept and comprising five aisles of thirteen bays with a semicircular
chancel end and a double ambulatory, originally without radial chapels though these were
later added (length 118 m, width 41 m, height 37.15 m). The elevation, however, is different.
There were no galleries to counteract the thrust of the huge vaults and the architect evidently
did not dare to entrust their support solely to flying buttresses, which had not been sufficiently
tested by this period. They were in fact first used on a large scale in Laon Cathedral and in
Notre Dame itself. The solution adopted was to make the inner side aisles higher than the
outer, so high indeed that the supports of the wide nave arcades measure 17 m. The elevation
of the nave, with a triforium and a fenestration storey, is repeated in the inner side aisles. A
perfect piece of scaffolding might have been created had not the sexpartite rib vaults of the
nave necessitated the retention of the square plan. As in Notre Dame, the articulation of the
walls is extremely delicate; here in fact even less of the wall surface remains *(ill. 116)*. – That
Bourges Cathedral did not become the prototype for classical Cathedral Gothic was due to
this rather particular construction. Nevertheless, it did inspire several French and more particularly Spanish churches, as for example the 33 m high chancel of *Le Mans Cathedral*, begun
in 1217. Le Mans differs from Bourges, however, in having no triforium, thus eliminating the
last remaining area of wall. One can see from the exterior the multitude of buttresses and
flying buttresses extending up through several storeys which were necessary to shore up this
almost wall-less glass case *(fig. 103)*. These buttresses in fact represent the masses of masonry
that have been pushed out from the interior and from the shell of the building.

Chartres: the first of the classical High Gothic cathedrals

It was *Chartres Cathedral*, built at the same time as Bourges, that had the greatest influence on
future development *(ill. 117)*. The previous building had been destroyed by fire in 1194 with
the exception of the west façade, and the new building begun immediately. Work proceeded
at a remarkable pace and the building was ready for vaulting as early as 1220. The final

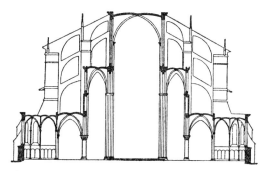

103 Le Mans Cathedral (after H. Koepf)

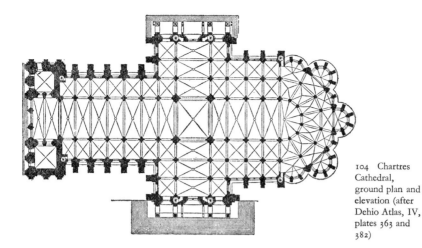

104 Chartres Cathedral, ground plan and elevation (after Dehio Atlas, IV, plates 363 and 382)

consecration took place in 1260. The cathedral has an extremely lucid plan comprising a three-aisled basilica, a three-aisled marginally narrower transept, and a five-aisled chancel with double ambulatory and five radial chapels. It measures 130 m in length and the nave is 16.4 m wide and 36.55 m high. The elevation is just as precise, with a shallow triforium above the high arcades and a tall, completely fenestrated clerestory *(fig. 104)*. Quadripartite rib vaults link the aisles in an uninterrupted series of bays; the alternation of columns and piers and the square system are finally abandoned. The powerful, uniform framework of the building rises firmly and tautly, and the nave and transept are keyed together with perfect regularity. The side aisle walls are also almost completely fenestrated, so that very little of the shell of the building remains. It is virtually 'dematerialized', achieving a degree of spirituality such as architecture had never succeeded in expressing before. Ultimately this form was derived from Roman architecture, via the Romanesque style, but it appears in complete contrast. Classical proportions, in particular, had by now been completely abandoned, for it had become impossible to apply the proportions of the human body to the columns, pillars and engaged columns of the Gothic cathedral. Also the tremendous increase in height had made the interior appear almost limitless, since the vaults lay in a perpetual, mysterious twilight produced by the stained glass.

Amiens: the prototype of classical High Gothic

Shortly afterwards the cathedrals of Reims (1210) and Amiens (1220) were begun. Adopting the plan of Chartres, they made it more delicate and at the same time reached an even greater height. *Amiens Cathedral* (length 133.5 m, width of nave 14.6 m, height 42.3 m) may be regarded as the purest realization of classical High Gothic *(ill. 118* and *fig. 106)*. During the course of building, it was decided to introduce a fenestrated triforium, a feature which was probably first used by Pierre de Montereau in building the nave and transept of St. Denis from 1231 onwards, and by which the last remaining wall surface was transformed into glass. – *Reims Cathedral* demonstrated how the entrance façade could be lightened and made to lose its concreteness *(ill. 119)*. Yet a comparison of the interior and exterior clearly shows how the whole

105 Reims Cathedral, west façade (after Dehio Atlas, IV, plate 412)

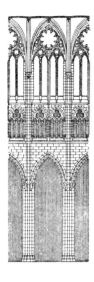

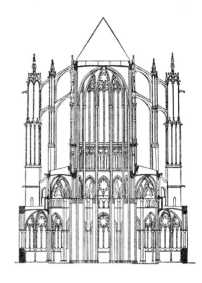

106   Amiens Cathedral, elevation (after H. Koepf)

107   Beauvais Cathedral, section (after H. Koepf)

fabric of the building has been dematerialized. In fact the greatest mass of masonry is concentrated in the façade, giving some of the sculpturing of the statue portals an almost Classical plasticity *(fig. 105)*.

The Sainte-Chapelle, Paris: a shrine of glass

The fullest expression of the concept of the glass case or shrine of light was achieved in the chapel of the royal palace in Paris, known as the *Sainte-Chapelle* and built by Pierre de Montereau *c.* 1243–8 *(ill. 120)*. The low ground floor has three aisles, while the upper floor consists of a single aisle and is extremely high (20.5 m, width 10.7 m, length 33 m). The walls are almost completely replaced by windows which rise above a low base, articulated with blind arcades and niches, right up into the vaults. The vaults themselves soar above this celestial shrine of light like a starry canopy.

Beauvais: the extreme increase in height

The choir of *Beauvais Cathedral* literally represents the zenith of classical Gothic architecture. The airy interior measures 47.6 m in height, while the width of the nave is only some 15 m *(fig. 107)*. The building was planned 1230–40 with the bays as wide as they are today, and begun in 1247. In 1284, however, some time after it was completed, the vaults collapsed and the bays had to be halved. The transept was erected *c.* 1500 at the very end of the Late Gothic period. The nave of the present cathedral is the old Carolingian basilica.

V The Dissemination of Cathedral Gothic

The influence of the classical Gothic style began to spread beyond the original sphere after 1230. The chancel of the five-aisled cathedral of Troyes, which had been begun before 1228, was given a fenestrated triforium *c.* 1235, and in 1240 Tours Cathedral was begun based on the same system.

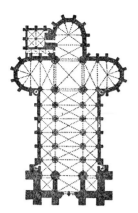

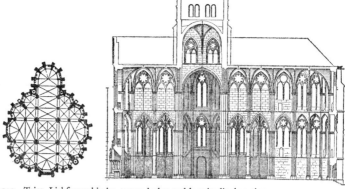

108　Marburg, St. Elizabeth

109　Trier, Liebfrauenkirche, ground plan and longitudinal section (after Dehio Atlas, V, plate 458)

Cologne and Strasbourg

Cologne Cathedral was begun in 1248 *(ill. 121)*. The chancel was complete by 1322, but the whole building was not finished until 1842–80 (length 136.5 m, width of nave 13.9 m, height 45.5 m). A novel feature was the linking together of the triforium and clerestory to form a vast single wall of glass. All structural sections and elements are of the utmost delicacy, emphasizing the insubstantial nature of the glass shell, and at the same time strengthening the impression of soaring weightlessness. Yet the building is in no way weak or imprecise; on the contrary, there is a springy, elastic clarity about its every line. – The elevation of the three-aisled nave of *Strasbourg Cathedral*, built 1250–76 *(ill. 122)*, was modelled on the most advanced example of the High Gothic, the nave of St. Denis, but since the proportions of width to height (1 : 2) were dictated by the late Romanesque east end, the resulting spatial impression is quite different.

Marburg and Trier: special architectural forms

The church of *St. Elizabeth, Marburg (ill. 123* and *fig. 108)* shows how the influence of the older German traditions upon the Gothic style gave rise to some highly individual forms which deviated from the classical system. Built 1235–83, it is a three-aisled hall-church with a triconchal east end. The triconchal structure was derived from Late Romanesque buildings in the Rhineland and the hall system was adopted from nearby Westphalian examples. In elevation, however, it departs from Romanesque tradition and follows the pure Gothic form as developed by the Soissons school, adopting the two storeys of fenestration without triforium. These form as it were a skin of glass stretched right round the walls. The shaping of the individual sections followed the example of Reims. – The *Liebfrauenkirche, Trier (ill. 124* and *fig. 109)* was begun shortly after 1235 and completed *c.* 1253. It replaced what remained of the Early Christian basilica, which had still been in use as late as 1233. As a centralized structure, it bore no relationship either to its predecessor or to French models, although the concept of the diagonal chapels and the formal apparatus (cf. S. Yved de Braisne, Soissons school) stemmed from there. The interior is characterized by a dramatic graduation in height rising from the single-storeyed corner sections through the two-storeyed arms and culminating in the

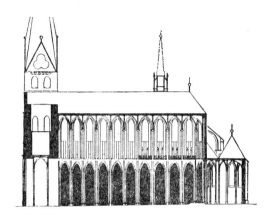

110 Lübeck, St. Marien, longitudinal section (after H. Koepf)

crossing which is 35.16 m high. Where areas of walls remain, as above the arcades of the cross arms, they appear like weightless, insubstantial membranes. The extremely slender columns are applied almost graphically.

Lübeck: brick construction

A two-storeyed elevation is also found in the brick basilica of *St. Marien, Lübeck (ill. 125* and *fig. 110)*. The building was begun as a hall-church probably soon after 1251, but was developed as a three-aisled basilica. It has no genuine transept and the chancel apse merges into the ring of chapels. The inspiration probably came from Soissons Cathedral and ultimately goes back to St. Denis. S. Marien was the first urban parish church to attempt to compete with the cathedrals in size and form, and represents the shift of initiative in church building which was to be characteristic of the Late Gothic period.

The Cistercians

The Cistercian monastery church at Altenberg near Cologne (1255–1379) represents a contradiction of the customary simplicity of Cistercian architecture since it was built according to the most fully developed Cathedral Gothic plan. A three-aisled columnar basilica with a transept, choir ambulatory and ring of chapels, it has a three-storeyed elevation including a triforium and open buttress work. The only concession to Cistercian principles is the absence of towers and of any decoration. The tracery window that almost completely fills the entrance wall was not added until after 1379.

Mendicant friars

The churches built by the orders of mendicant friars which were founded all over Europe from 1230 onwards were never without a certain grandeur. Despite every effort to achieve the greatest simplicity and to reduce all elements to a bare necessity, the spaciousness of these three-aisled vaulted basilicas almost invariably gave them an impressively monumental character. The Dominican church of *S. Maria Novella, Florence (ill. 126)*, begun some time before 1246, is a typical example. Despite individual peculiarities, all the following churches (and there are many other examples) share an international language of expression by virtue of the fact that they were designed for preaching and thus required a clear, open interior which

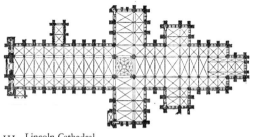

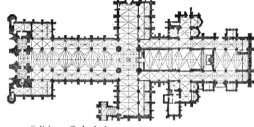

111   Lincoln Cathedral   112   Salisbury Cathedral

would allow the preacher to be seen from all parts of the building: viz S. Francesco, Bologna, 1236, the Dominican church of SS. Giovanni e Paolo, Venice, 1246, and the Dominican church at Regensburg, *c.* 1260.

English High Gothic: Lincoln and Salisbury

Not only was the High Gothic style adopted earlier in England than anywhere else, it was also much more decisively transformed into an individual mode of expression. Its newness is particularly apparent in the nave and Angels' Choir of *Lincoln Cathedral (ills 127, 128* and *fig. 111).* The ten-bayed nave and side aisles were begun in 1192 and were virtually complete by 1233. The original Gothic chancel end was pulled down and the three-aisled straight-ended Angels' Choir erected between *c.* 1255 and 1320, increasing the overall length to 146 m. The retention of two transepts goes back to the tradition of Cluny III, and cloisters and a freestanding chapter-house were added for the monastery to which the cathedral was attached. The nave is extremely broad in proportion to its height and has widely spaced arcades. Every line and form is very precise. The typically Norman division of wall-surfaces and the articulation of the masonry has been developed to the maximum extent without, however, creating an actual skeleton as was done in France. This is typified in the construction of the vaults. Sexpartite and quadripartite rib vaults are here transformed into something that no longer bears any relation to any systematic type of elevation. The concept of the rib vault as the apex of a skeletal framework is denied completely by the longitudinal rib and the clusters of six diagonal ribs which fan out from each pillar, introducing a linear decorative element in place of the rigorous logic of the vertical system of construction. The possibilities inherent in this system were grasped very quickly at Lincoln itself and are displayed in the Angels' Choir. This type of graphic abstraction, peculiar to England, is known not unjustly as the Decorated style. – Somewhat similar is *Salisbury Cathedral (ills 129, 130* and *fig. 112).* Of all the English High Gothic cathedrals, Salisbury gives the most uniform impression owing to the fact that it was built in an extremely short space of time, between 1220 and *c.* 1270. In plan it conforms fairly closely to Lincoln, comprising two transepts and a straight chancel end and having an overall length of 144 m. The east end constitutes a Lady Chapel, itself a typically English feature which generally adjoined the retrochoir. The exterior as well as the ground plan makes it clear that the central crossing divides the nave from the presbytery. The central point of the crossing, almost exactly at the half-way point, is emphasized on the exterior by a 123 m spire, and on the interior by a vertical shaft of space into which the four arms of the building flow. – The English church most strongly indebted to the French Gothic is Westminster Abbey, begun in 1245.

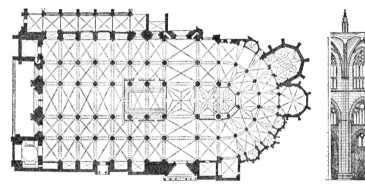

113   Toledo Cathedral,
ground plan and elevation

Spanish High Gothic

Of the three most important Spanish cathedrals founded in the thirteenth century – Burgos, Toledo and Leon – it was Leon that most closely followed the classical French form, like Cologne Cathedral with which it was roughly contemporary. *Toledo*, on the other hand, begun in 1224, was modelled on Bourges and Le Mans, and itself shows the derivation of later Spanish developments *(ill. 131* and *fig. 113)*. It is a five-aisled basilica with side aisles graduated in height, a non-projecting transept and a double ambulatory with a semicircle of shallow chapels. The elevation is in three storeys, with the triforium and clerestory fenestration linked even more closely than at Cologne.

Italian Gothic

Lastly, the way in which French Cathedral Gothic was adapted in Italy is shown by *Siena Cathedral*, begun in 1229 *(ill. 132)*. It comprises a hexagonal domed crossing, which extends beyond the width of the nave and draws together the transept arms and the chancel in a most unusual way, and a rib-vaulted nave of five bays with side aisles. The elevation is in two storeys divided by a continuous bracketed cornice. Alternating courses of two different colours in the supports and walls emphasize the horizontal character of the building. Verticality and the idea of the skeletal framework are both rejected. Similarly the façade, which has no towers, bears very little relation to the interior but constitutes an independent frontispiece, although with its three portals, galleries and rose windows, it clearly follows the scheme developed in the French cathedrals. – Far more Gothic in character is the church of *S. Andrea, Vercelli (ill. 133)*, which was begun *c.* 1219 possibly by the architect Benedetto Antelami. Even so its proportions, the

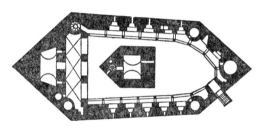

114   Kaub, near Koblenz, Palace

115   Goslar, Imperial Palace (after H. Koepf)

weight of its members, the domed crossing and the composition of the exterior give it an appearance which is closer to Early Gothic and even Romanesque than to High Gothic, and which is similar to many contemporary German churches.

Castles and fortresses

For the first time since the Roman period secular architecture can also be discussed – not actual dwelling-houses, for these, if one disregards monasteries, had not yet achieved artistic form, but institutional buildings associated with emperors and kings. Pride of place is taken by the *Castel del Monte, Apulia,* built by Frederick II *c.* 1230–40 *(ill. 135).* Two storeys, each comprising eight trapezoid rooms, are grouped around an octagonal court 35 m in diameter. The outer corners are stressed by octagonal towers containing staircases, bathrooms and other utility rooms. The overall diameter is 80 m. Details of the articulation indicate a debt to French Gothic, but the building as a whole was probably inspired by Islamic architecture of the Omayyad period. – Among German palaces that continued the Carolingian-Ottonian tradition through the twelfth and thirteenth centuries, those of *Goslar (fig. 115),* Gelnhausen, *Kaub (fig. 114),* Eger and the Wartburg near Eisenach should be mentioned. – The principal fortresses of this period are the fortress of Eltz on the Moselle, the Castle of the Counts of Flanders, Ghent, and Conway Castle in Wales. Their appeal is due not so much to artistic considerations as to the romantic associations they conjure up. The same considerations may be applied to the fortified towns, of which particularly impressive examples are preserved at Avila, Angers and Aigues Mortes. – The earliest urban architecture worthy of mention began first in Holland and Italy towards the end of the thirteenth century, and will be mentioned in the next chapter.

8 Late Gothic

Characteristics: Late Gothic architecture made use of the same elements as Early and High Gothic but moved away from the radical character of the pure, articulated supporting structure. Walls became more solid again, and larger surfaces appeared. Interiors became more lucid and precise. Proportions were no longer exaggeratedly stretched, though they did not return to the purity of Classical tradition.
Late Gothic decoration – tracery work, pinnacles, gables, net-vaulting etc. – was particularly rich.

Materials: Freestone, brick, marble (in Italy) and wood.

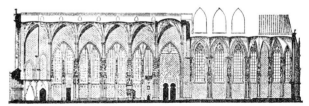

Vienna, Cathedral of St. Stephen, longitudinal section

Schwäbisch-Gmünd, Heiligkreuzkirche

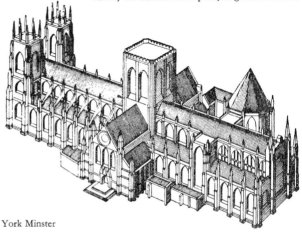

York Minster

By the end of the thirteenth century, the Gothic forms developed in France had been accepted throughout Europe, establishing a common architectural language that was more homogeneous than at any previous period in history. The discipline of classical High Gothic was quickly abandoned and new lines of development began which were to assume very different forms in different countries. The principles of dematerialization and incorporeality, however, were adhered to everywhere. Though buildings became more solid in appearance with more of the wall surface remaining, the walls themselves did not become any heavier but appeared like thin membranes. There was less emphasis on height and spatial units were more clearly defined, more 'earthly' as it were, though without actually becoming firm plastic shapes; there was still a certain transparency, a certain lack of logic about them. Decorative elements became richer and were often distributed over expansive surfaces with a sort of linear abstraction. – Secular architecture, particularly that of the middle classes, began increasingly to rival the hitherto undisputed leadership of church architecture. Towns began to assume an importance they had not had since Classical times.

So many fourteenth- and fifteenth-century buildings have been preserved that our selection must be even more limited than before. A survey of individual lines of development in different countries would obscure the fact that many of them ran parallel to each other. The best approach is to examine a cross-section every fifty years or so, which will in fact reveal some quite astonishing parallels. On the whole it is true to say that Late Gothic architecture was most abundant in England and Germany. France, after its pioneering work and the splendours of the twelfth and thirteenth centuries, produced comparatively little. The Late Gothic architecture of Spain was certainly magnificent but its development was rather biased in one direction. Italy continued to treat the Gothic style in a most un-Gothic way and was the first country to produce an entirely new mode of architectural expression in the Renaissance of the fifteenth century.

I About 1300

England: linear abstraction

The development of the Late Gothic style found its most homogeneous form in England. Originality was limited to changes of decorative detail; no new solutions were explored for the building as a whole. The systematic skeletal structure continued to be modified in favour of the sort of linear abstraction apparent in the case of Lincoln Cathedral and which was

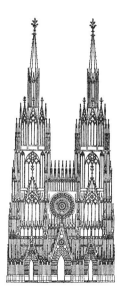

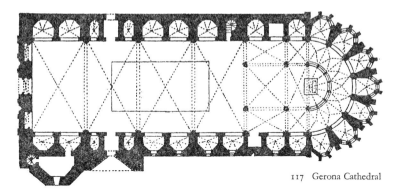

117 Gerona Cathedral

without structural logic. Alterations were begun in 1275 to the three-bayed Lady Chapel of the Norman *Exeter Cathedral (ill. 134)*. By the beginning of the fourteenth century, the eight bays of the three-aisled presbytery had been added, and the nave was completed before the middle of the century, giving the cathedral the typically English elongated plan. The elevation comprises three storeys in the classical Gothic tradition but is relatively low, with the pillars of the arcades spaced widely apart. The dissolution of all the members into individual sharply linear units is seen at its most extreme in the palmate fan vaults with their continuous central rib.

Germany: plane walls

A parallel to this extremely linear treatment can be seen in a related tendency in the façade (begun 1276) of *Strasbourg Cathedral (ill. 136* and *fig. 116)*. This was the use of planes, particularly in the two lower storeys. The original plan envisaged a continuous upward movement with each new form arising from the preceding form, and each storey from the storey below. In the two lower storeys, however, this plan recedes into the background, giving way to static sections, because a thin screen of free-standing tracery work is set like a transparent plane in front of the walls. The north tower was built by Ulrich von Ensingen of Ulm. It was begun in 1402 and completed in 1439. – The retention of tall church towers represented the continuation of an ancient heritage, although their number was reduced to the two towers of the typical High Gothic façade. Occasionally only one tower was built. In that case, it was made particularly tall, as displayed for example by the crossing tower in England and the façade tower in Germany.

Single-tower façades

In terms of beauty of form and audacity, the single-tower façade of *Freiburg Cathedral (ill. 137)* was never surpassed. The tower was erected between 1270 and 1350 and is 115 m in height. The flat surfaces of the lower section emphasize the richness of the hollowed-out octagon with its four corner towers and the intricately perforated spire. – The façade tower of Ulm Cathedral is modelled on Freiburg, but is even higher (162 m) and more elaborate. It was not completed until the nineteenth century. – Single-tower façades also occurred in Holland. The powerful tower of *St. Rombout, Mecheln*, begun in 1341 *(ill. 138)*, is not hollowed out like the tower at Freiburg but achieves its lightness by the wealth of Late Gothic decoration applied to the outer skin.

Quasi-pictorial wall compositions

The planes and lines which appeared on the Strasbourg façade found a uniquely magnificent expression in the west façade of the contemporary Cistercian church at *Chorin* in the Mark of Brandenburg (1273–1334, *ill. 139*). Despite the limitations of brick construction, which does not lend itself easily to rich decoration, this quasi-pictorial frontispiece, divided into three parts lying in different planes, gives an impression of severity and elegance at one and the same time. It is a genuine composition, springing from an appreciation of abstract beauty. An astonishing parallel is the chancel wall of the Franciscan church of *S. Croce, Florence*, which was begun a year or two after the Chorin church and was built over roughly the same period. Here, however, it occurs not on the exterior but inside the building *(ill. 140)*. S. Croce is a three-aisled basilica with an open roof, a transept and a narrow chancel with five rectangular chapels on each side. The windows in the chancel end and the windows of the narrow side chapels, which are on different planes, appear to be drawn forward into the same plane as the windows in the wall between chancel and nave, so that the whole of this wall, 19.5 m wide, gives the impression of an artistic composition. Providing as it were a screen of light for the sanctuary, it is the crowning glory of this eminently simple hall-like basilica. The powerful continuous bracketed cornice emphasizes the broadness of the interior, although the spacious nave is higher (34.5 m) than Notre Dame and almost as high as Reims.

Spain: departure from the skeletal structure

The transition from the transparent planes and the fluidity of the skeletal structure again led to a related composition in *Palma de Mallorca Cathedral*, begun in 1298 or 1300 *(ill. 141)*. This three-aisled basilica has no transept and terminates in three apses which are lower than the nave. The wall surface above them is filled with large rose windows, creating a sort of grand tripartite interior frontispiece. The side aisles are 30 m high and the nave is 40 m high, imparting the aspect of a hall-church to the cathedral, the more so since the arcades are extremely widely spaced and the smooth, slender octagonal pillars allow an almost unimpeded vista. In Barcelona Cathedral, begun in 1298, the side aisles were built even higher, leaving only a narrow strip of small round windows in place of a clerestory. Some time later, in 1312, the basilican chancel, ambulatory and radial chapels of *Gerona Cathedral* were begun *(ill. 142* and *fig. 117)*. When it was decided in 1417 to continue the building under Guillermo Boffig, an enormous hall-like nave was added, measuring 62 x 23 m, with the result that, as at Palma, the wall between chancel and nave formed an interior 'frontispiece' with three graduated arch openings and three round windows. The rib vaults of this nave are among the most audacious constructions of the entire Middle Ages. Their span of 23 m is almost exactly that of the vaults of the Basilica of Constantine, Rome. – The same striving after a well-ordered, expansive composition characterizes the façade of *Orvieto Cathedral*, begun *c.* 1310 by Lorenzo Maitani and Andrea Pisano on the model of Siena *(ill. 143)*.

France: brick Gothic

French architecture at this time had not yet freed itself from the discipline of High Gothic, and it was in that spirit that the great cathedrals of Rouen, Tours, Orléans, Bordeaux and many others were built, beginning in the thirteenth century and continuing into the fifteenth and sixteenth centuries. Only two, those of Albi and Toulouse, were remarkable for their originality, and they found no successors. *Albi Cathedral* (1282–1390, *ill. 144)* is a single-aisled brick building. Extremely spacious within (width 19.5 m, height 32 m), it lies in the tradition of southern French architecture, although its structure is unique. The buttresses were brought inside the building and chapels placed between them which originally extended right up to the vaulting. The walls thus appear to be segmented by lamellas, and this sharpness of line is echoed in the framework of engaged columns and ribs. The exterior is completely plain and gives the cathedral the appearance of a fortress. A more complete contradiction of classical Cathedral Gothic could hardly be imagined. Almost contemporary (1294–1340) is the *Jacobin church, Toulouse,* another brick building with a double nave divided by slender round pillars and surrounded by shadowy chapel recesses and soaring fenestration *(ill. 145)*. The central pillar of the polygonal chancel supports a stellar vault. The forms of this church, a long wide hall divided by pillars, is rather like that of a monastic refectory.

Florence Cathedral

The width and spaciousness of the interior of S. Croce, Florence, also characterized the cathedral of *S. Maria del Fiore* which was begun in 1296, probably by Arnolfo di Cambio, and was intended to match the largest of the Gothic cathedrals *(ill. 146* and *fig. 118)*. The new self-awareness of the Florentine middle classes made them demand of their episcopal church the same grandeur as other Italian city states had done long before. The originally smaller design was extended to its present size (length 154.9 m, width 40.6 m, width of nave 16.5 m, height 41.4 m) by Francesco Talenti from 1357 onwards. In height, it is very close to the cathedrals of Amiens and Cologne, but because of the widely spaced arcades of the four bays (Amiens has ten bays, Salisbury twelve) and the horizontal line of the bracketed cornices, this is not apparent. Also, although the size and strength of the walls and pillars are considerable, any

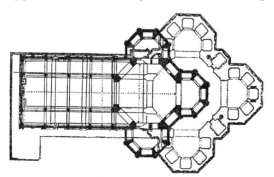

118   Florence Cathedral

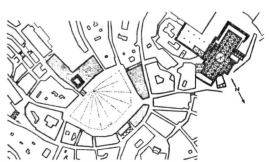

119   Siena, Palazzo Pubblico (left-centre) and Piazza

impression of heaviness or solidity that they might have given is removed by their having been treated as surfaces. The unification of the interior is furthered by the centralized arrangement of the east end, which resembles a triconchal structure. This creates a clearly defined, almost physical feeling of space that is a long way from the transparent intangibility of the Gothic style, and anticipates the treatment of space in the Renaissance. A feeling of compactness also characterizes the exterior which has neither façade towers nor projecting buttresses *(ill. 147)*. The campanile was probably designed by Giotto, and built, as was then current, separate from the church. The pattern for the decoration of the external walls was furnished by the multi-coloured marble incrustations of the Romanesque baptistery which stands opposite.

Italy: secular building
The same sensitive treatment of space, the same compactness and use of planes were applied to the many secular buildings erected in Italy at about this time. As the city republics of northern and central Italy increased in wealth and power during the thirteenth and fourteenth centuries, many of them built city halls and palaces. Artistically speaking the *Palazzo Pubblico, Siena* (1298–1348, *ill. 148* and *fig. 119)*, is one of the most perfect buildings ever constructed. The two side wings, which originally had only two storeys, meet the four-storeyed central section at a slight angle, making this section and the tall tower rise even more commandingly above the broad base. The smooth wall surfaces are articulated with delicate rows of windows, blind arcading and crenellation. The angle formed by the wings embraces the piazza which rises in the shape of an amphitheatre towards the tall buildings that encircle it. The fourteenth- and fifteenth-century palaces which survive there each possess the same articulation and arrangement of windows as the Palazzo Pubblico, enclosing the piazza with an evenly formed surround of wall-surfaces. The piazza itself is no chance creation but a deliberate spatial arrangement – an arena for assemblies and festivals that was the secular counterpart of the churches of Tuscany. Compared to Siena the Palazzo Vecchio, Florence, also begun in 1298, appears much more aloof, more like a fortress. – Not all city halls followed the same form. Owing to its quite different constitution, the city hall of the republic of Venice, the *Doge's Palace (ill. 149)*, was indeed much more like a royal palace. The laguna wing (length 71.5 m) was built 1309–40, and the piazzetta wing (length 75 m) was completed in 1442 by Giovanni and Bartolommeo Bon, who also built the Porta della Carta, the main portal between the palace and St. Mark's Cathedral. The fact that large and comparatively solid walls are supported by two completely perforated storeys of arcades and loggias (an apparent reversal of the normal logic of elevation which presupposes a solid base supporting somewhat lighter upper storeys) no longer appears as unusual as it does at first sight if we consider the church architecture of the period. In fact, the large surfaces of wall do not seem heavy at all but are like thin, almost weightless planes, an impression which is even increased by the patterns of coloured lozenges that cover them almost like embroidery. The building is inherently Gothic in this respect. – Apart from the city republics of Italy, the Flemish cities played the largest part in ushering in the rich bourgeois culture of the fourteenth and fifteenth centuries, and one of the most important Flemish secular buildings is the Cloth Hall, Ypres, begun in 1302. It is an elongated building, very simple in form, comprising three storeys. The sole decorative element is the tall tower, a symbol of bourgeois power anticipating the later Flemish belfries.

120 Marienburg

Castles

Castles, those further secular buildings of the Middle Ages whose picturesque ruins the eighteenth-century Romantics found so attractive, had not as a rule assumed a genuine architectural form by this period. They were still designed primarily for defence. Among the few exceptions were the castles built by the Order of Teutonic Knights, which since they combined the functions of castle, monastery and palace, occupy a rather special position. The *Marienburg* on the river Nogat (1274–80, *fig. 120*) is a good example. In 1318–25, it was enlarged to become the residence of the Grand Master and a reception and banqueting hall, the *Grosser Remter*, was added *(ill. 150)*. It was divided into two aisles by three slender octagonal granite columns, a pattern which, as we saw in the case of the Jacobin church, Toulouse, was derived from monastic refectories. The ribs rise like palms to form a complex system of stellar vaults, a feature that was undoubtedly introduced from England and which subsequently spread throughout Germany, becoming more and more intricate. The somewhat earlier double-aisled hall of the Castle of the Landgrave, Marburg an der Lahn (33 × 14 m), still possessed simple rib vaults.

II About 1350

England: the Perpendicular style

The tendencies we have mentioned so far became more pronounced as the century went on. This is particularly noticeable in the choir and presbytery of *Gloucester Cathedral (ill. 151)*. Alterations to the eastern part of the Norman building were begun in 1332. The eleventh-century arcades and galleries were retained but the clerestory was completely rebuilt. A lattice of vertical and horizontal rods masks the whole height of the walls, creating two even surfaces that are less like walls than like some giant cage. The vault is so rich in imaginative decoration and linear movement that it appears like a sort of intricately carved lid. The palmate fans branch out into an involved yet regular network of ribs applied to the whole surface of the vault. The east end of the cage is formed by a single wall of glass 11.6 m wide and 22 m high. The Perpendicular style as developed in Gloucester Cathedral replaced the Decorated style and determined the course of English architecture for more than 200 years. – A supreme

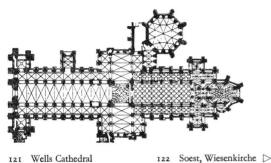

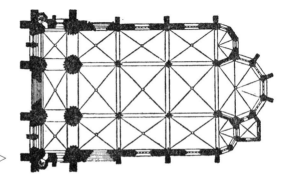

121   Wells Cathedral   122   Soest, Wiesenkirche ▷

example of the abstract and occasionally abstruse imagination of English architecture during the Late Gothic period are the interior abutments of the crossing tower of *Wells Cathedral* which were erected in 1338 *(ill. 152* and *fig. 121)*. Such a solution, completely denying the spatial relationship of nave, transept and presbytery, would undoubtedly never have occurred to a continental architect.

Germany: hall-churches

The architectural development which led in England from Exeter to Gloucester involved a process of defining and unifying the interior without introducing any greater solidity or corporeality to the walls. The same result was achieved in Germany with the hall-church. The *Wiesenkirche, Soest (ill. 153* and *fig. 122)*, was built at the same time as the alterations were being made to Gloucester Cathedral. Spatially the three bays of the three aisles form almost a cube (length 27.8 m, width 24.4 m, height 24 m) with three apses let into the end wall. All the walls, with the exception of the façade wall, are completely replaced by windows, so that the church constitutes a sort of glass shrine like the Sainte-Chapelle, Paris. But the character of the Wiesenkirche is completely different. The sharpness and tension of the skeletal type of structure have completely gone and the surfaces and structural members appear to grow into one another. This is particularly noticeable in the supporting members; instead of consisting of a core with engaged columns individually applied to it they have become unities whose smooth, fluent surfaces are gently recessed or decorated with graphic lines that lead, uninterrupted by capitals, right up into the vaults. – The hall-chancel of the *Heiligkreuzkirche, Schwäbisch-Gmünd*, with its ambulatory and chapels between the buttresses *(ill. 154)* was begun in 1351, probably on the model of the Cistercian church at Zwettl (1343–83). It directly adjoins the nave, also a hall-structure built *c.* 1320, with no transept in between. The line of the tall, smoothly rounded pillars is crossed by the line dividing the two storeys, so that the vertical, horizontal and circular dynamics of the interior achieve a satisfying balance. Outside, the lower storey of the chancel forms a continuous rounded curve. Schwäbisch-Gmünd was the prototype for many Late Gothic chancels in Germany – St. Lorenz, Nürnberg, for example, dating from the mid-fifteenth century – but it was not the only form that was developed. There was a noticeable change, too, in the cathedrals built during this period. The Cathedral of *St. Veit, Prague*, which was begun by Matthias von Arras in 1344, continued by Peter Parler and not completed until this century, adopted the classical Gothic plan and elevation. It has a chancel ambulatory ringed with chapels, and three storeys with fenestrated triforium *(ill. 155)*. But there is a quality of relaxation about the interior which has little connection with the austere solemnity and awe-inspiring height of thirteenth-century cathedrals.

The Alhambra, Granada

At this point, while still remaining within the confines of Europe, we take a somewhat surprising leap into a completely different world – the contemporary Islamic civilization of the Iberian Peninsula – to look at the *Alhambra, Granada*. We mentioned the Suleiman Mosque at Istanbul in an earlier chapter; the Alhambra is another example of a style of life that puts the Western civilization of the period in its right perspective. In comparison with this pleasure-palace of the Caliphs – the Lion Court *(ill. 156)* dates from 1354–91 – the secular architecture (not of course the sacred architecture) of the whole of western Europe, interpreted as an expression of the standard of living of its practitioners, appears unimaginative and even barbaric.

III About 1400

Dwelling-houses

It was not until after 1400 that any kind of refinement began to appear in the secular life of Europe. It happened first in Italy and the *Ca' d'Oro, Venice*, begun in 1421 by Giovanni and Bartolommeo Bon, is a landmark in this respect *(ill. 157* and *fig. 123)*. It was no accident that the Venetians led the field in this development for they had long been in contact with the Islamic East through their commercial activities. The Ca' d'Oro is a delightfully asymmetrical building with one part of the façade left more or less solid, while the other larger part is completely perforated with arcades and loggias. Colourful marble incrustations and gilding add

123   Venice, Ca' d'Oro

124   Milan Cathedral, section (after H. Koepf)

to the lively fluency of the Late Gothic decoration. Many features of the building – the use of planes, the lightness of the walls, the appearance of weightlessness and the richly graphic interplay of lines – are the same as those used in church architecture. – In complete contrast to the festive gaiety and interior spaciousness of the Venetian house was the typical burgher's house in the North, like that of *Jacques Coeur, Bourges*, for example, which was built 1442–53 *(ill. 158)*. Relatively little attention was given to the façade, which faced on to a narrow street. A more important feature is the courtyard around which the various parts of the house are grouped asymmetrically, some of them with shallow-arched arcades. The main building has a slight bend in the middle and includes three tower-like structures of different shapes, each containing a spiral staircase. The principal storey contains a large hall, a chapel and the living rooms. An element of the fortified castle is still in evidence in the severe way in which the building is shut off from the outside world. Castles themselves, however, were changing during this period and becoming more and more like châteaux, after the manner of those built by the Teutonic Knights. *Pierrefonds near Soissons*, from the end of the fourteenth century, may be considered a good example since it was completely reconstructed by Viollet-le-Duc in the nineteenth century *(ill. 159)*. Rectangular in shape (84 × 70 m), it has four corner and four central towers. It is still essentially a fortress; the living-quarters do not pretend to serve more than a merely functional purpose and the representative or institutional associations of the building are expressed only in the orderly arrangement of the site as a whole. The French royal châteaux built in Paris in the fourteenth century (Vincennes, Louvre, Bastille) followed the same system, as did all châteaux up until the end of the fifteenth century (the moated Château Sully on the Loire).

Late Gothic in Italy
Around 1400, a certain intensification of the Gothic style such as had occurred in Venice made its appearance in other Italian towns outside Tuscany. The Cathedral of S. Petronio, Bologna, which was begun in 1390 and never completed, was intended to outstrip even Florence. The three-aisled nave – the only part that was built – measures 57.68 × 132 m and is 44.27 m high. It follows the model of Florence both in its supporting members and in the span of the arcades (19.2 m) but it lacks the horizontal line formed by the bracketed cornice and the rows of side chapels, and as a result it has a completely different spatial character. – A few years earlier, in 1386, work had begun on the most astonishing of all Italian Gothic buildings, *Milan Cathedral (ill. 160)*. It was intended to surpass all the cathedrals of northern Europe and in fact, next to Seville Cathedral (1402–1506), it became the largest church building of the Middle Ages. At the beginning, famous German and French architects were engaged. They did not manage to hold their own against the Lombards, however, and a fierce quarrel broke out, which incidentally revealed a great deal about medieval construction methods. It consists of a five-aisled basilica with graduated side aisles *(fig. 124)*, a three-aisled transept with a domical vault over the crossing, and a three-aisled chancel with ambulatory and no chapels. The interior is extremely dark, brightening to a sort of twilight in the crossing and the chancel. In the strongest possible contrast is the over-elaborate splendour of the exterior, an outstanding example of that love of decoration which was such a feature of Late Gothic architecture everywhere. Over the centuries more than six thousand sculptures appeared on the building.

125   London, Westminster Palace, wooden ceiling of the hall

A hall-church at Landshut

Architecture in Germany during this period was centred almost exclusively on urban parish churches of the hall type. One of the most important is *St. Martin, Landshut (ill. 161)*, a brick building of considerable size (length 76.7 m, width 29.15 m, height 29.3 m) begun in 1387 by Hans Stethaimer. The smoothly finished polygonal pillars are 22 m high and only 1 m in diameter. This slenderness, together with the even wall-surfaces, emphasizes the lightness of the building and gives it a strongly vertical character, in contrast to the churches at Soest and Schwäbisch-Gmünd mentioned earlier.

Secular halls

A similar desire for unity and spaciousness led to the rebuilding (1394–1402) of the hall of the *Palace of Westminster, London (ill. 162)*, the last example of a Teutonic royal hall. The earlier hall, dating from the late eleventh century, had been the same size (72.5 × 20.6 m) but it had comprised three aisles. The unification of this enormous space was made possible by a wooden roof, the first really magnificent example of the newly invented hammer-beam roof *(fig. 125)*. The English preference for complex wooden structures, as used in country houses throughout the centuries, was not confined to secular buildings; large churches were frequently given wooden ceilings instead of stone vaulting (e. g. York and Ely cathedrals, among others). – The same striving after spaciousness brought about the creation of one of the most beautiful halls in Western architecture – the 'Salone' in the *Palazzo della Ragione, Padua (ill. 163)*. Its size (*c.* 79 × 27 m) was determined by the original building of 1218–19. This had been made higher in 1306, when loggias and an enormous keel-shaped wooden roof (height 26.72 m) regarded as one of the engineering marvels of the time were also added. The upper storey was divided into several sections. Both the upper storey and the roof were destroyed by a fire in 1420, and in the rebuilding the partition walls were omitted, creating this enormous hall.

IV About 1450 to the Sixteenth Century

Late Gothic in England

The desire for spaciousness and unification also dominated the final period of Late Gothic architecture. This is illustrated in a particularly impressive way by *King's College Chapel, Cambridge* (1446–1515, *ill. 164*), which continued the process that had been begun in the chancel of Gloucester Cathedral. The lattice walls of the Perpendicular style by their very nature allowed for little alteration to the transparent cage-like structure, but in the erection of the vaulting imagination was given free rein. A spate of new inventions testified to the English architect's enjoyment of abstract linear ornamentation. The Chapel of Henry VII in Westminster Abbey, St. George's Chapel in Windsor Castle and the Oxford Divinity School are three contemporary examples.

Germany: Late Gothic hall-churches

The same was true of hall-churches in Germany. One of the last pure Late Gothic buildings of this type was the *Annenkirche, Annaberg* in the Erzgebirge region of Saxony, which was built 1499–1520 *(ill. 165* and *fig. 126)*. In width (25 m) and height (20 m), it is very close to the Wiesenkirche at Soest, but the latter's severe and, in retrospect, almost ascetic elegance is here transformed into gay, festive beauty. It is the intricate net-vaulting that is chiefly responsible for this impression. The delicately formed ribs grow directly out of the smooth surfaces of the fluted octagonal supports at varying heights. – Consideration must be given at this point to the subject of coloured window-glass, which made such a decisive contribution to the appearance of interiors. The total area of window used had changed hardly at all since the thirteenth century, and might therefore have been expected to admit the same amount of light, but this was not in fact the case. In the thirteenth century tiny segments of dark glowing colour were used which dispelled most of the light and bathed the interior in constant twilight. As time went on lighter and lighter colours were used, and the segments of glass became larger.

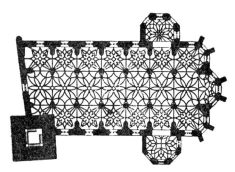

126 Annaberg, Annenkirche

Gradually the strange glowing twilight was transformed into a transparent blaze of colour until, during the fifteenth century, the colours became so light as to disappear completely, giving way to a delicate grey and a very pale yellow. The amount of light admitted to the interior became proportionately greater until finally it was very close to actual daylight.

Late Gothic in Portugal

At the same time as the Annenkirche, a hall-church was built at the *Monastery of Belem* near Lisbon (1500/02 to *c.* 1550, *ill. 166* and *fig. 127*). Again, in width (22.6 m) and height (*c.* 25 m), it approximately corresponded to the Wiesenkirche, although it is considerably longer, measuring *c.* 92 m externally. It is even longer than St. Martin, Landshut, although it matches it in the slimness (1 m) of its six octagonal supports. But the spatial proportions adopted from German hall-churches are here made to look even more expansive still. This impression is due in part to the contrast between the completely bare walls and the highly ornamented supports and intricate net-vaulting, giving the church a slightly precious character which finds its fullest expression in the south portal (width 12 m, height 32 m), which appears like an enormous piece of artistic carpentry and is probably one of the most richly ornamented portals in Western architecture. Comparable decoration is to be found in Spain, for example on the façade of S. Gregorio, Valladolid (late fifteenth century). This style, called Manueline in Portugal and Plateresque in Spain, is one of the most extreme examples of the Late Gothic passion for decoration.

Spain: secular architecture

The commercial towns of Spain enjoyed a period of great economic prosperity during the fifteenth century, and a large number of lonjas or commercial exchanges were built, some of which are still in use today. The *Lonja de la Seda* (Silk Exchange) at Valencia was built in 1483–98 by Pedro Compte. It is a three-aisled hall measuring some 36 × 21 m, and it has turned columns similar to those which were to be found at about the same time in German architecture *(ill. 167)*. According to a contemporary document what was required was a 'lonja molt bella, magnifica y sumptuosa, honor y ornament da questa insigne Ciutat'. Here again, in a secular building, we come across the sort of unified space enclosed by slim planes that was such a feature of Late Gothic architecture from 1300 onwards.

Spain: Late Gothic cathedrals

The last Islamic principality in Spain was conquered towards the end of the fifteenth century, and for the first time the country was united under Christian rule. The long fight against the Moors had given Spanish Christendom a rather special character; there was still something of the medieval crusading spirit about it. As a result, Gothic Cathedrals continued to be built in Spain until the sixteenth century, long after cathedral building everywhere else had either lost its importance or had begun, as in the case of St. Peter's, Rome, to reflect a completely new style of architectural thinking. In 1522–1615, the old *Cathedral of Segovia*, which had been destroyed during the revolution of the Comuneros in 1520, was replaced by a new building designed by Juan Gil de Hontañón. The new cathedral rivalled those of the thirteenth and fourteenth centuries *(ill. 168)*. It comprises three aisles (length 105 m, width 48 m, height

127 Belem, near Lisbon, Abbey Church

33 m) and a transept. The crossing dome is 67 m high, and the tower 110 m. The three aisles are graduated in the usual way, forming a structure between a basilica and a hall-church. The five arches of the nave arcades are so wide and so high that the side aisles merge with the nave to form a single, very broad unit of space. In addition a series of tall, deep side chapels allow the incorporation of a fenestrated clerestory in the side aisles as well as in the nave, giving the impression that the cathedral has five aisles. Palma Cathedral also gives this impression, but a comparison between the two buildings reveals the same kind of differences as noted between the Wiesenkirche and the Annenkirche. The simple planes and ascetic severity of Palma are here relieved by an intricate play of line.

France: the 'Style Flamboyant'

The conservatism of French religious architecture which we mentioned earlier is well illustrated by *St. Maclou, Rouen*, begun in 1434. On plan, it comprises three aisles, a transept and a chancel ambulatory lined with chapels. The elevation is in three storeys, based on the thirteenth-century model. Only the western vestibule (1500–14), with its polygonal shape and its elaborate Late Gothic decoration (an example of the so-called 'Style Flamboyant'), shows great originality and imagination *(ill. 169)*. Two churches built in Paris according to the classical schema were St. Séverin in the late fifteenth century, and St. Eustache during the sixteenth century.

Urban architecture

The elaborate appearance of the *Town Hall, Leuven* (Louvain), Belgium (1447–63, *ill. 170)*, built by Mathias de Layens, is a further example of the delight in decoration that characterized Late Gothic architecture. The building itself is completely regular in form. The architect obviously concentrated all his powers of imagination on the decoration, which transforms the building into a sort of vast reliquary. It is a perfect illustration of the way secular architecture developed out of religious architecture. – A brick building that displays the same line of development, although in a different way, is the *Town Hall, Stralsund (c. 1400, ill. 171)*. Its frontispiece is just one example among many that show the sort of aesthetic awareness that ultimately re-echoes the façade of the Cistercian church at Chorin. Its severe and at the same time elegant dignity was the perfect manifestation of the pride of the middle classes of the Hanseatic towns. By using brick, it was found that extremely beautiful effects could be achieved with the simplest materials, and the possibilities of building with brick were also exploited in fifteenth-century town gates. The *Treptower Gate, Neubrandenburg (ill. 172)* originated not so much from a need for defence, as from a desire to express the power and wealth of the town in a monument that would lend a fitting dignity and splendour to the reception of visitors. The harmony and balance of its articulation, which is entirely in one plane, is again reminiscent of the church at Chorin and also of the picture-wall in the chancel of S. Croce, Florence. We sense here not so much the exuberance of Late Gothic decoration, as the germ of a new aesthetic sensibility which was to lead *c.* 1420, at first only in Florence, to the beginning of the Early Renaissance.

9 The Renaissance

Characteristics: Renaissance architecture constituted a complete resumption of the elements of the Classical period (column, pilaster, entablature, tympanum, etc.) together with the Classical system of proportions, but without returning either to the structural principles of Greek architecture or to the massiveness of Roman architecture.
Interior and exterior were made to tally as far as possible, creating homogeneous compositions conceived almost like living organisms.
Decoration was used sparingly so as not to disturb the precision of individual parts and the clarity of the whole.

Materials: Mainly freestone.

Rome, St. Peter's

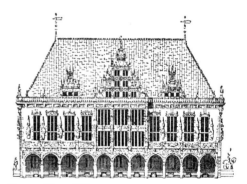

Bremen, Town Hall

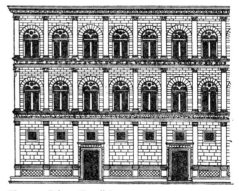

Florence, Palazzo Rucellai

Renaissance architecture began to develop in Florence *c.* 1420 and continued until *c.* 1770, a period of 350 years which in its unity matched the Gothic period from the twelfth to the sixteenth centuries. Its most characteristic feature was a new feeling for harmony and physical presence derived from the proportions of the human body. Space and mass merged into an organic whole which attained, by virtue of its beauty and inner consistency, a sort of ideal perfection. Buildings became distinct aesthetic phenomena and architects, originally primarily craftsmen, became artists. The individual man gained rights he had as yet never possessed. Symptomatic of this was the fact that even church architecture took on a more 'worldly' character. The term 'secular' cannot as yet be applied since Christianity, although it had lost the unity of the Middle Ages, still completely dominated the western world. Secular power, however, enjoyed equal status with the Church, and this was expressed in an extraordinary increase in secular architecture, challenging the hitherto undisputed authority of church architecture.

The new architectural thinking borrowed its formal apparatus from Classical Rome without, however, indulging in deliberate imitation. Creative energy was still strong enough in the West to evolve a completely independent style. Two factors determined the adoption of Classical elements as the basis of the new style. Firstly, in their stirring self-awareness, the Italians had begun to feel themselves the heirs of the Romans, whose monuments stood everywhere around them, and to resent the dark interlude of the Middle Ages imposed by the yoke of foreign barbarians (of the Goths, Gothic). Secondly, the emerging philosophy of humanism found its man-centred ideals confirmed in the philosophy and literature of the Classical period.

This final period of western Christian culture has been divided into Early, High and Late Renaissance (or Mannerism) and Early, High and Late Baroque (or Rococo). The purpose of these divisions is understandable in terms of clarity and ease of reference, although they do not correspond to what really happened, since developments took a very different course in each country. Between *c.* 1480 and 1520, for example, when the High Renaissance was at its peak in Italy, the rest of Europe was still completely dominated by Late Gothic. It was not until 1600, by which time Italy was already launched on the Baroque style, that the ideas of the Renaissance were really understood and assimilated elsewhere.

Fifteenth-century Florentine architecture poses a similar problem to the one encountered in connection with the beginnings of Early Gothic in the Ile-de-France. Is this to be considered a genuinely new style, or simply a particular variant of Late Gothic? Early Renaissance architecture did in fact have a great deal in common with Late Gothic, as Early Gothic had had with Romanesque, before it became during the period of the High Renaissance the perfect expression of the new architectural thinking. In accordance with the general fifteenth-century trend, the Florentine Early Renaissance was largely the creation of the middle classes, though the humanistic content of the new style rapidly assured its acceptance at all levels of society.

Filippo Brunelleschi

The pioneer architect Filippo Brunelleschi (1377–1446) began his career by putting the finishing touch to a Gothic building, and erecting the *dome of Florence Cathedral (ill. 173)*. The drum, which had already been begun, was completed in 1412–17, and the dome and lantern followed. The vaulting of the 43 m wide and 89 m high crossing was made possible by the erection of a double shell, and by doing without centring, which would have been extremely expensive and in any case hardly practicable in term of construction. The double dome was chosen for both constructional and aesthetic reasons; not only did it considerably reduce the load, but it also gave a different interior and exterior profile *(fig. 128)*. The slimmer shape of the outer dome gives an impression of soaring gently upwards. It is reinforced with eight marble bands and surmounted by a lantern which is thought to be the first occurrence of a 'reconstructed' Classical centralized structure. While the exterior appears firm and solid, the interior retains something of the insubstantial character of Late Gothic in the eight curved planes of the webs of the vault. The ribs are situated between the two shells.

The first piece of pure Early Renaissance architecture is a secular building – Brunelleschi's *Orphanage* (Spedale degli Innocenti) in Florence, built 1419–45 *(ill. 174)*. The whole building is arranged horizontally without in any way overstressing its stability. The arrangement of the slender delicate members is almost linear, forming a single apparently weightless plane.

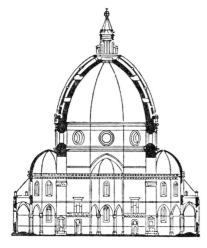

128   Florence Cathedral
(after H. Koepf)

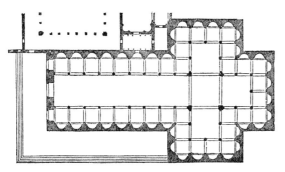

129 Florence, S. Spirito, ground plan and elevation

This is another echo of the Late Gothic spirit, although the architect did not derive his means of expression from that period but rather from the Florentine Pre-Renaissance and so indirectly from Classical Rome. – The same is also true of Brunelleschi's two basilican churches in Florence – S. Lorenzo, begun in 1421, and *S. Spirito*, begun in 1444. In both these churches, it appears as if the façade of the orphanage has been transferred onto the nave walls; they have the same delicate one-dimensionality, the same 'secular' character. They are flat-ceilinged basilicas, with transept and short rectangular chancel, and in plan are based on the square of the domed crossing *(fig. 129)*. The square system, however, is only apparent in the domical-vaulted side aisles, which are flanked by shallow chapel recesses, and lead without interruption around the transept arms and the square choir. Although the church is conceived horizontally, its horizontal, vertical and diagonal dynamics are so finely keyed as to achieve a serene stillness. The clear proportions, particularly in the height of the columns, are immediately perceptible to the human eye and sensibility. The concept of the lucidly self-contained building, based on the proportions of the human body, was to find its ideal expression in the form of the centralized structure. The eastern part of S. Spirito, with its Greek cross plan, already suggests this. The concept had in fact already been realized on a smaller scale in the old Sacristy of S. Lorenzo (1421–8) and again in a rather special way in the larger *Pazzi Chapel* in the cloisters of S. Croce (c. 1430–44, *ill. 175* and *fig. 130*). This is not a pure centralized structure, but a broad rectangular hall measuring *c.* 18 × 10 m with a central dome and a protruding square sanctuary. The form and articulation of the sanctuary are exactly projected onto the smooth side walls of the chapel in such a way as to form apparently identical arms of a Greek cross. The principle of perspective which lay behind this projection of lines onto flat surfaces can be readily understood if one imagines a section across an optical pyramid. It was Brunelleschi, in conjunction with the mathematician Manetti and others, who invented the science of centralized perspective. The flat, pictorially conceived walls of the Late Gothic style were given a new clarity and rationality of proportion which make them considered works of art in which each part corresponds to the next and is welded into an integrated whole. As a result of two conscious demands – for harmony ('concinnità') in the whole and beauty ('bellezza') in the individual parts – buildings were transformed into works of art. The sacred had become aesthetic and, since 'concinnità' and 'bellezza' were of God, the aesthetic could do it justice. – The centralized structure that Brunelleschi began in 1434 on the model of the Minerva Medica was never completed, but the idea was taken up in the chancel of SS. Annunziata, Florence, designed by Alberti.

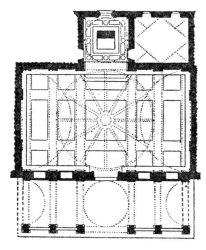

130　Florence, Pazzi Chapel

Leon Battista Alberti

Leon Battista Alberti (1404–72) was the first architect to consider himself deeply an artist in the new sense of the word. To Alberti the 'invenzione' was all; execution was something to be left to others. He began as a theoretician, and laid down the principles of architecture in his *De Re Aedificatoria* which he completed in 1450, and which was based on Vitruvius' ten-volume *De Architectura* rediscovered in 1414. Alberti then set out to put his ideas into practice in a number of secular and religious buildings. He built the *Palazzo Rucellai, Florence,* between 1446 and 1451 and used in its façade for the first time pilaster orders based on those of the Colosseum *(ill. 176* and *fig. page 122).* This façade is conceived uniquely as a frontispiece, and does not echo the structure of the interior. The entablatures do not even tally with the levels of the different storeys. It is a pictorial wall with a linear projection. The masonry does not appear to consist of courses of heavy blocks, but has an ornamental character. 'Bellezza' and 'ornamenti' (notably in the shape of pilasters and entablatures) were the principal elements of Alberti's architecture, treated in a mathematical way that was related to the intervals of the musical scale. The Palazzo Rucellai did not contain a court, though this feature was included in the *Palazzo Medici-Riccardi, Florence (ill. 177),* begun in 1444 by Michelozzo, and soon became the rule, recreating the Classical peristyle in a new form with the addition of arcades and loggias. The façades of the Palazzo Medici-Riccardi are articulated by means of three different treatments of the masonry corresponding to the three storeys; the lower storey being rusticated, the middle consisting of large blocks of stone and the top storey being smooth. A similar conjunction of smooth and rusticated masonry is found in the Palazzo Pitti (after 1460, designed by either Alberti or Brunelleschi) and the *Palazzo Strozzi (fig. 131)* (begun in 1489, probably by Benedetto da Maiano). The latter is distinguished by a heavy bracketed cornice which terminates the façade in an extremely powerful plastic manner. This feature as well as the novel regularity of the ground plan, showing how buildings were coming to be designed organically and as a whole, are distinctive of High Renaissance architecture. Alberti had already taken the decisive step in the direction of the organically conceived and articulated building in the façade and side walls of *S. Francesco, Rimini* (the 'Tempio Malatestiano'), which

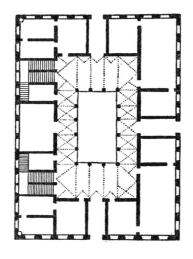

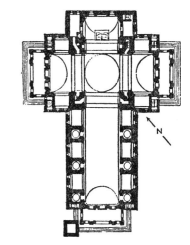

131 Florence, Palazzo Strozzi

132 Mantua, S. Andrea
(after Millon-Frazer)

he based on the triumphal arch of Augustus in Rimini *(ill. 178)*. The rebuilding of this Gothic church was begun in 1446–50, but never completed. At about the same time the façade of S. Maria Novella, Florence, was built to Alberti's design. By using old-fashioned marble incrustations but making them quite flat, Alberti gave his Classical temple façade the appearance of a three-dimensional sculptured structure projected onto an incorporeal surface. – Alberti employed Roman forms to an even greater extent in *S. Andrea, Mantua*, creating at the same time a type of church that was to have a decisive influence on the future *(ill. 180 and fig. 132)*. His design was for a large tunnel-vaulted hall-like church with three chapels, also tunnel-vaulted, down each side, exactly identical transept arms, a broad rectangular chancel and a dome on a drum surmounting the crossing. The design was drawn up in 1470, work was begun in 1472 under the supervision of Luca Fancelli, and with the eastern parts somewhat altered, the church was finally completed in 1732 with the erection of Filippo Juvarra's dome. The idea for S. Andrea was derived from Roman thermae and from the Basilica of Constantine. The grandeur of its interior, conceived in the Classical Roman tradition, would be even more striking without the later decoration. The walls represent a series of linked triumphal arches whose form, articulation and proportions are dictated by the façade. The façade itself terminates in a gable, as if a triumphal arch and the façade of a temple had been blended together. The identical articulation of façade and interior walls shows the typical Renaissance concern for architectural unity.

The Early Renaissance in Rome

After 1450, the Early Renaissance style began to spread to other parts of the country. The first 'modern' building in Rome was the *Palazzo Venezia*, built 1465–71 *(ill. 179)*. The unfinished two-storeyed arcades of the court were designed by Giuliano da Maiano, an architect who was influenced by Alberti. Visual echoes of the Colosseum and the Theatre of Marcellus are even more pronounced here. The earlier idea of projection onto a plane surface was already beginning to give way to the fully developed sculptural articulation that was to be characteristic of the High Renaissance.

Villas

The properly artistic development of the villa or unfortified country house also began in Florence. Around 1480 Giuliano da Sangallo (1445–1516) built the *Villa Medici, Poggio a Caiano (fig. 133)*, a simple but finely proportioned building rising above an arcaded base. Its only representative or display feature is the Classical temple façade set into the flat wall on the entrance side. Much more important is the regular distribution of the rooms around the central hall in four square corner blocks, each of which comprises a separate 'appartamento' of several rooms. This arrangement was to have a decisive influence on the domestic architecture of the future.

Centralized structures

Shortly afterwards, in 1485–91, Sangallo designed a pure centralized structure, *S. Maria delle Carceri, Prato (fig. 134)*. In this church, the Renaissance ideal of a regular and harmonious progression of space and mass from the centre outwards found complete realization, although the flat wall-planes and the linear character of all interior and exterior 'ornamenti' still belong stylistically to the Early Renaissance. The enrichment of architectural forms with vibrant activity did not occur in Florence but in Rome.

Town planning

The same desire for regular, harmoniously proportioned arrangements was expressed in larger complexes of urban architecture in Tuscany. In *Pienza*, a city founded in 1459–62 by Pius II, the façade of the cathedral, the bishop's palace and the Palazzo Piccolomini frame a trapezoid piazza. The city hall stands at the narrow end of the piazza, slightly east of the longitudinal axis *(fig. 135)*. The cathedral follows the form of a German hall-church. The Palazzo Piccolomini, designed by Bernardo Rossellino (1409–64), was modelled on the Palazzo Rucellai.

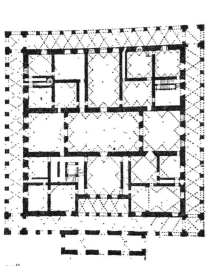

133 Poggio a Caiano, Villa Medici (after Millon-Frazer)

134 Prato, S. Maria delle Carceri (after H. Koepf)

1   Saqqara, the Step Pyramid of Zoser, Third Dynasty, *c.* 2750 B.C.

2   Giza, the Pyramids, Mycerinus (*c.* 2575 B.C.), Chephren (*c.* 2600 B.C.) and Cheops (*c.* 2650 B.C.)

3   Karnak, Temple of Amun, Eighteenth and Nineteenth Dynasties, 1570–1197 B.C.

4 Luxor, Temple of Amun, *c.* 1390 B.C.

5 Edfu, Temple of Horus, 237–212 B.C.

6 Deir el-Bahari, Funerary Temple of Queen Hatshepsut, *c.* 1500 B.C.

Warka, Inanna Temple, c. 1440 B.C.

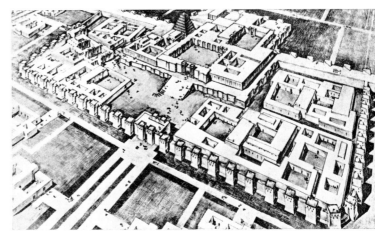

Khorsabad, Palace of Sargon II, 742–705 B.C.,
(reconstruction by Charles Altman)

Persepolis, Royal Palace, 518 to c. 460 B.C.

10 Knossos, Palace of Minos, c. 1650–1400 B.C.,
staircase in the east wing

11 Mycenae, Lion Gate, *c.* 1350–1300 B.C.

12 Corinth, Temple of Apollo, *c.* 540 B.C.

13 Aegina, Temple of Aphaia, beginning of fifth century B.C.

14 Paestum, Temple of Poseidon (after 480 B.C.) and Basilica (*c.* 550 B.C.)

15 Athens, Acropolis, the Parthenon, 447–432 B.C.

16 Athens, Acropolis, the Propylaea, 437–432 B.C.

17 Athens, Acropolis, the Erectheion, 421–406 B.C.

18

19

20

21

18   Delphi, Siphnian Treasury, *c.* 525 B.C., reconstruction of the façade, Museum of Archeolog
     Delphi

19   Athens, the 'Theseion', *c.* 449 B.C.

20   Athens, Choragic Monument of Lysicrates, *c.* 334 B.C.

21   Sounion, Temple of Poseidon, *c.* 440 B.C.

Epidaurus, Theatre, c. 350 B.C.

Nîmes, Maison Carrée, 16 B.C.

Cerveteri, Burial Chamber in the Tomb of the Reliefs, third century B.C.

25 Aegosthena, Fortress, third century B.C.

26 Herculaneum, House of Neptune and Amphitrite, view of the Nymphaeum, first century B.C.

27 Tivoli, Villa of Hadrian, 125–35 A.D.

28 Praeneste, Sanctuary of Fortuna Primigenia, beginning of first century B.C., reconstructed model, Museum of Archeology, Palestrina

Tivoli, Temple of Sibylla, beginning of first century B.C.

30 Baalbeck, Temple of Venus, second and third centuries A.D.

Baalbeck, Temple of Bacchus, second century A.D.

32 Split, Palace of Diocletian, c. A.D. 300

33 Rome, Basilica of Constantine, *c.* A.D. 310 to 320

34 Rome, Colosseum, A.D. 72–80

Saint-Rémy, Mausoleum of the Julii,
beginning of first century A.D.

36 Miletus, Market Gate, reconstruction, *c.* A.D. 160, State Museum, Berlin

Rome, Arch of Constantine, A.D. 312–15

38 Nîmes, Pont du Gard, beginning of first century A.D.

39 Rome, S. Sabina, 422–32

40 Rome, S. Maria Maggiore, 432–40

41 Ravenna, S. Apollinare Nuovo, beginning of sixth century

42 Antioch, Syria, the Turmanîn, second half of fifth century

Rome, S. Costanza, *c.* 350

44   Rome, S. Stefano Rotondo, 468–83

Ravenna, Orthodox Baptistery, first half of fifth century

46   Ravenna, Mausoleum of Galla Placidia, *c.* 425

47   Milan, S. Lorenzo Maggiore, *c.* 355–72

48   Ravenna, S. Vitale, *c.* 525–48

49   Constantinople, SS. Sergius and Bacchus, *c.* 525

50   Constantinople, Hagia Sophia, 532–7

Kiev, Cathedral of S. Sophia, 1018–37

52   Lorsch, Gate-Hall of the Monastery, 767–74

53   Phocis, Monastery of Hosios Loukas, first half of eleventh century

54 Aachen, Palace Chapel of Charlemagne, *c. 792–805*

55 Corvey, Abbey Church, 873–85

56 Hildesheim, St. Michael, 1010–33

Asturias, S. Maria de Naranco, *c.* 750

58   Essen, Cathedral, *c.* 1000

59   Maastricht, Liebfrauenkirche, *c.* 1000

60   Nivelles, Ste. Gertrude, 1000–46

61   Gernrode, Convent Church of St. Cyriakus, 961–5

62   Paderborn, St. Bartholomew Chapel, 1017

Trier, Cathedral, 1017–47

64 Tournus, St. Philibert, c. 950–1120

Bernay, Abbey Church, 1017–40

66 Ripoll, Spain, S. Maria, c. 1020–32

67 Church at Earls Barton, Northamptonshire, *c*. 1000

68 Speyer, Cathedral, begun *c*. 1030

69 Como, S. Abbondio, 1027–95

70 Cologne, St. Maria im Kapitol, 1030–65

71   Venice, St. Mark's, begun *c.* 1050 or 1063

72   Pisa, Cathedral with Baptistery and Campanile, 1063–fourteenth century

73 Santiago de Compostela, Pilgrimage Church, *c.* 1078–1128

74 St. Savin-sur-Gartempe, nave, *c.* 1095–1115

75 Fontevrault, Abbey Church, *c.* 1100–19

76 Caen, St. Etienne, *c.* 1063 to after 1077

77 Autun, St. Lazare, 1116–32

78 Hersfeld, Abbey Church, 1037

79 Jumièges, Abbey Church of Notre Dame, 1037–66

80 Paulinzella, Abbey Church, 1112–32

81 Fontenay, Cistercian Church, 1139–47

82 Maria Laach, Benedictine Abbey Church, 1093 to *c.* 1177

83 Vézelay, Ste. Madeleine, 1120–1201

84 Milan, S. Ambrogio, eleventh to twelfth centuries

Pavia, S. Michele, after 1117–55

86 Cologne, Church of the Apostles, *c.* 1200

87 Maursmünster, Monastery Church, c. 1150

88 Mainz, Cathedral, eleventh to thirteenth centuries

89 Lucca, S. Michele, west façade, c. 1239

90 Florence, S. Miniato al Monte, 1060/70–1207

91   Florence, Baptistery of S. Giovanni, *c.* 1060–1150

92   Monreale, Cathedral, begun 1174

93   Toulouse, St. Sernin, 1095–1135

94   Périgueux, St. Front, begun *c.* 1120

95   Nevers, St. Etienne, begun 1063

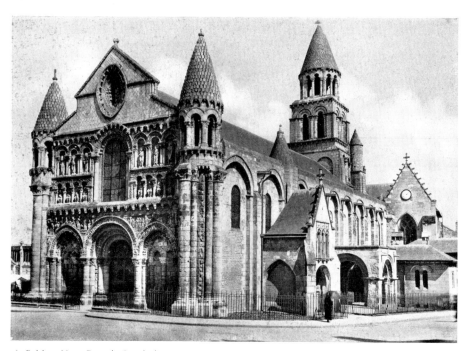

96   Poitiers, Notre Dame la Grande, begun *c.* 1100

97   Durham, Cathedral, 1091 to c. 1130

98   Durham, Cathedral

99   Ely, Cathedral, c. 1087 to twelfth century

100 Tournai, Cathedral, begun *c.* 1116

101 St. Denis, Abbey Church, 1231

102 Rome, S. Maria in Trastevere, 1138

103 Chartres, Cathedral, west façade, c. 1140–64

104 Sens, Cathedral, after 1130–68

105 Noyon, Cathedral, begun c. 1150

106   Paris, Notre Dame, west façade, c. 1163–97

107   Paris, Notre Dame, nave

108   Poitiers, Cathedral, 1166 to fourteenth century

109   Paderborn, Cathedral, nave, 1225–80

110 Alcobaça, Cistercian Church, after 1178–1223

111 Fossanova, Cistercian Church, 1187–1208

112 Maulbronn, Monastery Church, 1178 to after 1210

113 Limburg an der Lahn, Seminary Church of St. Georg, 1220–80

114 Canterbury, Cathedral, 1175–1400

115 Assisi, S. Francesco, 1228–39

116 Bourges, Cathedral, c. 1190 to after 1250

117 Chartres, Cathedral, 1194–1260

118 Amiens, Cathedral, 1220–58

119 Reims, Cathedral, 1211 to c. 1290

120 Paris, Sainte-Chapelle, c. 1243–8

121 Cologne, Cathedral, 1248–1322 and nineteenth century

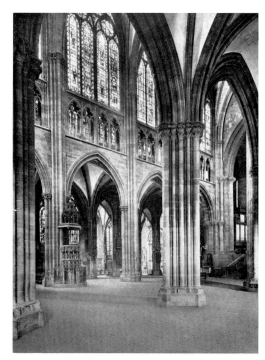

122 Strasbourg, Cathedral, 1250–76

123 Marburg, St. Elizabeth, 1235–83

124 Trier, Liebfrauenkirche, after 1235 to c. 1253

125 Lübeck, St. Marien, begun after 1251

126 Florence, S. Maria Novella, nave, *c.* 1278

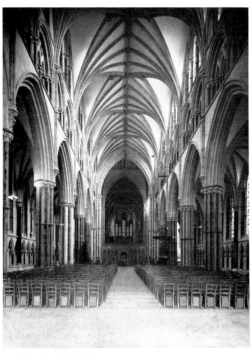

127 Lincoln, Cathedral, nave, 1192–1320

128 Lincoln Cathedral, Angels' Choir

129 Salisbury, Cathedral, west façade, 1220 to c. 1270

130 Salisbury, Cathedral, nave

131 Toledo, Cathedral, begun before 1224

132 Siena, Cathedral, begun 1229

Vercelli, S. Andrea, begun *c.* 1219

134 Exeter, Cathedral, *c.* 1275 to *c.* 1350

Apulia, Castel del Monte, *c.* 1230–40

136 Strasbourg, Cathedral, west façade, 1276–1439

137 Freiburg, Cathedral, 1270–1350

138 Mecheln, St. Rombout, begun 1341

139 Chorin, Cistercian Church, 1273 to after 1334

Florence, S. Croce, 1294/5–1442

141 Palma de Mallorca, Cathedral, c. 1300 to seventeenth century

142 Gerona, Cathedral, view of chancel and nave, 1312 to seventeenth century

143 Orvieto, Cathedral façade, begun *c.* 1310

144 Albi, Cathedral, 1282–1390

145 Toulouse, Jacobin Church, 1294–1340

146 Florence, Cathedral of S. Maria del Fiore, nave, 1296–1446

147 Florence, Cathedral of S. Maria del Fiore

148 Siena, Palazzo Pubblico, 1298–1348

149 Venice, Doge's Palace, 1309–1442

150 Marienburg, Grosser Remter, 1318–25

151 Gloucester, Cathedral, 1089 to fourteenth century

152 Wells, Cathedral, c. 1191–1338

153 Soest, Wiesenkirche, 1331–76

154 Schwäbisch-Gmünd, Heiligkreuzkirche, *c.* 1320 to sixteenth century

155 Prague, Cathedral of St. Veit, begun 1344

156 Granada, the Lion Court of the Alhambra, 1354–91

157 Venice, Ca' d'Oro, *c.* 1421

158 Bourges, House of Jacques Coeur, 1442–53

159 Pierrefonds, near Soissons, nineteenth century (late fourteenth century)

160 Milan, Cathedral, begun 1386

161 Landshut, St. Martin, begun 1387

162 London, Hall of the Palace of Westminster, 1394–1402

Padua, Palazzo della Ragione ('Il Salone'), 1218 to fifteenth century

164 Cambridge, King's College Chapel, view towards the choir, 1446–1515

165 Annaberg, Annenkirche, 1499–1520

166 Belem, near Lisbon, Monastery, c. 1500–51

167 Valencia, Lonja de la Seda (Silk Exchange), 1483–98

168 Segovia, Cathedral, 1522–1615

169 Rouen, St. Maclou, begun 1434

170 Leuven, Town Hall, 1447–63

171 Stralsund, Town Hall, *c.* 1400

172 Neubrandenburg, Treptower Gate, fifteenth century

173 Florence, Dome of the Cathedral, 1412–46

174 Florence, Orphanage, 1419–45

175 Florence, Pazzi Chapel, c. 1430–44

176 Florence, Palazzo Rucellai, 1446–51

177 Florence, Palazzo Medici-Riccardi, begun 1444

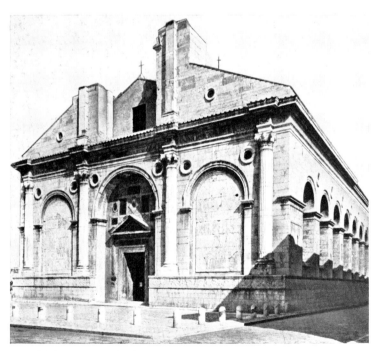

178 Rimini, S. Francesco, façade, c. 1450

179 Rome, Palazzo Venezia, 1465–71

180   Mantua, S. Andrea, 1472 to eighteenth century

181   Venice, Palazzo Vendramin-Calergi, *c.* 1500

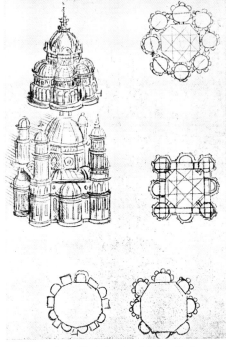

182   Leonardo da Vinci, drawing, Windsor Castle

183 Como, Cathedral, 1519 to eighteenth century

184 Rome, Tempietto of S. Pietro in Montorio, 1502–3

185 Rome, Palazzo Vidoni-Caffarelli, c. 1515–20

Rome, Palazzo Farnese, 1541

7 Rome, St. Peter's, view from the west, 1506–1626

188 Rome, Capitol, 1538–1654, copperplate engraving by Etienne Dupérac, 1569

189 Palmanova, Italy, view of the town

190 Rome, Il Gesù, 1568–83

191 Venice, Libreria Vecchia, 1536–82

192 Venice, S. Giorgio Maggiore, 1566–1610

193 Vicenza, Villa Rotonda, c. 1550

194 Château de Chambord, begun 1519

195　Paris, Louvre, Lescot's building is on the left, 1546–63

196　Escorial, near Madrid, 1563–89

197　Heidelberg, Castle, Ottheinrichsbau, 1556–1608

198   Antwerp, Town Hall, 1561–5

199   Augsburg, Town Hall, 1615–20

200   Hameln, Rattenfängerhaus (Pied-Piper's House), 1602

201 Munich, St. Michael, 1583–97

202 Wollaton Hall, Nottinghamshire, 1580–8

203 London, Banqueting House, 1619–22

Rome, S. Carlo alle Quattro Fontane, façade, 1662–3

205 Rome, S. Agnese, Piazza Navona, 1653–72

6 Rome, Piazza of St. Peter's

207 Venice, S. Maria della Salute, 1631–56

208 Paris, Val-de-Grâce, 1645–62

209 Rome, Palazzo Barberini, 1625

210 Paris, Maisons-Laffitte, 1642–6

211 The Hague, Mauritshuis, 1633–44

2 Château of Vaux-le-Vicomte, near Paris, view from the park, 1656–61

213 Château of Versailles, seventeenth to eighteenth centuries

214 Paris, Place Vendôme, 1698

215 Paris, Dome of Les Invalides, 1680–91

216 London, St. Paul's Cathedral, view from the west, 1675–1710

217 Turin, Palazzo Carignano, 1679–92

218 Turin, S. Lorenzo, 1666–87

219 Prague, St. Nikolaus auf der Kleinseite, 1703–11

220 Vierzehnheiligen, Pilgrimage Church, 1743–72

221 Granada, Cartuja (Charterhouse), 1724–64

Murcia, Cathedral façade, 1737

223 London, St. Martin-in-the-Fields, 1721–6

Paris, St. Sulpice, 1733–54

225 Salzburg, Church of the Jesuit College, 1694–1707

226 Turin, the Superga, 1717–31

227 Blenheim Palace, 1705–24

228 Vienna, Belvedere of Prince Eugene, north façade, 1721–3

Melk, Benedictine Monastery, 1702–38

230 Dresden, Zwinger, 1711–22

Berlin, Château, 1698–1706 (destroyed)

232   Würzburg, the Residenz, staircase, 1719–44

233   The Caserta, near Naples, staircase, 1752–74

234   Rome, Palazzo della Consultà, 1732–7

235　Paris, Hôtel Amelot, c. 1710

236　Versailles, Petit Trianon, 1762–4

237　Paris, the Panthéon, 1755–92

238 Chiswick House, London, begun 1725

239 Bath, the Circus, 1754–75

240 Paris, St. Philippe-du-Roule, 1769–84

241 Bordeaux, Grand Théâtre, 1773–80

242 London, 7, John Adam Street, 1768

Berlin, Brandenburger Tor, 1789–94

244 Twickenham, near London, Strawberry Hill, *c.* 1750–70

245 Paris, Barrière de la Villette, 1784–9

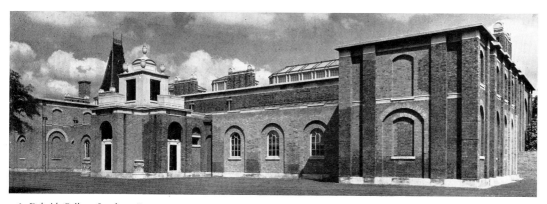

246 Dulwich Gallery, London, 1811–14

Baltimore, Md., Catholic Cathedral, 1805–18

248 Walhalla, Regensburg, 1831–42

Gilly, design for the Memorial to Frederick the Great in Berlin, 1797

250 Würzburg, Women's Prison, 1809–10

251 Naples, Teatro S. Carlo, façade, 1810–12

252 Berlin, Neue Wache, 1816–18

253 Munich, Glyptothek, 1816–34

254 Berlin, Schauspielhaus, 1818–21

255 London, British Museum, 1824–47

256 Edinburgh, High School, begun 1825

257 London, Cumberland Terrace, 1826-7

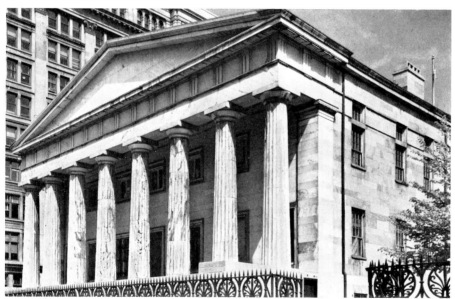

258 Philadelphia, Pa., Merchants' Exchange, 1832-4

259 London, Houses of Parliament, begun 1840

260 Paris, Ste. Madeleine, 1808–43

261 London, All Saints', Margaret Street, 1849–59

262 Paris, Ste. Clotilde, 1846–57

263 Potsdam, Friedenskirche, 1845–8

264 Edinburgh, Cathedral, 1874–9

265 Schwerin, Palace of the Grand Duke, south side, 1844–57

266 Hanover, Opera House, 1845–52

267 Paris, Bibliothèque Ste. Geneviève, 1843–61

268 London, King's Cross Station, 1851–2

269 London, Crystal Palace, 1850–1

270 Paris, the New Louvre,
north-west wing, 1852–7

271 Paris, the Opéra, 1861–74

272 Brussels, Palais de Justice, 1866–83

273 Berlin, the Reichstag, 1884–94

274 Scarborough, Grand Hotel, 1863–7

275 Milan, Galleria Vittorio Emmanuele II, 1865–77

276 Amsterdam, Rijksmuseum, 1877–85

277 Chicago, Reliance Building, 1890–4

278 Buffalo, N.Y., Guaranty Building, 1894–5

Paris, Sacré-Coeur, 1874 to *c*. 1900

280 Amsterdam, Stock Exchange, 1898–1903

281 Brussels, Solvay House, 1895–1900

282 Glasgow, School of Art, 1897–1908

283 Barcelona, Casa Milá, 1905–7 .

284 Chicago, Robie House, 1909–10

285 Brussels, Palais Stoclet, 1905–11

286 Vienna, Steiner House, 1910

287 Vienna, Postsparkassenamt (Post Office Savings Bank), main hall, 1904–6

288 Berlin, A.E.G. Turbine Factory, 1909

289 Alfeld an der Leine, Faguswerke, 1911

Dessau, Bauhaus, 1925–6

291 London, Piccadilly Hotel, 1905–8

Neubabelsberg, near Potsdam, Einstein Tower, 1919–21

293 Hook of Holland, Workers' Housing Estate, 1926–7

294 Utrecht, Holland, Schröder House, 1924

295 Brno, Tugendhat House, 1930

296 Paris, Notre Dame du Raincy, 1922–3

297 Ronchamp, Notre Dame du Haut, 1950–5

Berlin, Philharmonie, 1960–3

299   Paimio, Finland, Tuberculosis Sanatorium, 1929–33

300 Rome, Stazione Termini, 1947–51

301/02 New York, TWA Building, John F. Kennedy Airport, 1956–62

Tokyo, Olympic Hall, 1964

Montreal, German Pavilion at EXPO '67

305 Montreal, Habitat 67, 1967

306 Rio de Janeiro, Ministry of Education and Health, 1937–43

307 Caracas, Edificio Polar, 1953–4

Düsseldorf, Phoenix-Rheinrohr Building, 1959–60

309 New York, United Nations Building, 1947–50

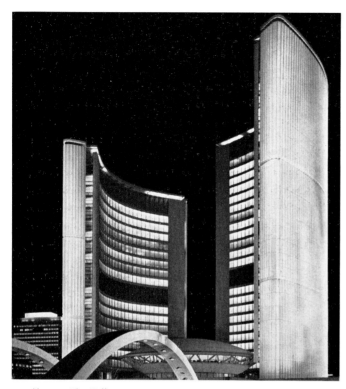

310   Toronto, City Hall, 1958–65

311   Berlin, Hansa Quarter, 1957

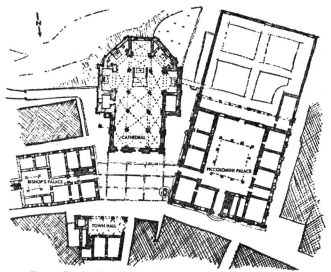

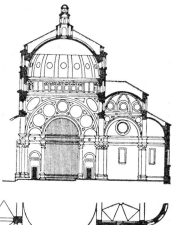

135 Pienza, Piazza Pio (after Millon-Frazer)

136 Milan, S. Maria delle Grazie, elevation and ground plan (after H. Koepf)

The Early Renaissance in Venice

Northern Italy was still dominated almost exclusively by Late Gothic during most of the fifteenth century. The Early Renaissance spread there only very slowly, and even when it did it was rarely in a pure form. Towards the end of the century, however, the new style was adopted in the North in a highly individual way. The *Palazzo Vendramin-Calergi* on the Grand Canal, Venice, built *c.* 1500 and probably designed by Mauro Coducci and Pietro Lombardi differed from the Florentine type in the break-down of its façade *(ill. 181)*. The columns of the upper storeys project slightly beyond the flat plane of the lower storey. The windows are concentrated towards the central axis, and the sections of wall which appear before the end windows are repeated at the angles and neatly terminate the composition on both sides. The façade forms a harmonious entity typical of the High Renaissance, but also shows a strong connection with the past in its lightness and in the Gothic form of the windows.

Bramante in Milan

In Lombardy, the Early Renaissance remained imbued with the Late Gothic passion for decoration. The transition from Early to High Renaissance occurred in the work of Donato Bramante (1444–1514), who worked in Milan from the seventies until 1499. Although he never in fact built a pure centralized structure there, except for the tiny sacristy of S. Maria presso S. Satiro (*c.* 1480), his thoughts revolved constantly around this one idea. He came close to realizing it in the eastern parts of his two basilicas, S. Maria presso S. Satiro and S. Maria delle Grazie. In the first, he used a trick of perspective to simulate a deep tunnel-vaulted chancel on a flat wall. *S. Maria delle Grazie* is not quite a pure solution either, since the eastern apse does not directly adjoin the crossing like the side apses, but has a square dome-vaulted bay in between *(fig. 136)*. Nevertheless both from the interior and from the exterior, an impression of a perfectly centralized building is imparted. The articulation and decoration, however, is conceived in lines and planes, and remains within the Late Gothic/Early Renaissance style.

Leonardo's designs for centralized structures

We must turn at this point to the work of *Leonardo da Vinci* (1452–1519) who lived in Milan between 1482 and 1499, and was closely associated with Bramante. Although he was not responsible for any buildings there, with the exception of work related to the fortifications and military engineering, for which he was engaged, he did occupy himself with a large number of designs, particularly for centralized churches. A manuscript sheet in *Windsor Castle (ill. 182)* shows two examples of plans with corresponding sketches. In a wealth of different compositions, Leonardo developed the most luxuriant elevations from circular, square or octagonal ground plans. His designs had a harmony between interior and exterior that was equally evident irrespective of the angle from which the building was viewed, and in their plasticity and organic development, they even surpassed the work of Bramante. The architectural ideas of both men, which soon made their influence felt far beyond Milan, were so similar that it is impossible to trace such influences back to either of them alone. This is shown by the chancel of *Como Cathedral (ill. 183)*. Christoforo Solari delivered his model for the rebuilding of the eastern part of the cathedral in 1519, and it was a complete expression of both Bramante's and Leonardo's ideas. It was altered somewhat in the execution, and was not completed until the erection of Filippo Juvarra's dome in 1730–70.

Bramante in Rome

The new ideas about centralized structures reached their most decisively influential stage in Rome, where Bramante moved in 1499. His *Tempietto*, in the courtyard of *S. Pietro in Montorio*, was built in 1502–3 *(ill. 184)*. The Tempietto perfectly exemplified the new architecture, and in its classic purity and simplicity was never surpassed. It followed the form of a Roman circular temple, a justifiable choice since it was designed to commemorate the martyrdom of St. Peter. That it is not simply a copy but an entirely new creation is due to certain fundamental changes that transformed the static character of Roman architecture into a dynamic vitality typical of the West. There is a sweeping upward movement from the circular stylobate of three steps through the base, columns, entablature and balustrade to the free-standing core, terminating in the dome and lantern. This dynamic of growth determined the way the whole building was treated and is particularly noticeable in the upper storey. Vertical movement is balanced by horizontal circular movement in such a way as to create an impression of complete repose, informed nevertheless with a subtle tension. The vibrant life filling the building demanded a similarly organic treatment of its surroundings and Bramante's plan envisaged the transformation of the court into a circular portico which would echo the form and movement of the Tempietto. The fact that this was never carried out somehow diminishes the effect of the building. Bramante was a master of building courts as we can see from the cloisters of S. Maria della Pace, Rome (1500–04), and even better from the Belvedere Court in the Vatican (begun in 1503). – The crystalline precision of the Tempietto is shared by another centralized structure, *S. Maria della Consolazione*, near Todi (1506/8–1608) *(fig. 137)*, which Bramante may also have designed. It too combines a sense of relaxed self-containment with a powerful upward movement. Horizontal and vertical articulations stress this dual character of dynamic

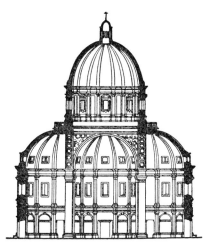

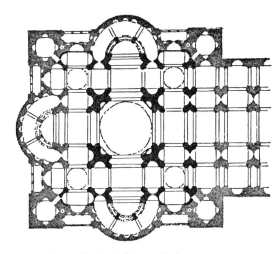

137 Todi, S. Maria della Consolazione (after H. Koepf)

138 Rome, St. Peter's, Bramante's plan

tension and harmonious composition. Even without knowing the form of the interior, it can be read clearly from the exterior, so perfectly does this building express the organic principle of growth outwards from the centre.

The foundation stone of the new *St. Peter's, Rome*, designed by Bramante, was laid by Julius II on 18 April 1506 *(fig. 138)*. On plan, it was a Greek cross within a square, with ambulatories around the semicircular ends of the arms projecting beyond the square in shallow arcs. The remainder of the interior consisted of smaller domed centralized structures. There were to have been towers above the strongly constructed corner rooms. Instead of the flat wall-surfaces that had been usual up until then, the ground plan reveals a sculptural approach, with recesses and niches articulating every part of the wall-surface. There is an organic development from the centre to the outer members, but the building could not have conveyed this impression if it had been completed as planned. Some of the members were too thin, too interrupted by niches and too cut off from the interior as a whole. By the time of Bramante's death in 1514, the crossing piers with their connecting tunnel arches were completed, and some of the abutment pillars had been begun. The Roman system of casting was used for the tunnels, which could not in fact have been constructed otherwise. Under Bramante's immediate successors, the first of whom was Raphael, no further building took place but a number of new plans were drawn up, alternating constantly between the centralized structure and the basilica. The only significant changes were made by Antonio da Sangallo (1485–1546). In 1543, he laid a new floor 3.5 m above the level of Constantine's basilica, creating the 'grottoes', and walled in the outer niches of the crossing piers, which simplified the line of the piers and strengthened them at the same time.

Raphael
Raphael (1483–1520) made his most impressive debut as an architect with the *Palazzo Vidoni-Caffarelli, Rome (ill. 185)*. This was built *c.* 1515–20, and was indebted to Bramante's Palazzo Caprini-Raphael, a building which has not been preserved. The ground floor is rusticated,

and the upper storey is strongly articulated with coupled columns and balustrades, terminating in a powerful cornice. The third storey is an unfortunate later addition. The urgent strength of the building is due in great part to its emphatically horizontal composition. A three-storeyed building which adopted the same type of articulation was the Palazzo Uguccioni, Florence, begun in 1550.

Antonio da Sangallo

In contrast to the gaiety of Raphael's palace, the *Palazzo Farnese, Rome*, designed by Antonio da Sangallo, seems austere and reserved *(ill. 186)*. It is a powerful three-storeyed block articulated only by the continuous rows of windows. The fifteenth-century treatment of walls as planes has here given way to a firm mass of masonry, which pushes out the windows in an almost sculptural way so that they stand solidly on the bracketed cornices. By the time Sangallo died in 1546, the outer walls were almost finished and two storeys of the façades around the court were complete. Michelangelo was entrusted with the completion of the palace, and it was he who added the powerful bracketed cornice on top, stressed the central axis with a richly articulated window, and completed the third storey of the court façade, decisively altering their dynamic character in the process. He also planned to open up the rear wing and to draw a longitudinal axis through the building right across to the other side of the Tiber, but the plan was never carried out.

Michelangelo

In the same year, 1546, Michelangelo was put in charge of *St. Peter's (fig. 139* and *fig. page* 122*)*. The size of the building had been largely determined by the parts already erected (length and width 137.5 m, diameter of dome 42 m), but the form was still undecided. Michelangelo's achievement was to draw all the parts together in such a way that they formed an architectural unity. By eliminating Bramante's imprecise outer members and the corner towers, he simplified the interior and made it cohere with the shell. He also reduced the number of recesses and niches in the shell, restoring an even flatness to the walls and giving the interior a more powerful

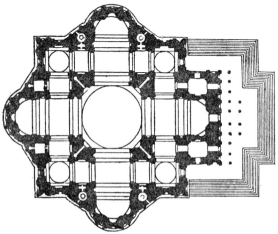

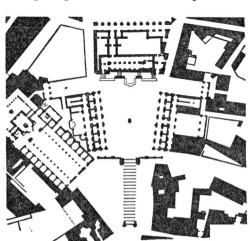

139   Rome, St. Peter's, Michelangelo's plan

140   Rome, Capitol (after Millon-Frazer)

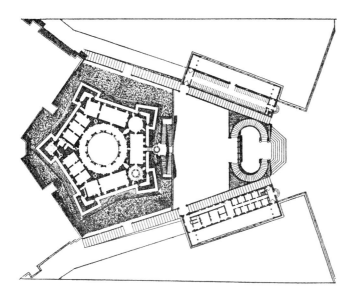

141 Caprarola,
north of Rome,
Palazzo Farnese

142 Rome,
Villa Giulia

definition. The tensely sculptured impact of these walls can be seen to its best effect in the view of the exterior from the west *(ill. 187)*. Previously, Michelangelo had only had the opportunity of designing small interiors such as those of the Medici Chapel (1521–34) and the Biblioteca Laurenziana, Florence (begun 1526), but with St. Peter's he could make free use of his ideas. The dynamism of the individual forms and within the body of the building is so much more vibrant than had been the case in the past, that an impression of actual passionate movement is evoked, and in this respect Michelangelo paved the way for the Baroque style. The dome, 132.5 m high to the top of the cross, was erected in 1588–90 by Giacomo della Porta (1539–1602). Carlo Maderna (1556–1629) added the basilican nave in 1607–17, bringing the overall length of the building including the portico to 211.5 m. The façade measures 114.69 m in width and 45.44 m in height.

What Michelangelo had built for the Pope as the spiritual ruler 'urbis et orbis' in St. Peter's, he built for the 'urbs' itself in the *Capitol (ill. 188)*. Work on the new complex began in 1538 with the erection of the equestrian statue of Marcus Aurelius which provided the centre and the axis around which the whole site was planned. It was completed in 1644–54 with the Palazzo Nuovo (now the Museo Capitolino). The building on which it was modelled, the Palazzo dei Conservatori, had been begun in 1563. These two palaces, together with the Palazzo dei Senatori, enclose a trapezoid whose narrow side faces the town and gives onto the flight of steps, the 'Cordonata' *(fig. 140)*. Within the trapezoid piazza, Michelangelo placed an oval design. This design is most important for it stresses the latent tensions and dynamics contained in the oval, and at the same time directs them towards the palaces which press in from three sides. There are similar tensions in the designs of the palaces themselves. Enormous two-storeyed pilasters like those used in St. Peter's appear to support the entablature, creating an impression of static calm. But within the storeys, columns crowd against the pilasters below and windows appear to push against the entablature above, transforming the façade into a veritable battleground of dynamic activity. Architectural thought having reached the point where entire towns came to be regarded as a single organism, the theories evolved during the fifteenth century were in fact realized during the course of the sixteenth century in the shape of such homogeneous urban complexes. *Palmanova* in the Veneto, laid out in 1593 according to the ideas of Vincenzo Scamozzi, was one of the earliest foundations to give practical expression to the principle of total centralization *(ill. 189)*.

Vignola

The *Palazzo Farnese, Caprarola*, was built in the same spirit *(fig. 141)*. It was begun in 1559 by Giacomo Barozzi da Vignola (1507–73) on the foundations of a fortress dating from 1521. The solid pentagonal exterior encloses a two-storeyed circular court with open arcades and loggias. A spiral staircase in the left-hand corner of the entrance side connects the storeys. Wide flights of steps lead up from the town through the trapezoid ante-court to the entrance of the palazzo. The whole complex is as it were crystallized out of the amorphous forms of its natural surroundings and of the little town below. The idea of the circular court with its two open storeys had been used before in Charles V's palace at Granada, begun in 1527 by Pedro Machuco, a former member of Bramante's circle in Rome, but there it had been placed within a square. Whereas palaces and castles had to fulfil a principally representative role as seats of authority and power, the many villas built around this time were given a much more intimate character. But here again requirements changed and the simplicity of the Villa Farnesina and the Villa Madama in Rome gave way towards the middle of the century to ever more elaborate structures like the Villa d'Este, Tivoli, and the *Villa Giulia, Rome* (1550–5, *fig. 142*). More and more importance was attached to the process of crystallization which drew out of the amorphous forms of nature first a formalized garden and second an organic architectural structure. A type of geometrically strict landscape gardening began to appear which was to find its culmination in seventeenth-century France.

The disciplined and dignified architectural context which Vignola had realized for secular life found its religious counterpart in his Jesuit church of *Il Gesù, Rome*. The foundation stone was laid in 1568 and the church was vaulted in 1576. Giacomo della Porta's façade was completed in 1583. During the Counter-Reformation, there was a tendency to return to the traditional longitudinal ground plan and the form chosen for Il Gesù was that of a hall with side chapels and a transept *(fig. 143)*. In the eastern part of the church, however, with its prominent crossing dome, the architect could still indulge his delight in the centralized structure. What Alberti had attempted in S. Andrea, Mantua, here found its classic solution. As a result of its perfect fusion of a centralized structure with a longitudinal building, its organic unification of space and mass and the dignity of its overall composition, Il Gesù became the prototype for many seventeenth- and eighteenth-century churches. The organic principle is particularly clear in the façade *(ill. 190)*. This develops upwards along the dominant central axis, and at the same time grows sideways in succeeding strata, linking horizontal and vertical lines in an indissoluble unity.

Sansovino in Venice

With the advent of the High Renaissance, Rome had become the artistic capital of the West. After Rome, the most important centre was the Veneto, with Venice and Vicenza. Florence

143 Rome, Il Gesù

144 Venice, S. Giorgio
Maggiore (after H. Koepf)

had begun to recede into the background. In Venice too, it was a native of Florence, trained in the school of Rome, who brought the High Renaissance to full architectural fruition. This was Jacopo Tatti (1486–1570), known as Il Sansovino. In 1536, he began the *Libreria Vecchia* opposite the Doge's Palace, giving final shape to the Piazzetta which opens towards the lagoon *(ill. 191)*. The building was completed in 1582 by Vincenzo Scamozzi (1552–1616). It comprises two storeys, and is only two bays deep. The balustrade is decorated with statues. The Libreria Vecchia recalls Michelangelo's palazzi on the Capitol, the only difference being that it is gay, expansive and relaxed in character. The characteristic majesty of Rome is replaced by splendour of decoration. The same basic design was continued around St. Mark's Square, so that together with the Piazzetta, these became the two most magnificent festive settings in the whole of Western urban architecture.

Andrea Palladio

Vignola's summing-up of the experiences of the first generation of Renaissance architects amounted to a virtual 'canon' of theory and practice. What Vignola had done for Rome, *Andrea Palladio* (1508–80) did for Northern Italy. His principal theoretical work, the *Quattro*

145 Vicenza, Palazzo Chiericati (after H. Koepf)

Libri dell' Architettura of 1570, together with Vitruvius and Vignola's book on columns, formed a part of the equipment of every architect up until the nineteenth century. Palladio's most important church is *S. Giorgio Maggiore, Venice*, begun in 1566 and completed by Scamozzi in 1602–10 *(ill. 192)*. Like Il Gesù, it is a combination of centralized and longitudinal structures, but here the longitudinal body comprises three aisles. The connection between the two structures is established by a repetition of the same formal elements – pilasters, half-columns and entablatures – in progressively larger units. These reappear on the façade, which consists of a high temple pediment supported by columns, and a wider wall set slightly behind with its own pediment corresponding to the basilican section of the church *(fig. 144)*. Palladio used the same arrangement in the church of Il Redentore, Venice, begun in 1577. – Among the various palaces Palladio built in Vicenza, the *Palazzo Chiericati* (1550–7) stands out for the way in which it anticipates the Baroque style *(fig. 145)*. In this building, Palladio abandoned the traditional form of the solid mass, so that only the projecting central part of the upper storey formed the façade, and he set the wings and the entire lower storey back behind open colonnades (compare also the arcades which he added to the Basilica, Vicenza). – Palladio was responsible for a number of villas, but only the *Villa Rotonda, near Vicenza*, which was begun *c.* 1550 *(ill. 193)* can be mentioned here. In plan, it is a square with an inscribed circle. Columned porticos in the form of Classical temple fronts stand on all four sides of the square. The regularity of the exterior is matched by the arrangement of the interior around the circular domed hall. In the Villa Rotonda, the private man's small country residence finally received artistic form. The architectural ideals of the Renaissance have never been more cogently expressed than in Palladio's introductory words to the *Quattro Libri*. 'Beauty shall result from order and from the relationship of the whole to the individual parts, of the parts to each other and of the parts back to the whole; let form appear as a whole and perfect body in which each member corresponds to every other and in which all are necessary to fulfil the intention.'

III French Renaissance

The adoption of the Renaissance style outside Italy from 1500 onwards was by no means an even process. Secular architecture took the lead while church architecture still clung at first to Late Gothic forms. France was the first country to prove receptive to the new ideas. While in Italy, François I had been quick to grasp the representative possibilities of Italian Renaissance architecture. He called upon the services of several other Italian architects besides Leonardo, and began by having several châteaux built on the Loire. François I was the first European monarch to be obsessed by that passion for building which was to capture so many rulers during the Baroque period.

The Châteaux of François I
François I's most elaborate undertaking, the *Château de Chambord*, was begun in 1591 but never completed *(ill. 194* and *fig. 146)*. The actual architect is not known, but Domenico da Cortona, a pupil of Giuliano da Sangallo, almost certainly had some part in it. The central core and the round corner towers were evolved from the keep or donjon of medieval castles but no hint of the fortress remains in the garden façade with its regular, open, horizontal formation. The

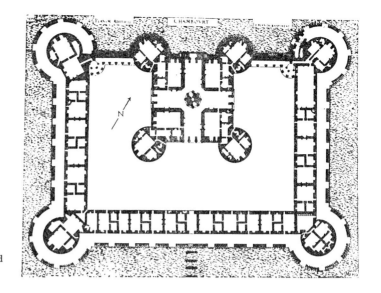

146 Château de Chambord
(after Millon-Frazer)

Gothic profusion of the superstructure stands in strong contrast to the façade. More than 300 turrets, chimneys, gables and dormer-windows surround the 36 m high central tower which rises above the double spiral staircase connecting the floors. The staircase stands at the focal point of four large halls which form a Greek cross. The idea for this magnificent edifice may possibly have come from Leonardo himself, although the regularly laid out residential units or 'appartements' in the corners of the square may have been designed by Domenico da Cortona, who would almost certainly have known about those in the Villa Medici at Poggio a Caiano.

When François I moved his court nearer Paris, he commissioned Gilles Le Breton to build the Château de Fontainebleau, which was begun in 1528. Two notable features of it are the curved flight of stairs designed by Jean Ducerceau in the Cour du Cheval Blanc, and the Galerie François I to which it leads. This gallery, which measures 5 × 58 m, served as the model for similar elongated rooms incorporated in other châteaux. They were decorated with frescoes and were later used as picture galleries. – In 1548, Philibert de l'Orme began the Château d'Anet, the three-winged layout of which had a great influence on future châteaux. – It was also François I who in 1528 pulled down the medieval château on the site of the *Louvre* and employed Pierre Lescot to begin a new building in 1546. The west wing (*ill. 195*, the portion on the left) was complete by 1555 and the south wing by 1563. Contrary to Italian practice, the court façades were left solid. The building is articulated with three projecting segmental gables. Lescot, who had fully absorbed the principles of Renaissance architecture, gave them a new interpretation which moved away from sonorous abundance in favour of a quiet, restrained elegance. If Lescot's building had been completed as planned around a square, it would have occupied only a quarter of the present Cour du Vieux Louvre. The extension of his design was begun under Louis XIII by Jacques Lemercier (*c.* 1585–1654), and was completed during the seventeenth century. Louis XIV, after rejecting Bernini's design, had the east façade built in 1667–74 by Claude Perrault (1613–88). Meanwhile work had been in progress since 1564 on the Palais des Tuileries which lay to the west of the Louvre. The architects were Philibert de l'Orme and Jean Bullant. The Palais was connected to the Louvre by wings and galleries built under Napoleon I and III which completed the enclosure of the whole site. The destruction of the Palais des Tuileries in 1871 opened up the longitudinal axis, which then continued through the Place de la Concorde, the Champs Elysées and the Place de l'Etoile to lose itself in the distance in a manner that would never have been permitted by Renaissance or Baroque architects.

IV The Renaissance in Other Countries

Spain

One of the most magnificent realizations of sixteenth-century architecture, the *Escorial near Madrid (ill. 196)*, returns to the strictest form of the Renaissance conception. A combination of château, monastery and centralized church, it embraces in a unique way the secular architecture of the Renaissance and the religious architecture of the Counter-Reformation. It was built under Philip II in 1563–89 by the architects Juan Bautista de Toledo and Juan de Herrera, and is a completely regular composition enclosed within a rectangle. The ground plan is in the shape of a grid with a large number of courts lying on either side of the central axis. The vertical emphasis reaches its climax in the high drum and dome of the church. In plan, the church is longitudinal but from the interior it appears as a centralized structure based on a Greek cross. The entire complex is built of granite throughout, and the august majesty of its composition extends down to the smallest detail.

Germany

Compared to the Escorial, the Ottheinrichsbau (built in 1556, *ill. 197)* in *Heidelberg Castle* resembles an ornamental exhibition-piece by a highly skilled craftsman. It is a three-storeyed wing comprising ten bays grouped in five pairs. Pilasters, half-columns, windows and statue niches form a dense arrangement which looks less like a building than a rich piece of pure

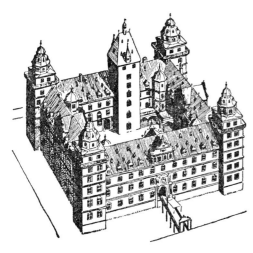

147   Aschaffenburg Castle (after H. Koepf)

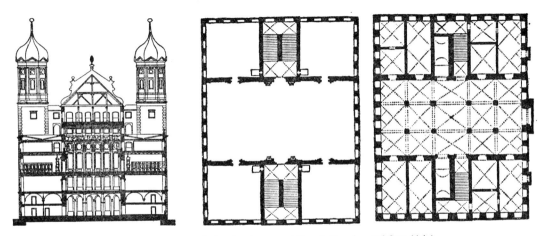

148 Augsburg Town Hall, elevation and ground plan showing ground floor (left) and second floor (right)

decoration. This impression is caused by the fact that, although both architecturally and orna-mentally the Ottheinrichsbau is exemplary, the architect seems to have had no direct experience of Italian buildings. Only in the Friedrichsbau (built 1601–7 by Johannes Schoch, *ill. 197,* extreme left) did architectural structure and ornamentation blend into a unity, with vertical and horizontal articulations being made more plastic and the whole composition becoming stronger and more alive. *Aschaffenburg Castle (fig. 147)* was built in 1605–14, immediately after the Friedrichsbau, and in the words of the architect Georg Ridinger it was to be a 'heroic opus of princely grace'. It was the first regularly laid-out German château to be based on French models. Apart from the inner and corner towers, the only vertical stress is provided by the three-storeyed gables in the centre of the side walls.

Towns Halls

The middle classes too took up Renaissance architecture for new buildings of a representative or institutional nature, and this occurred in the commercial centres of Flanders before it occur-red in Germany. In 1561–5 Cornelis de Vriendt built *Antwerp Town Hall (ill. 198),* a building that was long to serve as a model for other towns on the northern coasts. The horizontal dynamics of the wide four-storeyed façade are concentrated towards the centre in the three richly articulated bays of the projecting gable structure, which then sweeps them violently upwards. – One of the most splendid and original accomplishments of bourgeois architecture was the *Town Hall, Augsburg,* built in 1615–20 by Elias Holl and intended according to him to embody a 'heroic ideal' *(ill. 199* and *fig. 148).* In plan it is a rectangle measuring 45 × 35 m and containing a cross. The presence of the cross is indicated in the elevation by a basilica-like clerestory with gable ends and by two lateral staircase towers. The central part consists of three large rooms one above the other and extending from front to back. The topmost of these is the so-called 'Golden Hall' or banqueting hall. Its richly carved and gilded wooden ceiling is suspended from the rafters so that despite the enormous size of the room (length 32.5 m, width 17.3 m, height 14.2 m), it was not necessary to interrupt it with supports. All the utility rooms are regularly distributed in the corners of the rectangle on either side of the staircases. This carefully planned organic arrangement made the building extremely functional and ensured an admirable homogeneity between interior and exterior. The 'heroic' strength which its architect gave it invites comparison with the Escorial. – Mention must also be made of Bremen Town Hall as rebuilt by Lüder von Bentheim in 1609–13 *(fig. page 122)*.

Middle-class houses

A large number of sixteenth- and early seventeenth-century burgher houses have been preserved, including many half-timbered structures, but we shall have to limit ourselves to one example which may be considered typical of Germany and the Netherlands – the *Rattenfängerhaus or 'Pied Piper's House', Hameln an der Weser*, built in 1602 *(ill. 200)*. The gabled structure of such houses, which were often very narrow, was a heritage of Late Gothic, but the individual elements were governed by the formal language of the Renaissance. Their decoration appears to have sprung from an inexhaustible imagination and where entire rows of houses have been preserved, as in Ghent and Antwerp, they display a plethora of completely individual solutions.

Church architecture in Germany

Church architecture took a subordinate role during this period, but it too showed evidence of the lingering influence of Late Gothic not only in France and Spain (Segovia is a prime example) but also in Germany. The few new Protestant foundations such Bückeburg Church and the Marienkirche, Wolfenbüttel, dating from the early seventeenth century, were hall-churches with rib vaults (Bückeburg) and a wealth of Renaissance decoration. The first German Jesuit church, *St. Michael, Munich (ill. 201)*, was fundamentally different. It was built in 1583–97 by Wolfgang Miller and Friedrich Sustris, and was influenced by Il Gesù, Rome. The deep chancel directly adjoins the tunnel-vaulted nave which is more than 20 m wide and has four tunnel-vaulted chapels on either side. The absence of a true transept and domed crossing shows that the concept of the centralized structure, the chief preoccupation of Renaissance architects, was still totally alien to Germany.

England

Renaissance architecture reached England rather later than the rest of Europe, and when it did it was for some time used in conjunction with the Late Gothic Perpendicular style. For example, the large grid-shaped windows of *Wollaton Hall, Nottinghamshire (ill. 202 and fig. 149)*, built in 1580–8 by Robert Smythson, are reminiscent of heavily fenestrated churches such as King's College Chapel. The design of the house, however, was an extended version of a design in the third volume of Sebastiano Serlio's treatise on architecture, first published in Venice in 1540. The treatment of the articulation was derived from the fourth volume, published in 1537, and other features were taken from Jan Vredeman de Vries' *Architectura* (1563) and *Compartimenta* (1560). All these ideas were blended into a homogeneous and original building which develops organically from the central hall outwards, and which both in ground plan and elevation presents a rich composition.

If Augsburg Town Hall can be said to represent the complete assimilation of Renaissance architecture in Germany, the corresponding building for England is the contemporary

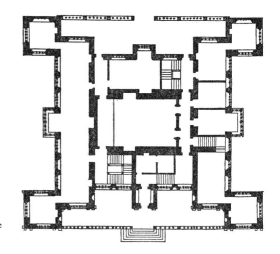

149　Wollaton Hall, Nottinghamshire

Banqueting House in Whitehall, London, designed by Inigo Jones (1573–1652) and built in 1619–22 *(ill. 203)*. Influenced by Palladio, from whom he adopted the two-storeyed order of the façade with its central projection, Jones created a building of classical perfection, balancing stasis and movement in an entirely Renaissance manner to form a harmonious organism. This link with the work of Palladio was to be of the greatest importance for seventeenth- and eighteenth-century English architecture.

Characteristics: Taking up the same architectural elements as the Renaissance style, Baroque used them in greater profusion and in a more plastic and fluent manner.
Interiors were given greater force though they never completely lost their definition. Structural members were given a similar fluency of line by means of projections and recesses, curved walls, etc., giving buildings increasingly the character of living organisms.
Once again sculpture and painting formed an integral part of architecture.

Materials: Mainly freestone.

Dresden, Zwinger

◁ Munich, Theatinerkirche

By the time Elias Holl in Augsburg and Inigo Jones in London had brought the Renaissance style to fruition in their respective countries, Italian architects had already evolved the Baroque style, of which the principal sources were St. Peter's, the Capitol and Il Gesù. The plastic and organic conception of space and mass which characterized these buildings formed the basis of the new style but tensions which had formerly been latent were now liberated. Implied movement became transformed into a fluent dynamism, though still within the context of the formal language of the Renaissance. – Once again so much has been preserved from this period of architecture, that our survey of it must necessarily be extremely limited. The best approach would seem to be that which we adopted for Late Gothic architecture; rather than consider each country in isolation, we shall take a number of cross-sections and examine the related and divergent developments which these reveal.

I High Baroque Church Architecture

Borromini
The decisive step towards High Baroque was taken in *S. Carlo alle Quattro Fontane, Rome (fig. 150)*, designed by Francesco Borromini (1599–1667). The church was begun in 1638 and the façade *(ill. 204)* was added in 1662–3. This incorporates all the same elements as the façade

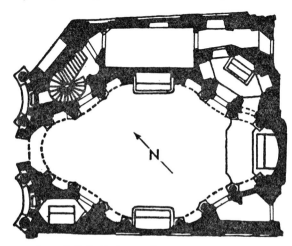

150   Rome, S. Carlo alle Quattro Fontane

151   Rome, S. Maria della Pace

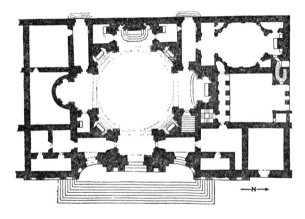

152   Rome, S. Agnese (after Millon-Frazer)

of Il Gesù – columns, niches, entablatures and pediment – but the flat planes of the sixteenth-century church are replaced by an undulating movement. The walls curve in and out, the entablatures follow their flowing line, the cornice and balustrade are thrust upwards by the oval design, and in the centre a structure like a tabernacle is forced out in a convex counter-curve. All this reflects the action within the interior of the church. The central elliptical cylinder of space becomes visible as such only in the vault. Below, it is split into four sections which constitute a rhomb with each angle extended to form a bay. The symmetry of the interior is so obscured by these constantly changing dynamics, that the building appears to be incessantly changing its shape. In a different way, Borromini achieved a similarly pulsating vitality in wall-construction and spatial relationships in S. Ivo della Sapienza, Rome (1642–60). – *S. Agnese, Rome*, a centralized church begun in 1652 by Girolamo (1570–1655) and Carlo Rainaldi (1611–91) was conceived in much the same spirit *(ill. 205 and fig. 152)*. A year later, in 1653, Borromini took over direction of the work, only to hand it back to Carlo Rainaldi in 1657. The church was completed in 1672. Niches at the four corners of the domed central square transform this square into an irregular octagon, and at the same time form a diagonal cross between the arms of the larger Greek cross. The eight columns that surround it constitute as it were the joints of the various spatial units. The façade swings inwards in a flattened curve, appearing to draw the Piazza Navona into itself. Most unusually for Rome, this façade has two towers, like the one planned by Bernini for St. Peter's but only partially executed. It plays a very important part in the shaping of the piazza surround, for the towers relieve the isolation of the dome on its high drum, and form together with it a rich group whose vertical emphasis is introduced by the obelisk of Bernini's Fountain of the Four Rivers. These accents give the elongated piazza, which took its shape from the Circus of Domitian, a very high degree of animation.

Pietro da Cortona

The façade of *S. Maria della Pace, Rome* (1656–7, *fig. 151*), designed by Pietro da Cortona (1596–1669), is also related to the space adjoining it. On the ground floor, an oval colonnaded portico bulges out, flanked by concave wings. The central portion of the upper storey returns to a convex curvature. The articulation of the whole building is extremely sculptural and is saturated with movements which develop right out into the surrounding streets. – Bernini's treatment of S. Andrea al Quirinale, Rome (1658–70) was rather more restrained but otherwise basically the same.

Bernini

The most magnificent example of this type of organic fusion of a piazza and an architectural structure is the *Piazza of St. Peter's, Rome (ill. 206)*, created by Gian Lorenzo Bernini (1598–1680). Bernini set out to modify the effect of the somewhat unfortunate proportions of the Cathedral's façade by placing before it the trapezoid 'piazza retta' which is 90 m deep and slopes downwards away from the façade. The 19 m high colonnades on either side converge towards the open end, so that this measures 27 m less than the façade end. In this way Bernini produced two complementary effects. Firstly the relationship between the colonnades of the 'piazza retta' and the façade itself, which the eye unconsciously assimilates, makes the façade appear narrower than it is, and secondly the height of the colonnades together with the rising slope stresses the vertical thrust of the façade and makes it appear higher. The tensions set up by this arrangement are released in the free elliptical sweep of the 'piazza obliqua', the axes of which measure 142 and 196 m. The arms of this piazza are also 19 m high and consist of four rows of columns. The way in which they open towards the Borgo not only gives the visitor a ceremonial reception but seems to draw him inwards and upwards towards the Cathedral itself. – In the 'Scala Regia' (1563–6), the main entrance to the Vatican in the base-line of the northern colonnade of the 'piazza retta', Bernini introduced an outstandingly successful piece of trick perspective, making the narrow shaft of the staircase appear like a grand triumphal arch.

Venice

S. Maria della Salute, Venice, built between 1631 and 1656 by Baldassare Longhena (1592–1682), represents in its own way a solution to the problem which had dominated architecture since the sixteenth century, namely the combination of centralized and longitudinal structures. But in the present context, it is the exterior which concerns us more *(ill. 207)*. Because of the position of the church on a point of land between the Grand Canal and the Canal della Guidecca, the intricate group formed by the main dome above the octagonal central space and the smaller chancel dome with its two flanking turrets assumes great importance in relation to the aspect of the city. The church was carefully designed to accord with St. Mark's Cathedral and S. Giorgio Maggiore, and to constitute a further landmark for the benefit of visitors arriving from the sea. As a result, it forms an integral part of the total organism of the city and provides a triumphal approach to the main artery and processional way of Venice – the Grand Canal.

Paris

In comparison with the Italian architecture of the period, the Church of the *Val-de-Grâce, Paris (ill. 208)*, built in 1645–62 by François Mansart (1598–1666) and Jacques Lemercier (1585–1654), is a great deal more restrained, yet in its extremely sculptural conception it is a perfect example of Italian-influenced High Baroque. There is no movement in the walls, however, and the building as a whole remains true to the Renaissance principle of contained dynamics.

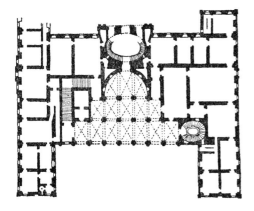

153 Rome, Palazzo Barberini

II High Baroque Secular Architecture

Rome

Italian palace architecture moved in the same direction as church architecture, although for practical reasons imagination was contained within certain limits. The design for the *Palazzo Barberini, Rome (ill. 209)* was drawn up in 1625 by Carlo Maderna. Borromini worked on the building for a time, and Bernini completed it in 1663. It departed from the normal ground plan of Roman palaces in having two wings jutting out towards the city and in having no interior court *(fig. 153)*. The central building is linked to the wings by means of lower and slightly recessed extensions which take on the same form as the wings. With its open ground floor and its two loggia-like upper storeys, it resembles the court façade of earlier palaces turned to face outwards. The exterior space flows into the arcade and is progressively narrowed down, penetrating the entire ground floor. The main hall and the oval garden hall form the central spatial axis of the piano nobile. The extensions which link the central building with the wings both contain staircases. The one on the right, a spiral staircase, was designed by Maderna. The other was by Bernini and was the first staircase in Rome to absorb exterior space so completely into itself. Prototypes for such staircases had existed since the second half of the sixteenth century in palaces in Genoa (e.g. the Palazzo Doria-Tursi, built after 1564 by Lurago), where the sloping ground had made spatial development on one plane impossible.

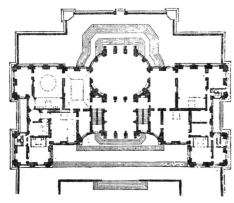

154 Château of Vaux-le-Vicomte

France

It is possible that the open three-winged form of the Palazzo Barberini was inspired by the châteaux architecture of France where it had been in use since the sixteenth century. The *Château of Maisons-Laffitte* near Paris (1642–6, *ill. 210*) by François Mansart is a clear and still relatively strict example of this form. Very much more complex is the *Château of Vaux-le-Vicomte* near Paris (1656–61, *ill. 212* and *fig. 154*), designed by Louis Levau (1612–70) in conjunction with André Lenôtre (1613–1700) who laid out the garden. The whole château consists of a series of 'pavillons' gradually increasing in depth and height and intricately bound together. They appear to radiate out from the powerful central axis of the square vestibule and the oval garden hall. On either side of this axis, the rooms succeed each other with perfect symmetry and all the rooms on the garden side have their doors on the same axis so that they form an 'enfilade' with an uninterrupted view from one end to the other. The whole organic composition stands on its own in an open space, untouched by the wildness of nature dominated only by Lenôtre's landscape gardening. Roads radiate out it across country in all directions. The very growth of the plants in the garden is dictated by it. The château has become an autocratic ruler. Versailles is only a step away.

Holland and Sweden

Compared with these developments, a building like the *Mauritshuis, The Hague* (1633–44, *ill. 211*), by Jacob van Campen (1595–1657) and Pieter Post (1608–69) represents a return to pure Renaissance architecture. The simple cube with its colossal pilasters is thoroughly articulated but in such a restrained manner that the impression given is a very severe one, alleviated only by a sort of delicate elegance. The Knight's House, Stockholm (1641–74), built by Jean de la Vallée and H. W. and J. Vingboons, is very similar in character.

III Louis XIV

Versailles

The buildings we have just mentioned simply ignore Italian developments in High Baroque, but the *Château of Versailles (ill. 213* and *fig. 155)* moves deliberately away from them. Versailles was intended to embody Louis XIV's absolutism in architectural form and thus to serve

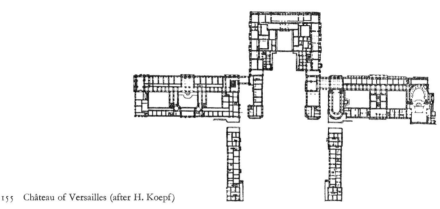

155 Château of Versailles (after H. Koepf)

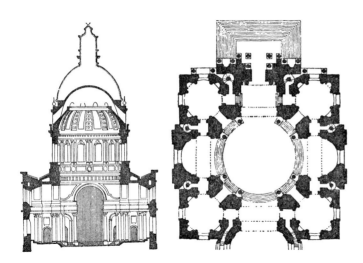

156 Paris, Dome of Les Invalides, elevation and ground plan

as a model for all monarchs. Its starting-point was the small three-winged château which Salomon de Brosse had built in 1623 for Louis XIII and which, contrary to the architect's wishes, had to be incorporated in the new building. Levau began mantling the wings in 1661, but the decisive alterations were not undertaken until 1668–71 with the addition of the two graduated court wings and the park façade, the width of which was determined by the outer edges of the court wings. Levau articulated this extended façade by erecting two corner pavilions, and connecting them by means of a terrace running along above the ground floor, setting the upper storey of the central block back by one axis and giving the building an organic unity like Vaux-le-Vicomte. At the same time, in 1667, Lenôtre began laying out the park. However, when Jules Hardouin Mansart (1646–1708) took over the work in 1678, he brought to it a different approach – one which had been developed by French architects as a result of their victory over Bernini concerning the design for the Louvre. He closed in the terrace between the corner pavilions, forming the Galerie des Glaces, and established the present continuous park façade which is only barely enlivened by the slightly projecting central portion. The dignity of the earlier façade, which had drawn its life and flexibility from the organism of which it formed a part, was replaced by a piece of pure representative display which already contained within it the seeds of formalization and rigidity. There is something slightly megalomanic about the almost infinite extension of the park façade by means of the two deeply recessed lateral wings to an overall length of 576 m. In 1699–1710, the Royal Chapel was added and beginning in 1742, a further enlargement took place under Louis XV in the shape of the two large wings to either side of the entrance court, constituting a sort of introduction to the site as a whole. The wing on the right was built by Jacques-Ange Gabriel (1698–1782) and the other, an exact copy of it, was completed under Louis-Philippe, the 'Bourgeois King', who reigned 1830–48.

The Dome of Les Invalides
No different from Versailles was the other enormous complex built by Louis XIV in 1671–91 to house 7,000 army veterans, comprising the Hôpital des Invalides and the *Dome of St. Louis*

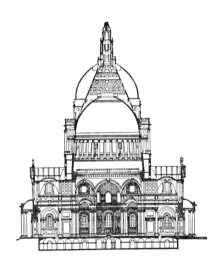

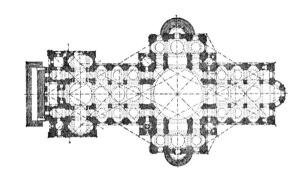

157 London, St. Paul's, elevation and ground plan

des Invalides. Modelled on the Escorial, the entire site measures 250 × 270 m and includes seventeen courts. The Dome (1680–91, *ill. 215* and *fig. 156*) was designed by Jules Hardouin Mansart. The ground plan, a Greek cross within a square, and the domed crossing recall St. Peter's, Rome, but the building differs from its model not only in its proportions and articulation, but also in the character of the centralized structure. It retains nothing of Michelangelo's forceful tension and very little of the dynamic movement of Italian Baroque. On the contrary, although perfect in the regularity of its geometrical and mathematical formation, it appears extremely rigid. The module is the radius of the central circle. It is repeated in the side arms of the Greek cross, so that these arms measure four times the module. The corner chapels measure one and a half times the module, making the diagonal axes five times the module. The distance from the floor to the base of the drum is equal to the diameter of the circle, and the height of the drum and interior dome are equal to one and a half times the diameter of the circle, so that the total height of the interior measures the same as the diagonal axes. The dome itself consists of three shells. The lower shell is left open and the eye travels through to the second closed shell. This is elliptical in shape, and is lit by the topmost row of windows visible from the exterior but invisible from the interior, making the vault look as if it is floating in a vacuum. The third and outer shell is carried on a wooden structure which supports the lantern. The same sort of majestic, rather rigid dignity is apparent in French urban architecture of this period, for example in Jules Hardouin Mansart's *Place Vendôme, Paris* (1698, *ill. 214*). Projecting pediments at the centre of the sides and above the angled corners give it the character of an articulated organism, but one which is so heavily armoured that it can hardly move at all.

London

Contemporary with the Dome of Les Invalides is *St. Paul's Cathedral, London* (1675–1710, *ill. 216* and *fig. 157*), designed by Sir Christopher Wren (1632–1723). It too competed with St. Peter's. It measures *c.* 157 m in overall length, and the distance from the floor to the top of the lantern is 111.65 m, being a perfect combination of longitudinal and centralized structures, and is completely consistent throughout both in ground plan and elevation. The building's height, size and arrangement of space are all organically evolved, and the structure possesses a high degree of rhythmic animation. The columns of the two-storeyed temple façade are grouped in pairs, and this coupling is repeated in the pilasters of the wings, which at the same time constitute a base for the Borrominiesque towers. The same type of articulation is continued around the entire building. In plasticity and movement, however, St. Paul's Cathedral falls short of Italian Baroque. It also falls short of French architecture in respect of physical presence, but resembles it in the classic calm of its members. The triple dome is similar to that of Les Invalides. In fact, both of them probably stemmed from a design which François Mansart made in 1665.

Guarino Guarini

The work of Guarino Guarini (1624–83) in Turin demonstrates how much English and French architecture differed from Italian in the last quarter of the seventeenth century. Stylistically, Guarini was the successor to Borromini but he far surpassed him in the mathematical precision and inventiveness of his buildings. The main portion of the *Palazzo Carignano* (1679–92, *ill. 217* and *fig. 158*) literally seethes with an organic flexibility of imagination bordering on the absurd. Immediately behind the central section of the façade, which curves out in the shape of an oval, two correspondingly shaped staircases lead to the upper storey and frame an oval vestibule. This oval cylindrical core projects above the top of the building. The oval façade is split from top to bottom, and represents two quarter ovals lying on either side of the portal axis. There is a vertical movement within the split which pushes up the line of the cornice as well. A fantastically convoluted pediment embraces the three main axes. Guarini's Church of *S. Lorenzo* (1666–87, *ill. 218* and *fig. 159*) is even more complex in form and is quite impossible to describe in the space of a few sentences. Its ground plan and elevation give rise to an infinity of spatial and formal constellations which appear in any number of different combinations. There is a similar wealth of movement in his Cappella della Santissima Sindone (1667–94) in Turin Cathedral.

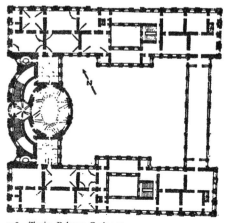

158   Turin, Palazzo Carignano

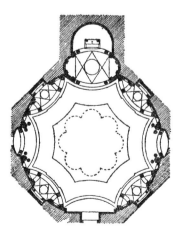

159   Turin, S. Lorenzo

246

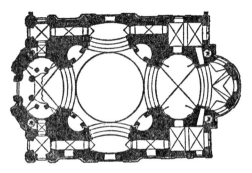

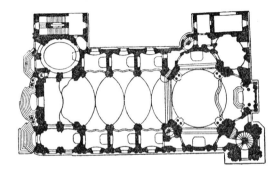

160 Gabel. northern Bohemia, St. Laurenz

161 Prague, St. Nikolaus auf der Kleinseite

IV Late Baroque Church Architecture

Italian architects in Germany

The kind of imaginative architecture begun by Borromini and more especially by Guarini was taken up most notably in Austria, Bohemia, southern Germany and the German part of Switzerland from the late seventeenth century onwards. With an almost explosive violence, these countries began to make up for the century of architectural development they had missed. The Thirty Years' War (1618–48) had made any kind of architectural endeavour unthinkable for most of the first half of the century, and another thirty years had been necessary to recover from it. But then a real passion for building broke out, directed almost exclusively by Italian architects. The Servitenkirche, Vienna, was begun in 1651 by Carlo Cannevale, the *Theatinerkirche, Munich (fig. page 238)*, in 1663 by Barelli and Zuccali, the Palais Czernin, Prague, in 1667 by Francesco Caratti, Passau Cathedral in 1668 by Carlo Lurago, the Stift Haug, Würzburg, in 1670 by Antonio Petrini and the Palais Liechtenstein, Vienna, in 1692 by Domenico Martinelli.

The first generation of German architects

The work of the first generation of German architects far surpassed that of all their predecessors combined. Johann Lucas von Hildebrandt (1668–1745) began the Church of *St. Laurenz, Gabel*, in northern Bohemia, in 1699 on a ground plan that would have been inconceivable before Guarini's S. Lorenzo *(fig. 160)*. Guarini's mathematical inventiveness, however, which tended towards the abstract, was endowed with substance and meaning by Hildebrandt. The same applies to an even greater extent to *St. Nikolaus auf der Kleinseite, Prague* (1703–11, *fig. 161)*, built by Christoph Dientzenhofer (1655–1722). The extreme flexibility of this building gives it a thoroughly festive air. The façade, like that of the Palazzo Carignano, consists of a central convex bulge, hollowed out with a concave recess, and sweeping concave wings. This undulating movement is communicated to the interior, which in plan is a simple rectangular hall with side chapels but in elevation is of extraordinary complexity, and gives the impression of a longitudinal oval intersected by three lateral ovals. This idea, too, originated with Guarini, who used it in a plan for the Theatinerkirche in Prague which he submitted in 1680 but which was never carried out. Kilian Ignaz Dientzenhofer (1689–1751) later added a large domed centralized structure to his father's nave *(ill. 219)*.

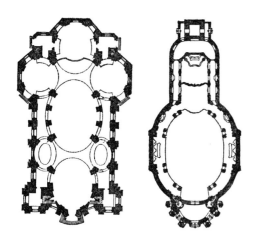

162 Vierzehnheiligen, Pilgrimage Church

163 Wies, near Steingaden, Pilgrimage Church

The second generation

What the first generation had initiated in relation to church architecture, the second generation continued and perfected. There are many examples from this period, but we shall consider only the *Pilgrimage Church, Vierzehnheiligen*, designed by Balthasar Neumann (1687–1753)
and built in 1743–72 *(ill. 220* and *fig. 162)*. In plan, it is a three-aisled basilica but the oval
extension of the nave around the pilgrimage altar transforms it into a centralized structure.
This form is repeated throughout in smaller longitudinal and lateral ovals which, together
with the abundant light and the wealth of colour and ornament, give a gay, lively pulse to an
interior that almost defies comparison with anything outside German architecture of the
eighteenth century. – This gay fairytale quality reaches almost delirious proportions in the
Pilgrimage Church, Wies (1746–54, *fig. 163)*, which was designed by Dominicus Zimmermann
(1685–1766). Here the interior stands in the greatest possible contrast to the modest, simple
exterior, which gives no hint of the fluent splendour within.

Spain

The only country to compete with Germany in decorative imagination, though in a very different way, was Spain. The development was rather slower there and reached a climax in 1724–
64 with the *Cartuja* (Charterhouse) at Granada *(ill. 221)*, particularly in the sacristy built by
Luis de Arévalo and F. Manuel Vasquez. Reminiscent of some Moorish palace or Indian temple,
it is a mixture of mathematical abstraction and tropical vegetation, both of which spell death
to any concept of the building as an organism. A similar dissolution characterizes the façade
of *Murcia Cathedral* begun in 1737 by Jaime Bort y Melía *(ill. 222)*.

England

A contemporary English church, *St. Martin-in-the-Fields, London* (1721–6, *ill. 223)*, designed
by James Gibbs (1682–1754) looks very different. It is rigidly rectangular in form with a
Corinthian temple façade standing in front and a Baroque spire, modelled on Wren's designs,
above it. Although the building remains a homogeneous organism, it has been robbed of all

248

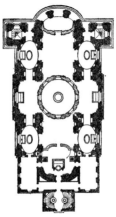

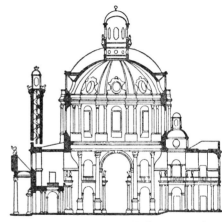

164 Salzburg, Church of
the Jesuit College

165 Vienna, Karlskirche (St. Charles Borromeus),
(after H. Koepf)

flexibility with the exception of the spire. The interior, a three-aisled hall-church with galleries, in-swinging pilaster walls in front of the chancel and enormous Palladian windows in the chancel end, is comparable to German Late Baroque in width, spaciousness and abundance of light, but the lack of colour and movement give it a completely different character.

France

In a slightly different way, the same is true of the façade of *St. Sulpice, Paris* (1733–54, *ill. 224*), which was designed by Giovanni Niccolò Servandoni (1695–1766) and placed before a nave of a completely different shape which had been begun in 1656. It has been pointed out that the present shape of the façade does not correspond to Servandoni's design, but dates from some twenty years later when it was decided to terminate it with a balustrade. Chalgrin's north tower was added in 1777. Although there is still some connection between the towers and the lower storeys, and between these and the rather different middle section, one can no longer talk in terms of organic growth, nor is there any lateral thrust from the centre outwards. The composition contains an element of Baroque drama, but it is incapable of animating the rationality of the whole and the rigidity of the individual parts.

Fischer von Erlach

Parallel to the gay, almost frenzied development of church architecture in southern Germany ran a stricter and more monumental vein represented by the work of *Johann Bernhard Fischer von Erlach* (1656–1723). Outside the church architecture of Italy, his *Church of the Jesuit College, Salzburg* (1694–1707, *ill. 225* and *fig. 164*) is one of the most powerful examples of High Baroque. It is a combination of centralized and longitudinal structures, with the accent on centralization. The square of the crossing, surmounted by a high drum and dome, is the spatial focus of the whole of the interior of the church, which is 75 m long and 38 m wide. The sculptured massiveness and powerful articulation of the colossal pilasters emphasize the loftiness of the interior, and convey an impression of almost heroic grandeur. The formative power of the

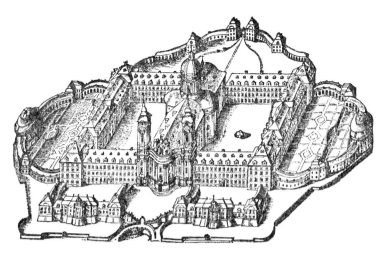

166 Weingarten, Benedictine Abbey, as planned in 1723

building is also revealed in the façade, which emerges forcefully between two towers. Fischer von Erlach worked for Bernini for a long time and his influence, as well as that of Guarini, can be seen in this church. The monumental façade was taken as the model for those of the monastery churches of *Weingarten* (1715–22, *fig. 166*) and Ottobeuren (begun in 1744). – In the Church of the Trinity, Salzburg (1690–1702), Fischer von Erlach discovered a slightly different way of increasing the monumentality of a building. He again applied a semi-oval façade to the relatively small elongated oval body of the church, but this time, inspired by S. Agnese, Rome, he made it swing inwards between two towers. His last church, the *Karlskirche, Vienna* (known as St. Charles Borromeus, 1715–23, *fig. 165*), constituted the sum of his entire experience of Classical, Renaissance and Baroque architecture. Two triumphal columns based on Classical models stand before the broad temple façade, with the drum and dome of the centralized structure rising behind. It is a practical demonstration of the kind of synthesis of architectural grandeur which he had formulated in his book *Entwurf einer historischen Architektur*, published in 1721. His enormous designs for the Hofburg in Vienna and the Palace of Schönbrunn were only partially executed.

German monasteries

The large number of monasteries built during this period represent a combination of ecclesiastical and secular architecture. The most splendid example is certainly the *Benedictine monastery of Melk, Austria*, begun by Jakob Prandtauer (1660–1726) in 1702, and completed by Josef Munggenast in 1738 *(ill. 229)*. The 320 m long main axis of the site terminates in the double-tower façade of the church which is framed by two converging pavilions linked by a deeply-curved gallery. This powerful sculptural composition is crowned by the 64 m high dome. The church follows the pattern of Il Gesù, Rome. A lively sense of movement informs the monumental plasticity of the whole organism, achieving a synthesis of the two possibilities of architectural expression represented by Hildebrandt and Fischer von Erlach. – The *Benedictine Abbey of Weingarten in Württemberg (fig. 166)*, begun in 1715 but only half built, went even

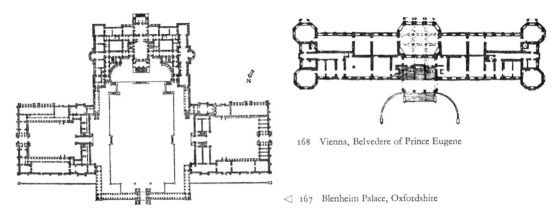

168 Vienna, Belvedere of Prince Eugene

◁ 167 Blenheim Palace, Oxfordshire

further than Melk in the intricacy and invention of its organic formation. The author of the plan, which looks like a magnificent ornamental showpiece, was probably Caspar Moosbrugger (1656–1723), who had drawn up a similar plan in 1703 for the monastery of Einsiedeln. As the man who introduced Italian ideas into south-west Germany, he occupies as important a place in the history of architecture as Fischer von Erlach and Hildebrandt, who did the same for south-east Germany.

The Superga

How much further High Baroque developed in Germany than in Italy can be seen in an Italian building that was contemporary with Melk and Weingarten and can be compared to them – the *Superga, near Turin* (1717–31, *ill. 226*). Its architect, Filippo Juvarra (1678–1736), was of the same generation as Balthasar Neumann. Although entirely Baroque in conception, in execution it is closer to the characteristic 'raison' of French architecture than to anything that had been built in Italy during the seventeenth century or that was being built in Germany during this period. It has a calmer, more classic quality, starting from the rectangular columned portico which forms the entrance to the site. This portico neither resolves the forward thrust of the powerful six-storeyed monastery block nor does it initiate any real movement itself. The hard lines of all the members of the building as well as the mathematical 'raison' which permeates it inhibit any feeling of life and growth.

V Late Baroque Secular Architecture

England

A good introduction to eighteenth-century secular architecture is provided by one of the best examples of High Baroque to be built in England, *Blenheim Palace, Woodstock, Oxfordshire (ill. 227)*. Blenheim was designed in 1705 by Sir John Vanbrugh (1664–1726) and completed in 1724 by Nicholas Hawksmoor (1661–1736). Both in form and in size, it competed with Versailles. The graduated wings link up with the large kitchen and stable courts to form an expansive 'cour d'honneur' *(fig. 167)*. Curved colonnades form the joints between the wings and the main block. The central axis formed by the Great Hall and the Garden Salon thrusts out powerful temple façades of pillars and columns in both directions. Two semicircular apses in the centre of the sides stress the ends of the lateral axis which follows the court façade. This axis has little importance in terms of the spatial construction of the building, and is only there to give greater geometrical regularity to the ground plan. Both ground plan and elevation are richly developed in exact symmetry and give the impression of an extremely flexible organism, but an essential element is missing. The building lacks a sense of presence and of coherent animation. Its flexibility appears mechanical and rattles and creaks in the joints – one might almost say 'hinges'. The entire building is too disturbed, too broken up; it disintegrates into individual parts which seem to have been piled together as a child piles wooden bricks. A typical example, and one could mention a great many, is the utterly inorganic way in which the wings are made to collide with the corner pavilions with no attempt at transition. There is probably not one single example of such an 'abstract' treatment in the whole of the Baroque architecture of the Continent. It was typical of England's pioneering role in the eighteenth century, in that it pointed the way towards the new architectural style of Classicism.

Germany

In contrast to Blenheim, the *Belvedere of Prince Eugene, Vienna* (1721–3, *ill. 228* and *fig. 168*), designed by Lucas von Hildebrandt on the French 'pavillon' system, constitutes a particularly lively organism. The triaxial central pavilion, with its broad high projecting mansard roof, dominates the graduated wings of the garden façade which terminate gaily in octagonal pavilions. The court façade follows the same principle in a slightly different way, and contrary to the French custom does not form a 'cour d'honneur'. The central pavilion not only forms the centre of the exterior aspect, but it performs the same function in the development of the interior as well. It combines the staircases leading from the garden and from the court up to the banqueting hall which lies above the 'sala terrena', and occupies the whole height of the pavilion. This functional and at the same time beautifully dignified centrepiece of the château perfectly embodies the principle of organic architecture. – The same gaiety of conception,

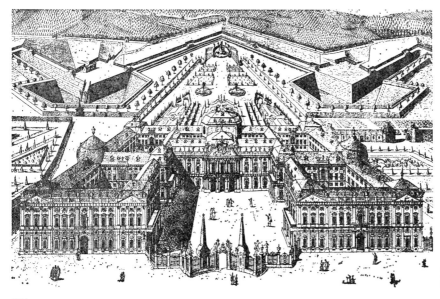

169 Würzburg, Residenz, engraving from 1760

252

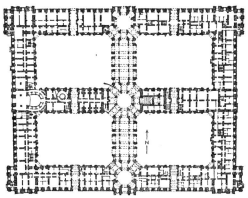

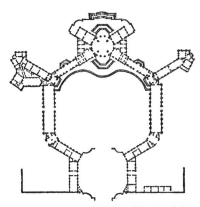

170 Naples, the Caserta

171 Stupinigi, near Turin, Royal hunting lodge

heightened to a frenzy of fluid corporeality, determined the form and character of the *Zwinger, Dresden* (1711–22, *ill. 230* and *fig. page 238*), a building which was designed by Matthäus Daniel Pöppelmann (1662–1736) expressly as a place in which to hold celebrations. It was only a small part of a huge plan to rebuild the royal palace in a series of four large courts starting from the open side of the Zwinger and going down towards the Elbe. In 1847–9 this open side was closed off in a most unfortunate manner by Gottfried Semper's gallery. At either end of the 204 m long lateral axis stand two-storeyed oval pavilions which were exuberantly decorated with sculptures under the direction of Balthasar Permoser. Here the concept of organic architecture is expressed quite literally in writhing torsos and luxuriant vegetation.

But there was a stricter, more majestic vein of secular architecture just as there was of ecclesiastical architecture. Its most perfect expression was the *Château built in Berlin* in 1698–1706 by Andreas Schlüter (*c.* 1664–1714) and since pulled down *(ill. 231)*. Contrary to Versailles and its successors, but in conformity with the tradition of Italian palaces, this huge building formed an enclosed rectangle. Michelangelo and Bernini were the dominant influences. All its members had the heavy fullness typical of High Baroque and appeared to grow out of the body of the building. – Balthasar Neumann achieved a classic synthesis of dignity and gaiety in the *Residenz, Würzburg*, built in 1719–44 *(fig. 169)*. The experience and advice of a large number of Austrian and French architects were called upon before the completion of the existing building with its 'cour d'honneur', four internal courts, numerous pavilions and dominant central structure containing the staircase and the imperial hall. The staircase *(ill. 232)* and hall were decorated in 1751–3 with Tiepolo's magnificent frescoes. In its compactness as well as in its extremely rich but perfectly organic articulation, the whole building could hardly offer a greater contrast to Blenheim Palace.

VI Conclusion

Italy

The last of the very large Baroque châteaux, the *Caserta near Naples (ill. 233* and *fig. 170)*, was begun in 1752 by Luigi Vanvitelli (1700–73) and completed a year after his death. The question has often been raised as to whether the Caserta, like St. Sulpice, Paris, is to be regarded

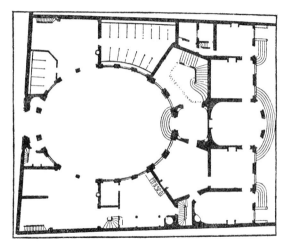

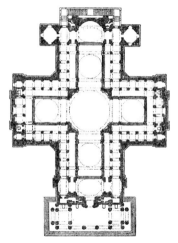

172   Paris, Hôtel Amelot

173   Paris, the Panthéon

as an early example of Classicism. Everything, however, tells against such a verdict. The staircase, which is the largest in Italy, the domed hall at the point of intersection of the arms of the cross, the articulation of the façade by means of projections, the regular disposition of the rooms, the detail – all these stand firmly in the Baroque tradition. Only the life has gone out of them, to be replaced by deathly cold boredom. The Caserta, far from being an example of a new spirit using the old forms, only shows the rigidity into which those forms had fallen.

In Rome, the wealth of examples all around encouraged a stronger adherence to tradition right up until the middle of the eighteenth century. Within that tradition, there was even something like a fresh development which might be termed 'Roman Rococo', and of which the most beautiful creation was the Piazza S. Ignazio (1727–8) by Filippo Raguzzini (c. 1680–1771). The gay relaxed quality of this piazza is also apparent in the work of Ferdinando Fuga (1699–1782), whose *Palazzo della Consultà* of 1732–7, compared with sixteenth- and seventeenth-century palaces, is all lightness and unburdened joy *(ill. 234)*. The dense composition of pilasters and window-surrounds in the façade is no longer an expression of dynamic structural tension, but represents rather a relaxed play of ornament on an indifferent surface. – The *royal hunting lodge of Stupinigi near Turin* (1729–33) by Filippo Juvarra, despite its highly imaginative ground plan *(fig. 171)*, is not so successful in creating a mood of gaiety. It is another example of the tendency which we observed in the Superga, Turin. The same mathematical striving after 'raison' obscures any feeling of organic presence and inclines towards a certain rigidity.

France

The French architecture of the same period presents a very different picture. After the epoch of Louis XIV, when architecture had been required to represent the grandeur and majesty of its patrons, life became more civilized and a quality of intimacy and comfort began to appear in the many small country residences and town houses of the eighteenth century. Germain Boffrand (1667–1754) began the *Hotel Amelot, Paris (ill. 235* and *fig. 172)*, shortly after 1710.

Using the limited space available in a quite exemplary way, both as regards functionalism and beauty, he created a perfectly harmonious organism. The court façade was given a certain dignity by the use of colossal pilasters, but it was not oppressive. All the members became delicate and flat, the masonry lost its density and a cultivated elegance informed the entire structure. A similar transformation occurred in the *Petit Trianon* (1762–4, *ill. 236*) built in the Park of Versailles by Jacques-Ange Gabriel, another building which has often been regarded as an early example of Classicism. Yet here again, everything was firmly within the Renaissance/Baroque tradition, only rather than appearing rigid like the Caserta, it had become so delicate and almost anaemic as to have lost all dynamism.

A similar problem of classification arises in connection with the *Panthéon* or Church of Ste. Geneviève, *Paris (ill. 237* and *fig. 173)*, designed in 1755 by Jacques-Germain Soufflot (1709–80) and completed in 1792. If Classicism is defined exclusively in terms of Greek antiquity, then the Panthéon does not belong to it, for Soufflot took all his ideas from the Renaissance and from Classical Rome. The centralized structure, based on a Greek cross, represented the Renaissance ideal. The drum and dome were modelled on Bramante's Tempietto. The graduated repetition of the temple façade at the sides is typically Baroque, as is the spatial complexity of the interior which bears no relation to the clarity of the ground plan. The only distinctive mark of a new stylistic tendency towards abstract nobility is the stereometric rigidity of the outer walls, which only took on this form when the windows were filled in during the French Revolution. While the windows were still there, the building had a certain presence. Certainly everything else about the exterior is rigid and inflexible too, but this is to be interpreted as a negative result of the dying concept of organic architecture rather than as positive evidence of the emergence of a new style.

England
Chiswick House, London (ill. 238), must surely be interpreted in the same way. Begun in 1725 by the Earl of Burlington (1694–1753) and William Kent (1685–1748), it was modelled on Palladio's Villa Rotonda, and as such represented a return to the ideas of Inigo Jones' English Renaissance. The contrast with Sir John Vanbrugh's exuberant Baroque is not in fact as great as at first appears. Kent's Holkham Hall, Norfolk, begun in 1734, resembles Blenheim Palace both in the intricacy of its symmetrical ground plan and in the 'abstract' way in which the various parts are joined together, but whereas Vanbrugh had given his building an element of imaginative cohesion, Holkham Hall is an extremely arid assemblage of blocks. 'Each section of a design is autonomous, related to the whole only by a general system of ratios and by strict symmetry.' (John Summerson, *Architecture in Britain 1530–1830*, London, 1953.) In this staccato rhythm, there is more than a hint of the later development represented by the work of Sir John Soane and by 'Revolutionary Architecture'. Kent's landscape gardening was even more influential than his architecture. Firmly rejecting the geometrical discipline so fashionable in France, he introduced the idea of the natural park, the so-called 'English Garden'. – This entirely new conception of the relationship between architecture and its surroundings was taken up again in the *Circus (ill. 239)* and the Royal Crescent, *Bath*, built in 1754–75 by John Wood the Elder (1704–54) and John Wood the Younger (1728–81). Instead of being treated as a regular self-contained organism, the town was opened right up to draw its natural

surroundings into itself. 'Nature is no longer the servant of architecture. The two are equals. The Romantic Movement is at hand.' (Nikolaus Pevsner, *An Outline of European Architecture*, London, 1960.)

Classicism and Romanticism ushered in a new era which marked the beginning of a total change in the architectural traditions of the West.

11 Romantic Classicism

Characteristics: Interior space, walls, ceilings and vaults were once again reduced to their simplest and most basic form in imitation primarily of Classical Greek but also partly of Egyptian architecture. There was little or no articulation and decoration.
The Renaissance and Baroque concept of buildings as flexible, living organisms was abandoned, and our terminology must change accordingly to include such epithets as 'rational' and 'abstract'.

Materials: Freestone, brick, wood and iron.

Potsdam, Nikolaikirche ▷

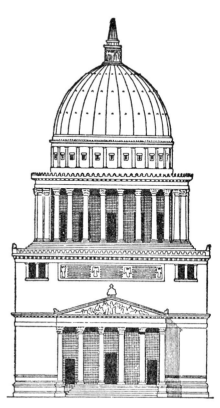

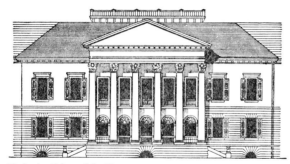

Karlsruhe, Palace of the Margrave

Gothic architecture, which was derived as we have seen from Romanesque and Carolingian architecture and ultimately went back to the Early Christian architecture of the Late Classical period, undoubtedly constituted the most original creative achievement of the Western Christian civilization. The Renaissance did not represent a real break in this continuity since it was based partly on the Romanesque 'Pre-Renaissance' of Tuscany, and for the rest upon pagan Classical elements which were understood and experienced personally as part of the legacy of the past. The new style which began to emerge towards the end of the eighteenth century, however, rather than growing out of a tradition experienced at first hand and passed down from one generation to the next, rested on an entirely new kind of historical consciousness and on an entirely new philosophical and ideological aesthetic, in short on theory and abstraction. Whatever we call this new style – Classicism and Romanticism or Romantic Classicism – it set out to give architectural form to certain ideas and feelings, with absolute beauty as an ethical norm, in accordance with the ideals which mankind had inherited once and for all from Classical Greece, and, together with absolute beauty, virtue and intellectual purity; the nobility and majesty of death, to which Egyptian architectural forms lent themselves; and an idealization of nature, a yearning for the inexpressible and a sense of melancholy at the transitoriness of life, as expressed in Neo-Gothic ruins and in Neo-Gothic architecture itself.

As a result of these philosophical, ideological (and no longer primarily Christian) demands, historical prototypes were chosen, though not at first in any deliberate way, even if a degree of deliberation was already inherent in the possibility of choice, and architecture moved radically away from the practice of treating buildings as physical organisms that had characterized the preceding Renaissance and Baroque periods. The idea of a building as a bodily 'incarination' to be appreciated through the senses came to be regarded as false and impure. Buildings were required to represent the mind and spirit, and it was in this sense that they became abstract. In addition to all this, there were certain new tasks for architecture to perform which had not existed before, but these we will mention in connection with the examples as they occur. The process of abstraction can also be explained better in the context of the buildings themselves.

I The Beginnings of Romantic Classicism

France

The new style did not, of course, make its appearance suddenly; it required a certain period of incubation. In fact, it is virtually impossible to distinguish with absolute certainty between those buildings that still represented the old style and those that heralded the new. However, a building like the Church of *St. Philippe-du-Roule, Paris* (1769–84, *ill. 240*), designed by J.F.T. Chalgrin (1739–1811), can perhaps be said to have made this transition if we compare it with St. Sulpice and the Panthéon in Paris and the Petit Trianon at Versailles. The new features are the return to the pure basilican plan, in this case complete with tunnel-vaulted nave, the total absence of any decoration, representing the new 'purity', the prevailing impression of rigid immobility, and a certain lack of massiveness about the building as a whole. This rigidity is not, as in the case of the Caserta and elsewhere, the effect of a moribund style but something quite deliberate. – In the *Grand Théâtre, Bordeaux (ill. 241)*, built in 1773–80 by Victor Louis (1731–1800), the foyer, reception and social rooms, staircases, auditorium, stage and dressing rooms are all contained within an elongated cube with no hint as to either their function or their arrangement being allowed to appear on the exterior. Before this rigid block stands an equally rigid colonnade, intended originally to surround the whole building, which would have turned it into an exaggerated peripteros, albeit more Roman than Greek in character. With this building the theatre became transformed into the 'temple of the muses', receiving an unchristian sanctification it had never possessed before. The same form was later used for churches and stock exchanges.

The significance of theory

The study of Greek architecture began in earnest around the middle of the eighteenth century. It had been completely ignored by previous ages, and even temples which were in the vicinity of much-visited towns, like those at Paestum near Naples, were only discovered during this period. The Doric columns without bases, particularly, created a great stir. Greek art was discussed in Winckelmann's *Geschichte der Kunst des Altertums* (History of Ancient Art) of 1764, the first history of art that can be called modern. At the same time, theoreticians were beginning to formulate the demands for a new architecture. One of the earliest and most emphatic of these was Carlo Lodoli (1690–1761), a Franciscan monk from Venice. He had given expression to his ideas as early as the 'forties, but they were not published until 1786, after his death, by Andrea Memmo under the title *Elementi di Architettura Lodoliana* (Principles of Lodolian Architecture). During his lifetime, however, his ideas had already influenced Francesco Milizia (1725–98). According to Lodoli, the chief requirements of architecture were that it should be functional and that it should do justice to its materials. Both points were in sharp contrast to the traditional ideas. The right use of materials had never concerned anyone before, but it now assumed the character of a moral demand for truth. Functionalism, too, departed radically from the concept of buildings as organisms, representing as it did a purely rational demand that a building fulfil its practical purpose in the highest possible degree, which again, on the moral level, amounted to truth. Similar ideas were expounded by Marc-Antoine Laugier, a Jesuit priest in Paris and a contemporary of Lodoli.

Noble simplicity and quiet grandeur

The idea of 'virtue' in a building demanded not only size and strength, but also simplicity and nobility. It was not required to represent anything in the institutional sense, but to display an attitude. Even when an element inherited from the Renaissance tradition was used, as for example in the triumphal gate, it was not endowed with the dramatic character of the Roman triumphal arch – unless there was an imperious will like that of Napoleon behind it (e. g. the Arc de Triomphe, Paris). For the ideal of 'noble simplicity and quiet grandeur', however, only Greek forms were suitable. The most beautiful example is the *Brandenburger Tor, Berlin (ill. 243)*, built in 1789–94 by Carl Gotthard Langhans (1732–1808). The Propylaea of the Acropolis, Athens, provided the model, although the Doric columns were given rather un-Greek bases, showing the lingering influence of the Baroque. The immobility of the structure, however, was something quite new. The connections between the gate and the guardhouse 'temples' on either side are not like natural, organic joints but more like hinges. The three parts are placed together in a functional relationship; they do not grow out of each other organically. The Brandenburger Tor is a construction rather than a physical presence. There is no appeal to the senses, only a sort of intellectual abstraction. The symbolic power of architecture had ceased to be something that could be appreciated directly and immediately by body, mind and spirit together and had become a completely abstract idea.

Robert Adam

Robert Adam (1728–92) belonged to the same generation as Chalgrin, Louis and Langhans. His most important piece of urban architecture, the Adelphi on the Embankment, London (1768–72), was pulled down in 1937. *No. 7, John Adam Street* is one of his few buildings to have survived *(ill. 242)*. It retains an echo of the Petit Trianon, although the differences between the two buildings are immediately apparent. The unusually elongated pilasters of the façade do not constitute a structural element but are applied almost like a quotation. There is also a hint of Rococo in the delicacy of the members.

Neo-Gothic

Another and at first sight irreconcilably different aspect of the new style was expressed very early on in *Strawberry Hill, Twickenham (ill. 244)*, a country house which was extended and gothicized *c.* 1750–70. The ideas were originated by the owner of the house, Horace Walpole (1717–97), the author of the first modern 'thriller', and the architect who executed them was William Robinson *(c.* 1720–75). Apart from the fantastic Neo-Gothic elements which were applied to it, the most significant thing about Strawberry Hill was the irregularity of its plan. Even the most fantastic of Late Baroque buildings still had a regular ground plan. 'In this imitation of the fortuitous, Walpole started something of more far-reaching significance than he can have guessed. He opened the door to the architecture of the Picturesque. (Summerson). The Picturesque style was related to the new attitude towards nature referred to in the last chapter in connection with the 'English Garden', and of course also to Romanticism. The abandonment of regularity and compactness in the layout, however, was far more prophetic, for it has become the most characteristic feature of twentieth-century architecture.

II Revolutionary Architecture

Architecture parlante

Equally prophetic was French 'Revolutionary Architecture', despite the fact that its principal advocates, L. E. Boullée (1728–99) and C. N. Ledoux (1736–1806), belonged to an older

174 Berlin, Werdersche Kirche, sketch by the architect, K. F. Schinkel

generation. Most of their ideas remained on paper, and in any case could hardly have been carried out given the technical means available at the time. This, too, was something quite new in the history of architecture. There had always been unrealized plans, but never before had there been unrealizable ones. It was a further sign of 'abstraction' that ideas no longer bore any relation to what was and what was not possible. The *Barrière de la Villette, Paris* (1784–9, *ill. 245*), one of Ledoux' designs that was actually carried out, is significant for the way it demonstrates just how deeply the new spirit had penetrated. Pillared façades are applied to all four sides of a flat square building on top of which has been added a cylinder with an open arcade. There is no question of any kind of interpenetration of the various parts of the building. All the openings – windows and arcades – are let sharply into the surface of the wall without any kind of sculptural surround, giving the mutually contradictory impressions that the walls consist on the one hand of simple layers of blocks, and on the other of some indefinable material that can be cut as if with a pair of scissors. The Barrière de la Villette is pure 'architecture parlante': a custom-house at the edge of a town must be stern and imposing in order to manifest the power of the state.

Soane

The new approach pioneered by Ledoux and Boullée in the 'seventies and 'eighties had a decisive influence on the work of the next generation. The Consols Office of the Bank of England, London, built in 1794 by Sir John Soane (1752–1837), differed from any centralized structure that had been built in the past in the 'incorporeality' of its outer shell. Indeed, this is so lacking in mass and weight that the interior space, no longer treated as a substance in itself, begins to flow out. The idea of leaving visible the cast-iron frame that supported the glass-work was as revolutionary as the purely linear treatment of the articulation, and an obvious anticipation of twentieth-century principles. An even more radical example of the new approach was Soane's *Dulwich Gallery, London* (1811–14, *ill. 246*), a brick building which in the juxtaposition of its various parts like a child's toy building blocks, represented the principle we observed in Blenheim Palace taken to the extreme. As an inevitable consequence, all incisions in the walls are left unframed, and the decoration is characterized by a sharply linear abstraction. – The same spirit that determined Soane's Bank of England appeared in a slightly less distinct form in the Roman Catholic *Cathedral of Baltimore, Maryland (ill. 247)*, built in 1805–18 by Benjamin H. Latrobe (1764–1820). Latrobe, an English architect trained

261

in England and Germany, had also submitted a Neo-Gothic design – 'one of the finest projects of the "Sublime" or "High Romantic" stage of the Gothic Revival; yet in its vast bare walls, carefully ordered geometry, and dry detail, it is also consonant with some of the basic ideals of Romantic Classicism. (H.-R.Hitchcock). Some time later, Schinkel also submitted two alternative designs, one Classical and one Gothic, for the *Werdersche Kirche, Berlin*, but in this case it was the Gothic design that was used (*fig. 174*). Obviously Classicism and Romanticism were not regarded as being incompatible. In America, Classicism achieved a surprising modernity. David Sears House (the Somerset Club), Boston, built in 1816 by Alexander Parris (1780–1852), anticipated the architecture of the early twentieth century.

Friedrich Gilly

There was a strong streak of the Revolutionary Architecture of France in the design which Friedrich Gilly (1772–1800) drew up in 1797 for the *Memorial to Frederick the Great* to be erected on the Leipziger Platz in Berlin (*ill. 249*). The main plan is related to the processional layout of Egyptian temple complexes, although the isolation of the central portion, stressed by the Doric temple which crowns it, is more reminiscent of the Acropolis. Other Egyptian features are the obelisks and sphinxes, and also the smooth cubic formations which occurred in neither Greek nor Roman architecture but only in the pylons and walls of Egyptian temples. The Egyptian element, with its connotations of the underworld and the realm of the dead, is confined to the lower part of the monument, the part which was to contain the Emperor's mausoleum. The Greek temple above provides a symbol of light and eternity. The rigid unadorned blocks which form the base collide head-on with the hypostyle halls placed between them. Every form is sharply cut, and joins the next without any transition. The openings look as if they have been punched out. The Emperor is not present as an image but as a pure idea, and the memorial by which he is glorified becomes a monument to some kind of supra-personal spiritual power manifest in him. There is no feeling of God's grace; this had always been bound up with Christian images, and there is not a single example of a Christian image left here. The sacred element, however, is not excluded. Although all the forms used are pagan forms, they spring nevertheless from sacred architecture. Reaching beyond the confines of the particular religion of Christianity, the building embraces a sort of world religion conceived in terms of a spiritual and ethical destiny. – We have devoted rather more space than usual to this example, because both in form and content it represents the revolutionary change which had occurred in human thought and feeling with almost programmatic clarity. Gilly's project found a successor in the *Walhalla, Regensburg (ill. 248)*, built in 1831–42 by Leo von Klenze (1784–1864). Another Greek temple towers above a substructure of stereometrically even terraces and flights of steps, but here the whole monument is given a natural setting. It, too, is highly abstract in intention, being dedicated to the German spirit.

'Architecture parlante' in Germany and Italy

The Women's Prison, Würzburg (1809–10, *ill. 250*), by Peter Speeth (1772–1831), was originally intended as a barracks. Its form, symbolizing power, authority and obedience, is certainly adequate to either case. The Doric temple façade let into the bare wall is strangely more reminiscent of Egyptian than of Greek architecture. The note of 'quotation' is characteristic.

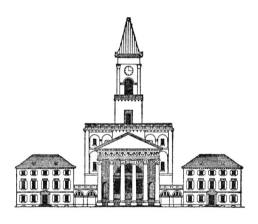

175 Karlsruhe, Marktplatz showing the Protestant Church (after H. Koepf)

The new approach to architecture was completely international in character, and our next example is from Italy – the façade of the *Teatro S.Carlo, Naples (ill. 251)*, built in 1810–12 by Antonio Niccolini (1772–1850). Here, the total absence of any connection between the various parts, in the sense of an organic development from the body to the members, is particularly striking. What takes its place is a sort of ordered community in which each part plays a different expressive role: the ground floor is all earnest austerity, the frieze has a delicate song-like quality, the upper storey is noble, measured and relaxed, and the attic proclaims the triumph of art with modest restraint. – Friedrich Weinbrenner (1766–1826) had the opportunity of erecting a whole complex of buildings in the new style in the *Marktplatz, Karlsruhe* (1804–24, fig. 175). Weinbrenner was influenced both by Revolutionary Architecture and by Gilly. Some of his earlier designs were far more daring than this one, but they all followed the same procedure as observed at work in the façade of the Teatro S.Carlo, each element of the composition being treated entirely in isolation (compare also the Palace of the Margrave, Karlsruhe, fig. page 257).

III The Climax of Romantic Classicism

Schinkel

Apart from Soane, the most important and certainly the most prolific architect of Romantic Classicism was probably Karl Friedrich von Schinkel (1781–1841). His *Neue Wache, Berlin* (1816–18, *ill. 252*), was designed entirely in the spirit of Gilly. It is basically a cube with smooth corner structures reminiscent both of a Roman fort and of Egyptian pylons. A Doric temple façade not only projects out in front of the building, but looks as if it belongs to a complete temple concealed within the cube. This intersection of forms might appear to have some connection with Baroque, but we shall see at once that it represents something entirely different if a simple experiment is contemplated. If, for example, one were to try to take away one pavilion from a Baroque château or extract one spatial cylinder from the Pilgrimage Church, Vierzehnheiligen, this would result in the killing and mutilation of the organism, but if in the case of the Neue Wache one could dislodge the temple from within the cube, neither of the two units would be damaged by the operation. This is certainly an abstract way of

263

explaining the conception of the Neue Wache, but then the idea of penetrating one structure with another was equally an abstraction. The intention was to symbolize both power and nobility, in accordance with the military ideals of discipline and honour to which the building was dedicated. The idea of the sacred, as handed down by the Christian tradition, had no more place here than it had had in Gilly's Memorial to Frederick the Great. – Nor did it have any part to play in another quite new form which architecture was called upon to create during this period – as a replacement, one might almost say, for the church – the museum or 'temple of art'. Not surprisingly, the *Glyptothek, Munich* (1816–34, *ill. 253*), which was begun in the same year as the Neue Wache, makes use of the same elements, a cube and a Greek temple. The architects were Leo von Klenze and Friedrich von Gärtner (1792–1847). The temple in this case follows the Ionic order, which was better suited to the spirit of a museum than the Doric. The cube, completely without windows, is decorated only with statue niches which 'sit' on the walls as if on the smooth surface of a lake, giving the impression that if the lake were not frozen they would swim to and fro. The interior bears no relation to the stereometric form of the exterior. The erection of the picture gallery (1838–48) by G. F. Ziebland (1800–73) opposite the Glyptothek, together with Klenze's Propylaea (1846–63), completed the Königs-platz ensemble. It is colder in its abstraction but also grander than Weinbrenner's Marktplatz in Karlsruhe.

The theatres at Bordeaux and Naples heralded the appearance of another new type of build-ing which, along with the museum, was to constitute one of the most important tasks which architecture was called upon to perform during this period and, indeed, ever since. Schinkel's solution for the *Schauspielhaus, Berlin* (1818–21, *ill. 254*) surpassed everything that had gone before. The building combines the use of expressive forms (Greek temple façade, pediment, etc.) with a new kind of structural functionalism. It represents a composition of separate stereometric formations which are themselves composed of a large number of self-contained parts. The beams that divide the windows do not give the impression of being extensions of the wall in the shape of pillars, but look like so many individual components, almost as if they were prefabricated parts that could be assembled in whatever form was required. The same applies to all the elements of the building – corner-pieces, columns, entablature and pediment. They have been chosen out of a box of bricks, as it were, to fulfil their particular function. The metaphor is deliberate for this 'Ankerbrick-box' later became part of the international currency of architectural terminology, though by then it had acquired a pejorative value for reasons which we shall examine in the next chapter. We must not, however, overlook the fact that it originally represented a genuine structural principle of the new architecture, seen in Schinkel's Schauspielhaus in its most creative form, where it is still pregnant with the noble ethos of Classicism.

England

The largest monument to Greek Classicism in England, the *British Museum, London (ill. 255)*, was begun in 1824, the same year as Schinkel's Old Museum, Berlin. Its architect was Sir Robert Smirke (1781–1867) and it was completed in 1847. The institutional nature of the building is expressed in the forty-eight Ionic columns of the south front, which represents the culmination of the strictly 'Classical' phase of European Classicism. – The same forms as were used for museums, theatres, churches and stock exchanges during this period were adopted also for centres of pure intellectualism such as academies and universities. A splendid example is provided by *Edinburgh High School (ill. 256)*, begun in 1825 by Thomas Hamilton (1785–1858). The central structure, a Doric temple, projects some way beyond lower side wings which terminate in cubic blocks. The entablatures of the side wings run immediately into the cubic blocks without transition (Blenheim Palace again!). The whole is composed of stereometric formations, and stands on a smooth unarticulated base, with a second lower 'base' fronting the street. The street curves at this point, but the building makes no concession to this. Large parts of Edinburgh even today constitute the most perfect example of Classicism in urban architecture. – *Cumberland Terrace (1826–7, ill. 257)* in Regent's Park, London, was designed by John Nash (1752–1835), an architect of the same generation as Sir John Soane. It uses Classicism in conjunction with the Picturesque style to create an effect that is reminiscent of Blenheim Palace. Once again, the extraordinarily prophetic role of this High Baroque building becomes even more apparent. The Picturesque element in Cumberland Terrace tied in very closely with Nash's plan for the whole of Regent's Park, which can be regarded as the first example of a 'garden city', an idea that has not lost its creative power even today. – Something of the same combination of freedom and formalism is present in the *Merchants' Exchange, Philadelphia (ill. 258)*, which was built in 1832–4 by William Strickland (1788–1854), the most talented American architect since Latrobe. Strickland's imaginative design had far more flexibility and charm than the pure Greek peripteros that was the favourite form for stock exchanges during the heyday of Classicism (compare those by A. T. Brongniart in Paris, 1808–15, and by Thomas de Thomon in St. Petersburg, 1804–16).

France

The form of a Roman Corinthian temple on a high base was chosen for the church of *Ste. Madeleine, Paris (ill. 260)*, to match the Roman character of the Arc de Triomphe. A church had been planned on the site since 1761, and it was finally begun under Napoleon I in 1808 by Pierre Vignon (1762–1828) – not, however, as a church but as a 'Temple de la Gloire'. It was changed back into a church in 1813, still keeping the original form, and was completed in 1843. The interior, which consists of a series of dark, solemn square bays vaulted with domes on pendentives, does not relate to the exterior. A similar discrepancy, the inevitable result of purely ideological intentions, also characterized the Grand Théâtre, Bordeaux, and the Glyptothek, Munich, as we have already seen. By contrast, the masterpieces of the two most brilliant architects of Romantic Classicism, Soane's Dulwich Gallery and Schinkel's Schauspielhaus, Berlin, assume an even greater importance.

Munich

The Ludwigstrasse, Munich, which was built principally between 1829 and 1840, marks the end of this first period of the new architecture, and even encroaches on to the next phase of stylistic development. The Ludwigkirche (1829–40) by Friedrich von Gärtner is a mixture of Early Christian and Romanesque architecture. The adjacent State Library (1831–40) was inspired by the Early Renaissance palaces of Tuscany, as were other buildings in the Ludwigstrasse, together with a few imitations of Italian Gothic. The unity of this broad, generous and elegant (even if somewhat arid) site stems from the repeated use of round arches. This so-called Round Arch style quickly spread to other countries besides Germany.

Although the high period of Classicism was over by *c.* 1830, its effects lingered on well into the second half of the nineteenth century, not only in theatres, museums, universities, parliament buildings and stock exchanges, but also in the more pretentious private houses and châteaux, though very few of the latter were built to any degree. Occasionally, even churches continued to assume the form of Classical temples. Since then, however, Classicism provided no new solutions which surpassed the creative achievements of the period 1780–1830, and we can dispense with further examples. By and large, after 1830 Classicism lost its separate identity in the welter of historical styles that dominated the next period of architecture.

Characteristics: During this period, architects drew not only upon every historical style from the Classical period to the Baroque, but also upon various non-European styles – principally those of Egypt and Mesopotamia but even including India, China, Japan and the world of Islam. These borrowed forms were used almost exclusively for the articulation of façades; actual construction and the treatment of space followed the principle of 'reasoned abstraction', very often exploiting the newly-discovered technical resources of iron and glass.

Parallel to this ran the development of new types of engineering structures which cannot be called architecture as such, but which already contained all the possibilities of the 'technological architecture' of the future.

Kaufbeuren, Town Hall

Paris, Eiffel Tower

The use of the term 'Historicism' to cover the period of architectural development from 1830 onwards is something of an *ad hoc* solution, since the term could have been applied equally to the first period of the new style, Romantic Classicism, which was also founded on the use of styles borrowed from history. However, after 1830, this borrowing process became more and more extensive, as we saw in the case of the Ludwigstrasse, Munich. Early Christian and Romanesque forms were added, then Italian Early Renaissance and Italian Gothic, until finally man's growing intimacy with his past increased the formal apparatus of architects to include every style from those of the ancient civilizations of Mesopotamia and Egypt to Late Baroque. This vast mass of adopted forms concealed what was taking place beneath the surface and was rarely allowed to appear, namely the new sophistication of construction techniques made possible by the use of iron and glass. It was the beginning of a disastrous estrangement between the architect and the engineer. The general opinion was that 'art' was the province of the architect; what the engineer produced was not 'art'. Consequently every element of a building which was either constructional or functional had to be dressed up by the architect in an artistically acceptable manner. This even led to the production of 'Gothic' machines.

Political and social power, even in the smallest communities, had now passed entirely into the hands of the democratic-capitalist middle classes. Population was increasing rapidly, towns were growing larger and industry, commerce and administration were expanding accordingly. There was an almost infinite number of new tasks for architecture to assume. At first, however, no proper form was found for them, and the new society had no alternative but to look for appropriate forms in the architecture of the past. Although it arose this time out of an entirely different view of the world and of mankind, the process was not unlike that which occurred at the beginning of Western civilization, when architectural forms were assembled from the Late Roman, Early Christian and Byzantine periods. Then, too, it had taken a long time for a properly individual style to emerge, although there had been elements of individuality from the very beginning; the older styles were not simply copied, but were used imitatively and to that extent creatively, as indeed they had been in the case of Romantic Classicism. The difference – and it was a fundamental one – was that in the early Middle Ages, it was the Christian faith with its awareness of the sacred that provided the driving force from which everything sprang, so that even the Baroque château was the expression of an order which was permeated by the sacred, whereas at the beginning of the nineteenth century, the sacred had been supplanted by the secular, as represented by human reason. It is certain that during the nineteenth century a large proportion of the population of Europe were devoted Christians, as is still the case today, and outwardly the Church still enjoyed a measure of power in many countries, but equally, the state, and the new order of society which it represented, were no longer imbued with the sacred to any significant extent but were secular in essence. Church architecture, far from being in a position to dictate the standard for architecture as a whole, was not responsible for a single creative idea, either during this period or during the previous period of Romantic Classicism.

I Neo-Gothic

London: the Houses of Parliament

If we begin this chapter with a Neo-Gothic building, it is because it illustrates particularly clearly the connection with the preceding period. The *Houses of Parliament, London*, a very large architectural complex indeed, were begun in 1840 *(ill. 259)*. The whole site measures 275 m in length and the height of the Victoria Tower is 103 m. The numerous wings of the building contain 1,100 rooms and enclose eleven courts. The architect was Sir Charles Barry (1795–1860), who prior to this project had worked as a Classicist. The interior was designed by A. Welby Pugin (1812–52). Gothic architecture had been characterized by an ordered lucidity which stemmed from the unity and integrity of the skeletal structure, by which the building was transformed into an insubstantial shell to provide an image of the Heavenly Jerusalem that was to come. The Neo-Gothic Houses of Parliament, however, present a highly unclear system of horizontal and vertical stereometric parts which can be understood only in an abstract and purely rational way. There is no question of a homogeneous skeletal structure here, and it is impossible to imagine any kind of homogeneous or interrelated spatial development taking place within the building. Nor, of course, is there any suggestion of the 'Heavenly Jerusalem'. The borrowed forms, all of them taken from church architecture, are given an exclusively secular designation – although one might perhaps speak in terms of a 'Worldly Jerusalem', since this was the seat of government of a world empire that was to play a decisive part in changing the political order of the world.

Churches

The abandonment of regularity in plan and elevation, which we observed in Horace Walpole's Strawberry Hill and which was taken even further in the Houses of Parliament, introduced new possibilities of freedom which were exploited in *All Saints', Margaret Street, London* (1849–59, *ill. 261*), an extremely original building designed by William Butterfield (1814–1900). A combination of church, school and rectory, All Saints' groups together a number of structures graduated in height on a relatively small site. There is a virtual impression of the twentieth-century about the irregular distribution of windows, conditioned by the different functions of the various parts of the interior. A further remarkable feature of Butterfield's Neo-Gothic style was its use of coloured bricks (red and black), matching the rich polychromy of the interior of the three-aisled church. Unlike the Houses of Parliament, which derived from the Perpendicular style, All Saints' took its forms from thirteenth- and fourteenth-century English Gothic, the sharp and abstract linearity of which combined well with the new style's essential lack of architectural 'sense'. – The Church of *Ste.Clotilde, Paris* (1846–57, *ill. 262*), by F.Ch. Gau

(1790–1853) and Théodore Ballu (1817–74), which in fact looks more like a cathedral, was also based on fourteenth-century architecture and more particularly on the French 'Rayonnant' style. In contrast to the Neo-Gothic architecture of Romantic Classicism and of Butterfield and other mid-nineteenth century architects, Ste. Clotilde is a clear example of the principal danger inherent in Historicism as it became better informed about the architecture of the past. This was the temptation to imitate the chosen style so exactly in every detail as to fall into a mechanistic approach which killed any form of imagination.

The contemporary *Friedenskirche, Potsdam* (1845–8, *ill. 263*), built to a design by Ludwig Persius (1803–45), is an excellent illustration of the range of Historicism. The church forms a part of an irregular group of buildings and is a copy of an Early Christian basilica, even including a real medieval apse mosaic from a Byzantine church on the island of Murano near Venice. The whole complex, however, 'is a masterpiece of the classically ordered Picturesque, rivalling Schinkel's Gardener's House in subtlety and elegance' (Henry-Russel Hitchcock, op. cit.). The Gardener's House, built in 1829–31 in the grounds of the château of Charlottenhof, Potsdam, was a supreme example of the trend towards asymmetry in Romantic Classicism.

Of the many Neo-Gothic churches built during the second half of the nineteenth century, only two can be mentioned here. The Votivkirche, Vienna (1856–79), built by Heinrich von Ferstel (1828–83), followed the path of faithful imitation laid down by Ste. Clotilde. *Edinburgh Cathedral* (1874–9, *ill. 264*), designed by the most famous Gothic specialist of the nineteenth century, G. Gilbert Scott (1811–78), is remarkable for a different sort of dryness and rigidity. More clearly than the High Gothic imitations, it reveals the abstract stereometric spirit which was at work beneath the surface.

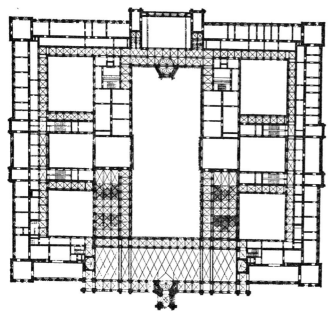

176 Vienna Town Hall (after Schmitt, *Handbuch der Architektur* [Handbook of Architecture])

Municipal buildings

The same trend towards a doctrinaire interpretation characterized the application of Neo-Gothic forms to secular buildings. In comparison with the Houses of Parliament, London, whose Picturesque style still contained an element of freedom, the *Town Hall, Vienna* (1872–83), by Friedrich von Schmidt (1825–91), is a typical example of the children's building–block architecture we have mentioned already in connection with Blenheim Palace and the Schauspielhaus, Berlin. Here, however, it is negative, mechanical, and totally lacking in imagination. A positive aspect of this extensive building is the perfect functionalism of the ground plan *(fig. 176)* which, in spite of its rigid symmetry, represents an extremely rational and effective use of space. – The link between Late Gothic architecture and the middle classes during the medieval period appears to have constituted a peculiar recommendation for the use of Neo-Gothic forms in municipal buildings and certain other buildings of a communal nature. Not only was the style favoured for town halls, for example, but also for post offices, schools and even railway stations. However, for buildings which were required to express the spirit of the state and society in a more meaningful way, such as theatres, museums, law-courts, hotels, etc., the more 'representative' styles of the Renaissance and Baroque periods were chosen.

II Neo-Renaissance

A theatre and a château

The restrained and elegant conception derived from Classicism and the Round Arch style and epitomized in Gottfried Semper's first Opera House, Dresden (1837–41), reached its climax in the *Opera House, Hanover* (1845–52, *ill. 266*), designed by G.L.F. Laves (1789–1864). It was typical of the architectural situation in the mid-nineteenth century that although Laves belonged to the same generation as Schinkel, his Opera House displayed little of the audacity and genius of the Schauspielhaus, Berlin. – A contemporary building, the *Palace of the Grand Duke, Schwerin* (1844–57, *ill. 265*) by G.A. Demmler (1804–86) and others, one of the now rare examples of aristocratic architecture on the grand scale, also illustrates the mid-century situation in two respects. On the one hand it took the Picturesque principle of total asymmetry to the extreme, and on the other, it borrowed its forms not from Gothic architecture or from the Italian Renaissance but from the 'style François I' of the French Renaissance. It has been claimed that Schwerin is an even more perfect example of this style than anything that was built in France, where the 'style Francois I' had been in fashion since 1830.

III The Architect and the Engineer

A library and a railway station

The discrepancy between engineering and architecture which we mentioned at the beginning of this chapter reached its most striking extent around the middle of the century. The sensationally daring *Bibliothèque Ste. Geneviève, Paris* (1843–61, *ill. 267* and *fig. 177)*, built by Henri Labrouste (1801–75), took up a position somewhere between the two. It is built on two storeys and constructed of iron and glass with a mantling of stone. Its use of the Round Arch style is noble and elegant, and incorporates the best qualities of Romantic Classicism. The reading

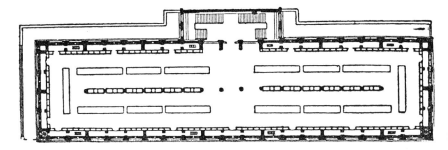

177 Paris, Bibliothèque
Ste. Geneviève

room on the upper storey is divided into two aisles and surrounded by an uninterrupted series of large arched windows. The glass vaults are supported by perforated iron reinforcing arches, which rest on corbels along the walls between the windows and on slim iron columns with tall pillar-like bases down the centre of the room. The sparse decoration goes back to the Classical period. As early as 1830, in a letter to his brother, Labrouste set down his belief that decoration, if it was to make sense and be really expressive, must derive from the construction itself. 'I often repeat to them [his pupils] that the Arts have the power to beautify everything, but I insist that they understand that in architecture the form of the building must suit the function for which it is intended.' Once again we come across the terms 'construction' and 'function'. Labrouste's ideas, far more radical than those of his contemporary, Semper, embraced everything demanded by Carlo Lodoli a century earlier. The new effects of space and light made possible by iron and glass construction were restrained in Labrouste's Bibliothèque Ste. Geneviève by the stone mantling, but in other buildings they were exploited in a purer form. One of the most successful and impressive solutions from this period is the façade of *King's Cross Station, London* (1851–2, *ill. 268*), designed by Lewis Cubitt (1799–1883). The two parallel iron-and-glass halls of the station receive a magnificent visual echo in the two enormous arches of the façade which rise between smooth square towers. The whole composition of the façade suggests a debt to Soane's revolutionary spirit.

Crystal Palace
An epoch-making building that may be regarded as a pure engineering structure was the *Crystal Palace, London* (built 1850–1 and destroyed by fire in 1936, *ill. 269*), which was designed by Sir Joseph Paxton (1803–65) for the International Exhibition of 1851 and built by the engineers Fox and Henderson in less than four months. It took so little time to erect because it consisted of standardized prefabricated units – cast-iron members, wooden arches and glass plates – which were assembled on the site. It consisted of a rectangular building (600 × 120 m) in three parts, graduated in height, with a 21 m high central roof, and an equally graduated transept with a vaulted glass roof 34 m in height. Most of the 3,300 columns and 2,300 plinths measured 7.87 m in height, and since the distance between the columns was also 7.87 m, this measurement constituted as it were the module of the building. Light and space could enter almost unimpeded and according to contemporary accounts, the impression given by the interior of the building was overwhelming, amounting to an entirely new architectural experience. Such a 'functional' experience of space is commonplace for people today, accustomed as they are to working in huge factories or offices and to using station booking-halls,

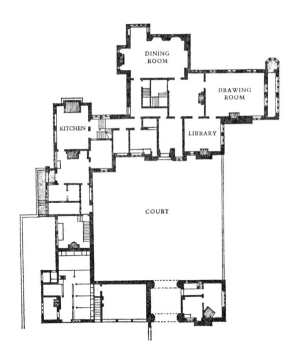

178 Leyswood House, Sussex

banks and other such functional interpenetrations of interior and exterior space, but at the time it was never for a moment suspected that the Crystal Palace could have anything to do with architecture. Another fifty years were to pass before engineering and architecture were reconciled.

Country houses

Equally important for the future was another development that began only a few years later, again in England, in country house architecture, arising out of the Picturesque tradition. In 1859–60 Philip Webb (1831–1915) built the Red House, Bexley Heath, Kent, for his friend William Morris. The importance of this house lay in the freedom implied in its utterly informal ground plan, which was dictated by the function of the various rooms, and in the absence of any decoration or articulation on the simple red brick walls. *Leyswood House, Sussex (fig. 178)*, begun in 1868 by Richard Norman Shaw (1831–1912), had an even greater influence on the next few decades, though at first this influence was confined to England and America. From our own viewpoint today, it is in many respects less 'modern' than the Red House, but in others – particular in planning and in its intensive fenestration – it is much more radical. There are possibilities in Leyswood House that anticipate Frank Lloyd Wright, Mies van der Rohe and other twentieth-century architects.

IV The Hypertrophy of Historicism

In the greatest imaginable contrast to the forward-looking character of the last few examples quoted, beginning with Labrouste's Bibliothèque Ste. Geneviève, was the contemporary

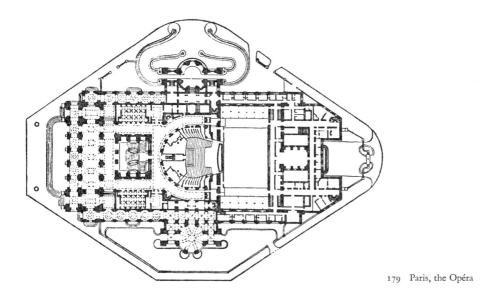

development of 'official' architecture during the Second Empire in France, the High and Late Victorian periods in England and the Wilhelmian period in Germany.

Paris: the New Louvre

This development was heralded by the north-west wing of the *Louvre, Paris (ill. 270)*, which was built in 1852–7 by L. T. J. Visconti (1791–1853) and H. M. Lefuel (1810–80) along the rue de Rivoli, leading to the Palais des Tuileries. Although elements were taken from the older part of the Louvre, the new wing did not imitate any particular historical style but represented a conglomeration of styles, chiefly Renaissance and Baroque. The 'pavillons', in particular, are garnished with a wealth of sculptured forms which appear to grow organically out of the body of the building but do not in fact do so. The volutes above the double columns of the corner pavilions are typical in this respect; they have no purpose whatever and merely serve to fill out the composition. Not the slightest hint appeared on the exterior of what lay behind the façade – two ministries, a library and stables. Since the splendour of the Second Empire was the admiration of the entire world, the New Louvre was taken as the model for a large number of buildings during the next few decades. In Paris itself, however, its influence was relatively small. There, this type of eclecticism was taken to far more imaginative lengths as the textbooks of style were ransacked for ever more elaborate combinations of forms.

Paris: the Opéra

A far more felicitous solution both in terms of overall composition and in the development of the ground plan was provided by the *Opéra, Paris* (1861–74, *ill. 271* and *fig. 179*), built by J. L. C. Garnier (1825–98). The Opéra was a climactic expression of the taste and way of life prevalent among the society of the time. In fact more than a third of the building was dedicated to social contact, including the huge vestibule, the imposing staircase and the large foyer. If one tries to imagine these rooms without their exaggeratedly eclectic decoration, with all the marble, porphyry, bronze and gilded stucco-work and all the candelabras, chandeliers and paintings stripped away, the grandeur of their construction and the originality of the spatial and structural concepts which they embody becomes much more apparent. The mixture of Renaissance and Baroque forms used in the Opera was taken mainly from the art of Venice.

Judicial buildings

Among the many architectural requirements of the modern state – ministries, offices for administration and the like, which had either not existed before or had played a subordinate role if they were not part of a royal palace or château – the building which housed the machinery of law was regarded as one of the most important, for the administration of justice lay at the very heart of an ordered society. This building was required to represent the sublime nature of justice, an idea which received one of its most imposing expressions in the *Palais de Justice, Brussels* (1866–83, *ill. 272*), built by Joseph Poelaert (1817–79). The stereometric composition in which the numerous parts of the building are bound together gives an impression of exceptional complexity. If one were to remove the confusing mass of borrowed formal elements which litters the building, the actual method of composition would be seen to correspond very closely not only to that of the Classicism of *c.* 1800 but also to twentieth-century architecture. As far as the formal apparatus of the building is concerned, it represents an extraordinary mixture of Baroque, Renaissance, Roman, Greek and Assyrian styles. This is indicative of the steadily widening scope of Historicism, which in other buildings was to extend to Islamic, Indian and Far Eastern influences until finally, it included the whole range of the architectural activity of mankind. Having in this sense developed a 'world architecture', European architecture then proceeded to become so in a literal sense by spreading the style which it had evolved throughout the entire world. The reason it was able to do this was that all the old high cultures which had run parallel to Western civilization had come to an end at about the same time as Western civilization itself during the course of the eighteenth century. This common decline cannot be attributed to suppression by force on the part of Europeans, but must be seen as a homogeneous process embracing the whole of humanity. We shall mention only two more examples, without further analysis, of buildings which are typical of the many huge 'judicial palaces' erected in almost every large town throughout the world during the last third of the nineteenth century. The Palazzo della Giustizia, Rome (1888–1910), by Giuseppe Calderini (1837–1916), was modelled on the Palais de Justice, Brussels, which indeed it closely resembled in the megalomanic aggressiveness of its forms, though Calderini did not manage to reproduce the fortunate composition of his model. In fact, the Palazzo della Giustizia represents a quite unique summary of the worst aberrations of Historicism. Not quite so disastrous but rather similar in its bombastic Neo-Gothic way is the *Reichstag, Berlin* (1884–94, *ill. 273*), built by Paul Wallot (1841–1912).

Culture and Society

The *Rijksmuseum, Amsterdam* (1877–85, *ill. 276*), by P. J. H. Cuijpers (1827–1921), is a mixture of Late Gothic, French Renaissance, sixteenth-century Dutch and Picturesque styles, distinguishing itself pleasantly from other contemporary buildings by its lightness and elegance of

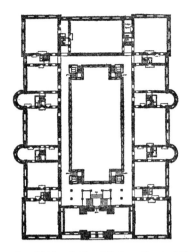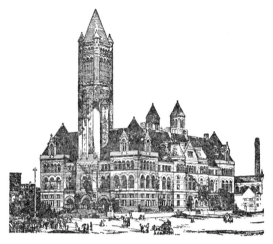

180 Pittsburgh, Pa., Allegheny County Jail, ground plan and view of exterior

design. In the two interior courts, an undisguised iron and glass construction was used, so that engineering and architecture appeared side by side without any connection in a way that was typical of this period. An example of how the pretentiously 'imperial' quality of Historicism seized upon any building no matter what its purpose is provided by the *Grand Hotel, Scarborough* (1863–7, *ill. 274*), designed by Cuthbert Brodrick (1825–1905). It was the first 'château-hotel' and its influence was far-reaching. The same tendency affected the large galleries that played an important part in urban life, particularly in Italy, combining the functions of passageway and utility and recreation area. The most impressive example is one which still stands at the centre of the life of the city today – the *Galleria Vittorio Emmanuele II, Milan* (1865–77, *ill. 275*), built by Giuseppe Mengoni (1829–77). The iron and glass construction of the roof stands in undisguised contradiction to the richly decorated façades. – Church building during this period was subject to the same compulsion towards pompous elaboration as we see from Paul Abadie's (1812–84) monumental invention, the *Sacré-Coeur, Paris* (1874 to *c.* 1900, *ill. 279*). Its commanding position above Montmartre makes it just as much a symbol of the city as the Eiffel Tower *(fig. page 267)*, which was built for the international exhibition in 1889 and is a pure engineering structure. The enormous gulf which existed between the two sorts of building during this period could hardly have a more striking demonstration. A few decades later, this gulf was to disappear completely. Meanwhile, in America, the first steps had already been taken to bring the two together.

V America

Architecture parlante

Before we go on to discuss the development to which we have just referred, let us take a look at another very different sort of building, extremely impressive in its way and somewhat reminiscent of the 'architecture parlante' of Romantic Classicism. This is the *Allegheny County Jail, Pittsburg, Pa.* (1884–8, *fig. 180*), designed by Henry Hobson Richardson (1838–86). Built of granite throughout, it has a sombre dignity which matches its purpo e well. It consists of a number of separate blocks linked together in the rather free manner typi al of the Picturesque style. The Romanesque overtones do not constitute a full-scale historical 'dressing', but are applied to the building like 'quotations' in the same way as we observed in the Revolutionary architecture of *c*. 1800. The resumption of this technique, which had fallen into disuse, was symptomatic of the new kind of clarity that was beginning to pervade architectural thought. This is true also of the Provident Life and Trust Company Building, Philadelphia, built in 1879 by Frank Furness (1839–1912), in which Gothic elements are used in such a personal and undogmatic way that the building bears less resemblance to nineteenth-century Neo-Gothic than to the stereometric imaginativeness of Romantic Classicism, particularly as interpreted by Soane, and at the same time anticipates in an entirely original way the fantastic creations of Antonio Gaudí. Both these buildings are astonishing feats of creative architecture. Europe produced nothing during this period to compare with them.

Skyscrapers

The *Reliance Building, Chicago (ill. 277)*, which was begun in 1890 with four storeys and increased to thirteen storeys in 1894, stands at the limit of Historicism and even transcends it. The horizontal bands between the storeys are a last echo of decoration borrowed from the past, but the fully developed skeleton construction represents the final bridging of the gulf between engineering and architecture. The engineer-architects were D. H. Burnham (1846–1912) and J. W. Root (1850–91). Immediately afterwards, in 1894–5, Louis H. Sullivan (1856–1924) and Dankmar Adler (1844–1900) created their masterpiece – the *Guaranty Building, Buffalo, N.Y. (ill. 278)*. The restrained geometrical ornamentation of the terracotta facing awakens no historical memories, and the decoration of the attic storey immediately beneath the roof-plate appears to be related to the exactly contemporary development of Art Nouveau. The treatment of the ground floor, with its virtually free-standing supports, was of tremendous importance for the future. On the one hand it permitted the unrestricted interpenetration of interior and exterior space which was to become a central principle of twentieth-century architecture, and on the other hand it raised the multi-storeyed skeleton construction off the ground in such a way as to give it, despite its enormous width and height, that impression of nonchalant weightlessness which again is one of the chief characteristics of the architecture of our time. This affirmation of the enormous architectural potential of techniques of construction which had formed part of the stock- in-trade of engineers for decades paved the way for the next phase of architectural development. During this phase, architects were to exploit the ideas which had lain dormant in Romantic Classicism in a much more creative and genuine way than Historicism had been able to do.

Characteristics: All the disguises of Historicism are abandoned and reason and abstraction (the conditions imposed by technique) appear unveiled and determine the character of architecture.

Rome ,Palace of the Olympics

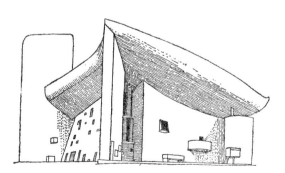

Ronchamp, Notre Dame du Haut

Alfeld an der Leine, Fagus Factory

During the last decade of the nineteenth century there was in various different countries – America, England, Belgium and Holland among them – a movement away from Historicism which is generally referred to by the terms 'Jugendstil' and 'Art Nouveau'. The movement began principally in the applied arts, and was chiefly directed towards a regeneration of ornamentation by freeing it from all traces of historical and naturalistic imitation. This led to a process of stylization which placed the main emphasis on clarity and purity of line. Hence the link with architecture, which, by acknowledging the new methods of construction made possible by iron, steel, glass and concrete, involved itself in similar demands for clarity and linearity of design. In fact once all historical dressing had been rejected and architecture had begun to obey the laws of construction, this clarity appeared almost automatically. It is no accident that some of the leading architects of the new style did not start off as architects, but as draughtsmen, illustrators, decorative artists, and even painters.

I The Period of Transition

Hendrik P. Berlage

The first architect whose work we shall examine, Hendrik Petrus Berlage (1856–1934), might equally well have appeared at the end of the last chapter, for in the final analysis his *Stock*

181   Hendrik P. Berlage, Amsterdam Stock Exchange

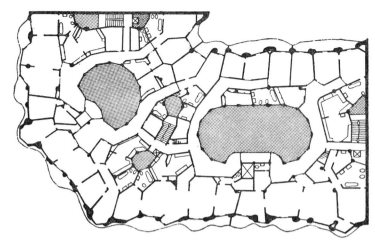

Exchange, Amsterdam (1898–1903, *ill. 280* and *fig. 181*), like Labrouste's Bibliothèque Ste. Geneviève, represents a combination rather than a synthesis of engineering and architecture. In Berlage's building, however, the architectural forms are relatively free of historical reminiscence, and the iron and glass construction of the large exchange hall is related more intimately to the spatial formation. Parallels have been drawn between this building and Richardson's work in America (compare *fig. 180*), but with equal justification we may say that it represents the flowering of seeds which had been sown by Romantic Classicism, and in particular by Soane. Berlage had a great influence in Holland during the next few decades.

Victor Horta

The contemporary work of Victor Horta (1861–1947) in Belgium was rather less influential, although it was considerably more radical. Horta was one of the principal representatives of Art Nouveau. This allegiance is chiefly apparent in the decorative mobility of the metal structures which were always clearly revealed in his interiors, a mobility which was applied to the ground plan just as much as to the elevation. The façade of his most homogeneous work, the *Solvay House, Brussels* (1895–1900, *ill. 281*), is given an animated rhythm by the use of slim iron elements in conjunction with the masonry. We cannot talk here in terms of a sculptured architectural body in the Baroque sense for the members and skin are too thin. This expression of weightlessness, which also characterizes the interior, corresponds to what we observed in the Guaranty Building, Buffalo.

Antonio Gaudí

Similar ideas had already been expressed in the work of the amazing Catalan architect, Antonio Gaudí (1852–1926), reaching a climax in his large block of flats, the *Casa Milá, Barcelona* (1905–7, *ill. 283* and *fig. 182*). It is so packed with movement that any kind of clearly comprehensible form seems to have disappeared completely. If any building can be called sculptural, it is certainly this one. But can it also be called an organic structure, and if so, where is the structure? The whole building appears to have been kneaded like clay, forming an abstract sculpture that has been compared to the work of Henry Moore. Gaudí's work anticipated a style which blossomed for a brief period in German Expressionist architecture and which has again emerged as a possibility in recent years.

Charles Rennie Mackintosh

In contrast to Horta and Gaudí, Charles Rennie Mackintosh (1868–1928) placed no great value upon the flexible ornamental line. His *Glasgow School of Art* (1897–9, north wing 1907–8, *ill. 282*) combines an asymmetrical ground plan and elevation (in the Picturesque tradition), with the use of firmly stereometric formations (Soane's influence again) and areas of wall largely dissolved by windows, creating a composition which is both forceful and at the same time extremely delicate in its proportions and its treatment of the various elements. Like Berlage's work but in a more modern way, it, too, illustrates an architectural approach that was already at work in Romantic Classicism. If we continue to point out this connection with Romantic Classicism, which was not necessarily present in the minds of the architects concerned, we do so in the conviction that the development of architecture since the period 1770–80 does in fact constitute a homogeneous 'style'. The acceptance of the role of technique which took place around 1900, far from representing a break in this style, brought it at last to full maturity.

Frank Lloyd Wright

The *Isidore Heller House, Chicago* (1897, *fig. 183*) by Frank Lloyd Wright (1869–1959) also stands in the Picturesque tradition which began with Strawberry Hill and led up to modern times through the development of the English country house by architects like Philip Webb and Richard Norman Shaw. One might even go so far as to say that there is an element of Historicism in Wright's building, for a distinct Japanese influence is detectable, not only in the contour of the roof but also in the ground plan, which for the first time decisively rejects the principle of division of rooms, connecting the hall with the dining and living rooms by means of wall openings which allow the rooms to flow into each other. The size and position of the rooms are determined by their function, and in turn dictate the shape of the exterior. Wright achieved an even greater degree of freedom, still within the context of a strict development of every part of the building according to the dictates of construction and function, in the *Robie House, Chicago* (1909–10, *ill. 284* and *fig. 184*). The terms 'abstraction' and

183   Frank Lloyd Wright, Isidore Heller House, Chicago

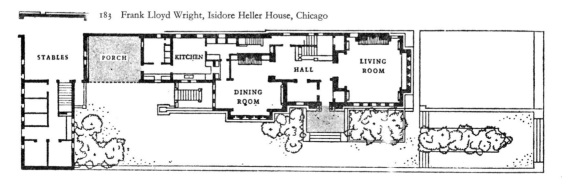

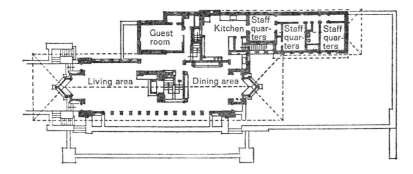

184   Frank Lloyd Wright,
Robie House, Chicago

'stereometry', derived from the contrast with the organic, corporeal nature of Renaissance and Baroque architecture, have been used frequently in this study but never, it would seem, with greater justification than in the case of this house. A complete fusion of exterior and interior space is brought about by an arrangement of cubes of various sizes and shapes. Even the surrounding space is brought into the house from all sides and used for its articulation. A detailed examination of the various stereometric formations of the building reveals an affinity with Schinkel's Schauspielhaus, Berlin, which had already contained all these possibilities in embryonic form.

Josef Hoffmann

The Viennese architect Josef Hoffmann (1870–1956) applied the same principles on a very much more extensive scale to the *Palais Stoclet, Brussels* (1905–11, *ill. 285*), although as a town house this could not be open to nature in the same way as Wright's villa. The walls and windows, both apparently made of the same insubstantial material, lie in exactly the same plane, which means that their roles can be interchanged, as demonstrated by the vertical window strip of the staircase tower. Although Hoffmann was a central figure of the Viennese 'Jugendstil' school, he rejected ornamentation almost completely.

Adolf Loos

Another Viennese architect, Adolf Loos (1870–1933), was even more radical in this respect. His *Steiner House, Vienna* (1910, *ill. 286)* is an even purer example of the stereometric approach than Wright's work. Note how the windows are cut cleanly in the almost two-dimensional wall. The parallel with Revolutionary architecture hardly needs pointing out.

Otto Wagner

Whereas Loos turned against any form of architectural ornamentation, even in theory (witness his book *Ornament und Verbrechen* [Ornament and Offence], published in 1908), Otto Wagner (1841–1918) began as Hoffmann did, firmly within the 'Jugendstil' school. His railway stations in Vienna, built between 1894 and 1901, along with Horta's work and the Paris Métro Stations built between 1898 and 1901 by Hector Guimard, represent the architectural climax of Art Nouveau. An echo of this linear animation is still present in the curves of the iron and glass construction of the main hall of the *Vienna Post Office Savings Bank* (1904–6, *ill. 287)* which, incidentally, shows how rapidly engineering technique and architecture became integrated during this period. If we compare this hall with the related one in the Stock Exchange, Amsterdam, completed only three years earlier, it becomes clear that the gulf had by this time definitely been closed. The façade of the building, however, with its touch of ornamentation, is again reminiscent of the Guaranty Building, Buffalo.

II The Synthesis of Technique and Architecture

Peter Behrens
The *A.E.G. Turbine Factory, Berlin* (1909, *ill. 288*), designed by Peter Behrens (1868–1940), was the first purely industrial building in the history of architecture. The front of the building, with its two corner pylons and projecting glass cube, is strongly reminiscent of Schinkel's Neue Wache (compare *ill. 252*) and other buildings and designs from the period of Classicism. In fact, Behrens and a number of other early nineteenth-century architects deliberately took up Classicism again because they recognized in it the beginnings of a new approach to architecture. When the Communist and National-Socialist dictatorships returned to the same source later, they were not stepping out of the mainstream of architectural development, but at the same time they did not introduce this kind of creative metamorphosis. In fact, they simply imitated, and in doing so they descended to the level of the democratic-capitalist middle-classes of the second half of the nineteenth century whom they hated so much. The steel frame that carries the panes of glass and spans the interior of the factory is left clearly visible, both in the façade and in the planes of glass in the side walls that follow the inclination of the outer edge of the pylons. The vertical line of the projecting glass cube of the façade is repeated in the concrete piers running down the sides, which serve to anchor the steel skeleton. The amount of light they inhibit is negligible. The gable of the façade reproduces exactly the contour of the steel and glass roof. The interior, because of its great height and width, is experienced not as a solid structure sitting firmly on the ground, but as an active creation that has been transformed into functions of space and light. This lively animation only becomes apparent when work is in full swing, with all the machines functioning and the cranes gliding to and fro.

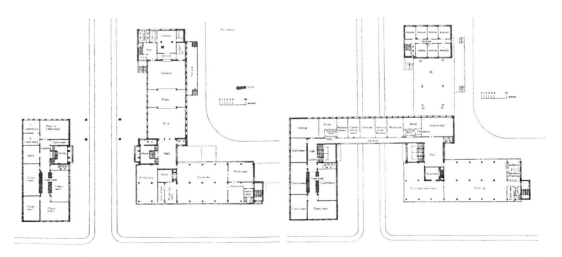

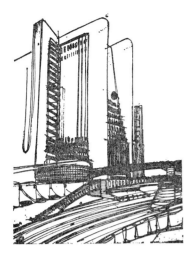

186 Antonio Sant'Elia, New Town Power Station,
sketch from the *Città Futura*

Walter Gropius

Walter Gropius (1883–1969), a pupil of Behrens, took his master's work a step further when in 1911 he built, together with Adolf Meyer, the *Faguswerke, Alfeld an der Leine (ill. 289* and *fig. page 278)*. Gropius' achievement lay in developing the site strictly in accordance with its function and the technical conditions imposed by the materials and method of construction without any recourse to 'symbolic' details like the façade of Behrens' Turbine Factory. Consequently, his factory consists of a perfect succession of stereometric figures differentiated by shape, colour and material according to their function. The administration block, which in terms of both function and structure constitutes the apex of the site as a whole, looks at first glance like a transparent box made entirely of glass. The vertical strips which rise smoothly out of the yellow-brick base suggest stability and order. They face the steel skeleton which supports and buttresses the building. The skeleton terminates in a roof beam from which the window strips are suspended, so that roof beam, windows and the dark horizontal bands of steel which mark the division of the storeys all lie in the same plane, projecting slightly beyond the skeleton and the base. This considerably heightens the impression of weightlessness. The concepts embodied here had been elaborated by Gropius since 1919 in his teaching at the Bauhaus (originally at Weimar), and received a further expression in the buildings which he erected for the Bauhaus in 1925–6 when it moved to Dessau. The influence of Gropius' *Bauhaus, Dessau (ill. 290* and *fig. 185)* has extended all over the world and the building has become a classic of architectural history, so we will do no more than refer the reader to the photograph and the plan.

Sant'Elia

The designs which the futurist architect Antonio Sant'Elia (1888–1917) drew up in 1914–16 were influenced to some extent by the Viennese architecture of the first decade of the century. The *New Town Power Station (fig. 186)* from his 'Città Futura' is reminiscent in many respects of Hoffmann's Palais Stoclet, Brussels, besides clearly pointing the way towards the Expressionism of the 'twenties and some of the achievements of the present day.

Official architecture

Until 1914, the majority of public and private architecture in Europe and elsewhere was still determined by a moderate degree of Historicism or at least by an approach which, although rejecting the pomp of Neo-Baroque, still clung to the idea that architecture and construction technique must be kept separate, since architecture was 'art' and needed a representative form. Among the many examples of this type of building, we shall mention only the *Piccadilly Hotel, London* (1905–8, *ill. 291*), by that same Richard Norman Shaw who a few decades earlier had been one of the pioneers of modern villa architecture. The Piccadilly Hotel combines a Classicistic colonnade with elements drawn from the Tuscan Early Renaissance and the Late Renaissance in the North, so that despite considerable simplification, it represents the same sort of conglomeration of styles as occurred during the last third of the nineteenth century.

III The Spread of Modernism

After 1918, the new functional approach to architecture began to achieve a wider currency, particularly in Holland and Germany. In France it gained less ground at first, and except for a very few examples, it did not penetrate England, America and other countries until considerably later. In the limited space available here it is impossible even to outline the extremely complex situation which arose as a large number of very different movements sprang up. Our selection must be confined to a few examples which illustrate certain trends.

Expressionism

In Germany, alongside the direction Behrens, Gropius and others had taken, a new kind of expressionist architecture emerged and flourished for a short time. Erich Mendelsohn (1887–1953) drew upon it for his *Einstein Tower, Neubabelsberg, near Potsdam* (1919–21, *ill. 292*). The original plan was for the building to be of cast concrete throughout, but it was later decided to build it of brick with a casing of cement. However, it still retained its plastic shape and in this respect it is related to Gaudí's Casa Mila, which was built of dressed stone, although the Einstein Tower is clearer and more compact in construction and does in fact look as if it were cast.

Housing estates

An element of the same imaginativeness of form can be felt in the *Workers' housing estate, Hook of Holland (ill. 293)*, built in 1926–7 by Jacobus Johannes Pieter Oud (1890–1963). The rounded corners of the end of each row may be an echo of the 'Jugendstil', but they are completely absorbed within the clarity and simplicity of the overall stereometric design. Proportions and details are handled with the utmost sensitivity, making this estate a masterpiece of a form of architectural development which entered its most crucial phase after the Second World War.

Private houses

The *Schröder House, Utrecht* (1924, *ill. 294*), by Gerrit Th. Rietveld (1888–1964), represents a very different line of development, combining as it does a rigorous interpretation of the 'abstract' ideals of the De Stijl movement with those of the contemporary Bauhaus (Mies van

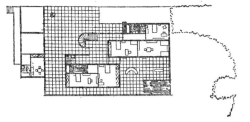

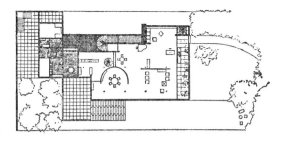

187 Mies van der Rohe, Tugendhat House, Brno, first floor (left) and ground floor (right)

der Rohe) and of Le Corbusier in Paris. The influence of Wright's pioneering work is clearly evident, but the Schröder House goes a good deal further. Here the abstract, geometrical, cubist approach achieved its most radical fulfilment. The *Tugendhat House, Brno* (1930, *ill. 295* and *fig. 187*), one of the masterpieces of Mies van der Rohe (1886–1969), employed the same approach but in a more mellow form which, without involving any compromises, made it more acceptable for general use. Van der Rohe had worked for Behrens in 1908, along with Gropius and Le Corbusier. The ground floor plan indicates a completely free treatment of the stereometric form, comprising a rectangle with numerous salients and re-entrants in order to do justice to the different functions of the living space. These demanded a room as large as possible, with a wide window-wall opening on to the garden, with which it is connected by means of terraces. The angular treatment of space, and the use of free-standing curved and straight walls made differentiation and articulation possible without destroying the unity of the whole. The effect which is achieved in a Japanese house by means of transparent movable screens was achieved here by similar means. The skeleton of the building stands in a free relationship to space. The upper storey does not repeat the lower, but is a different functional composition of small spatial and structural units serving as bedrooms, etc.

Churches

Le Corbusier built a number of similar villas in France during the 'twenties, but for an example of French architecture during this period, we shall examine first a quite different type of building – the church of *Notre Dame du Raincy, near Paris* (1922–3, *ill. 296*), by Auguste Perret

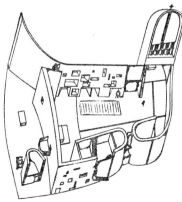

188 Le Corbusier, Notre Dame du Haut, near Ronchamp

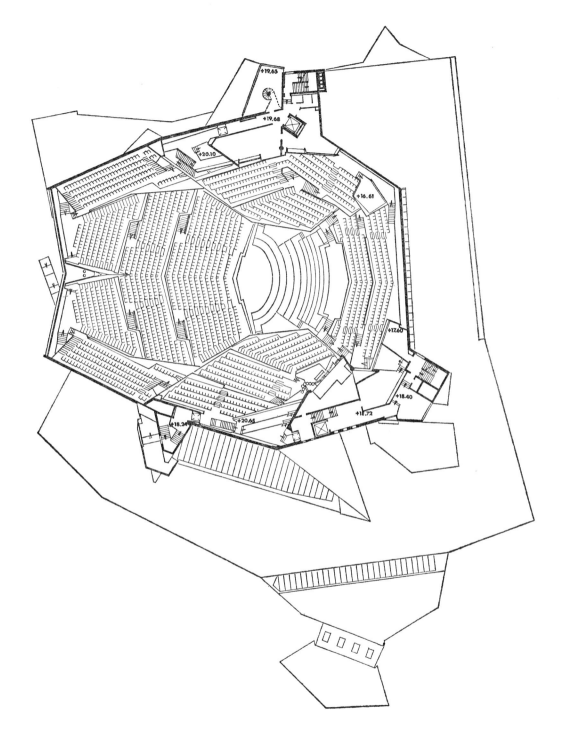

189   Hans Scharoun, the Philharmonie, Berlin

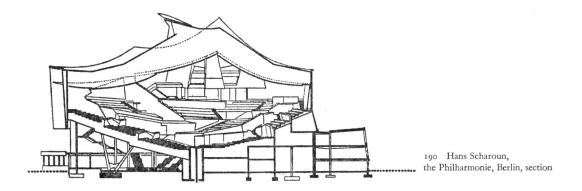

(1874–1954). With the help of concrete, now the most widely used of all building materials, church architecture here broke free from the chains of the Historicism with which it had been so closely connected, and joined the mainstream of modern architecture. Although the three-aisled layout was traditional and the idea of the glass wall went back to the aspirations of the Late Gothic period, the extremely slender concrete supports and the form of the vaults in Notre Dame du Raincy give an impression which is hard to define exactly, but which is utterly different from anything in medieval architecture. The modern technical spirit of functionalism, weightlessness and incorporeality is clearly at work here, but how effectively this spirit is capable of expressing the sacred is a question which church architects all over the world are now attempting to answer. – Some thirty years later, Le Corbusier (Charles-Edouard Jeanneret, 1887–1965) found a completely different solution, more in line with Mendelsohn's Einstein Tower, in his *Pilgrimage Church of Notre Dame du Haut, Ronchamp* (1950–5, *ill. 297* and *figs 188* and *page 278*). The interior is irregular in shape, widening from west to east and increasing in height from 4.8 m to 10 m. The overhanging roof of brown concrete consists of two separate shells, 2.26 m apart. On the south and east sides, the overhang is extended to give protection to the external altar and pulpit used for large assemblies of pilgrims. The south wall, which is pierced by a number of asymmetrically-arranged windows, consists, like the roof, of a double shell of concrete, with each shell cast in a different plane so that inside and outside offer a different inclination and curvature. The remaining walls and towers are built of dressed stone treated with a concrete spray. The towers accommodate separate chapels for private prayer. Every liturgical function has been considered in the building, and a form evolved which appears to be completely free and is reminiscent of some giant abstract sculpture. Notre Dame du Haut represents an attempt to discover a form for the sacred which does not deny the spirit of our time. By treating religion as a particular potentiality of the modern spirit, it raises it out of the ordinary and gives it a special prominence. Many people have expressed doubt as to whether the church does actually succeed in this, and whether in fact it really does represent a genuine manifestation of the sacred; however, to experience the building oneself is to become completely convinced, because of the spiritual power of the personality behind it.

The *Philharmonie, Berlin* (1960–3, *ill. 298* and *figs 189* and *190*) by Hans Scharoun (born 1893) testifies in a different way to the power of a creative personality to 'carry' the community.

The exterior is completely irregular in shape and looks like an enormous tent. It serves only as an envelope for the functions of the interior. This has two foci – the foyer with its staircases rising freely towards their destinations, and the concert hall itself, with ascending blocks of seats arranged all round the orchestral platform. Unlike Ronchamp, this building cannot be compared to a piece of abstract sculpture. Here it appears as if space itself has been moulded into a certain shape, and not merely one shape, for the form seems constantly to be changing. In a way, this fantastic vision of space represents a development of the possibilities inherent in the Expressionist architecture of the 'twenties. These seem to be far from exhausted, and may yet succeed in combating the rigidity which has undoubtedly beset the architecture of the present day.

With Ronchamp and the Berlin Philharmonie, we have already entered the period of the last few decades with its enormous increase of architectural activity. Never before in the whole history of mankind has so much been built in so short a time. It goes without saying that the vast majority of this has consisted, and indeed has had to consist, of standardized unimaginative constructions, but there have also been a great many valuable, creative, forward-looking achievements, so many in fact that it is impossible even to begin to undertake any kind of orderly survey of them in the space at our disposal. The selection which follows is inevitably a personal one, designed to include a few varied examples from as many different countries as possible in order to indicate the scope and the homogeneity of the architecture of today.

IV The Present Day

Specialized buildings
When the Finnish architect Alvar Aalto (born 1898) and his wife built the *Tuberculosis Sanatorium, Paimio* (Finland) *(ill. 299* and *fig. 191)* in 1929–33, there was virtually no stylistic tradition to go on. We shall leave aside the actual form and construction, since these, of course, used the architectural language which had been developed over the years since 1910, and examine only the functional organization of the ground plan. The six-storeyed main block, accommodating some 290 patients, faces south-south-west, and is met at a slight angle by the solarium, a terrace of free-floating balconies. Behind the main block, a shorter wing of the same height containing staircases and lifts leads back to the dining and recreation rooms. The medical units, offices and flats for doctors, nurses and other staff are situated in a lower wing that branches out at an angle from the connecting wing. Two lower buildings, again situated at an angle to the preceding wing, house the kitchens, laundry and power station. As purely practical and technical plants, these are completely separate from the sanatorium itself but still lie within the uninterrupted 'mechanism' of the functional order. The whole complex was designed with the help of numerous specialists to fulfil its purpose in the most efficient way possible, and the clarity and coherence of the proportions and articulation of every detail create an effect of great beauty.

How a purely functional building can achieve the highest degree of formal beauty and command of space and light is also illustrated by the *Stazione Termini, Rome* (1947–51, *ill. 300),* by Eugenio Montuori (born 1907) and his associates. The freedom of imagination which is

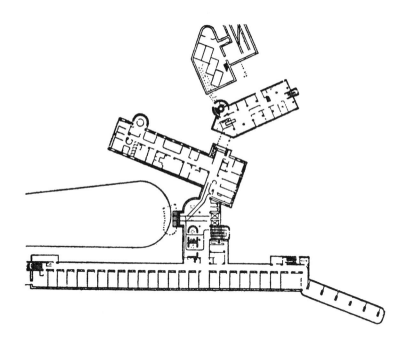

191 Alvar Aalto,
Tuberculosis Sanatorium,
Paimio, Finland

evident here and in the Berlin Philharmonie links with the expressionist tendencies of the years immediately following the First World War, although construction technique has become so immeasurably more sophisticated and audacious in the intervening period as to permit solutions which more than ever before convey an impression of total weightlessness and incorporeality. In the *TWA Building, Kennedy Airport, New York* (1956–62, *ills 301/02*), by Eero Saarinen (1910–61), these possibilities were even further exploited, and given a deliberately symbolic form to match the purpose of the site. Here the development which began with Mies van der Rohe takes a significant turn in the direction of greater expressiveness, and the building, which is constructed of four enormous concrete shells, assumes the form of a soaring bird. – A completely different building, yet one which has a similar lightness and suppleness of formation is the *Olympic Hall, Tokyo* (1964, *ill. 303*), by Kenzo Tange (born 1913). The only way to gain a true appreciation of the interior of this building is by actually experiencing it, or at least by studying a very much larger number of photographs than we have been able to include here. The same applies to any spatial formation, in fact, but particularly in the case of modern architecture where all the old horizontal and vertical constraints have been negated by advances in technique, and every arbitrary and unexpected movement seems to have been given free rein. This marvellous hall, made possible by new materials and new methods of construction, is the result of a close partnership of imagination with the most minute mathematical calculations. Once again, science and art form a unity, as they did for a brief period at the beginning of the Renaissance in the work of Leonardo da Vinci, and it is fervently to be hoped that this possibility, which at the moment is still limited to specialized architectural efforts of this kind, will extend to all kinds of building. Kenzo Tange himself has begun the process with his plans for expanding Tokyo out into the bay, plans which, if realized, will lead to the point where a whole urban complex with a population of millions will constitute a single work of art. – Another kind of specialized architectural task is the exhibition building, with a tradition going back to the Crystal Palace, London (see *ill. 269*). Although the Crystal Palace represented an exceptional technical feat for its time, it is not actually entirely true to describe it as epoch-making since at first it had no successors. The first really epoch-making exhibition building was Mies van der Rohe's German Pavilion at Barcelona (1929), which instigated a series of increasingly imaginative solutions. The most recent example, which is certainly in the same class as the TWA Building and Tange's Olympic Hall, is the *German Pavilion at* EXPO *67, Montreal (ill. 304)*, by Frei Otto (born 1925). Light building materials and pneumatic methods of construction have made possible the realization of the most unrestricted spatial fantasies.

Another type of imaginative development, which does not express itself in such linear movements in space but is no less free, is represented by the use of functionally determined arrangements of boxes, allowing for a wide variety of compositions reminiscent of the work of Wright, Mies van der Rohe and even of Rietveld. Completely new effects have been achieved, however, in the combination of open and closed sections. A case in point is the Town Hall, Tatebayashi, built in 1964 by Kiyonori Kikutake (born 1928), in which the manifold projections of the glass case play an important role. – *Habitat 67, Montreal (ill. 305)*, by Moshe Safdie (born 1938), a residential complex made up of 158 prefabricated living units and erected for EXPO 67, is related to Kikutake's building in terms of compositional approach, although it uses very different means and serves an entirely different purpose. It is an attempt at a solution to that apparently intractable problem of modern architecture – the combination of the tenement development and the private detached one-family house.

Skyscrapers
A feature of major importance in the architecture of large towns is the skyscraper, an American invention. From a number of very fine solutions in cities all over the world, it can be seen how this type of architecture has continually tried to free itself from the sort of rigid, unimaginative scheme which understandably accounts for the vast majority of these mass-produced buildings. It has not been an easy process. – In 1937–43, Lucio da Costa (born 1902) and Oscar Niemeyer (born 1907), with Le Corbusier acting as advisor, built the *Ministry of Education and Health, Rio de Janeiro (ill. 306)*, the pioneer building of modern Brazilian architecture. To the basic form – first designed by Mies van der Rohe in 1919 – of a skyscraper completely surrounded by glass, Le Corbusier had the idea of adding *brises-soleil*, a new solution which was not only functional, in view of the climatic conditions, but also aesthetically original. The enormous planes which are often so incredibly monotonous in such buildings are given here an extremely effective rhythmic animation. – The *United Nations Building (ill. 309)* has become a new symbol of New York. It was built in 1947–50 by Wallace K. Harrison (born 1895) and Max Abramowitz (born 1908), with the cooperation of an advisory committee which included Le Corbusier and Niemeyer. The thin slab, the broad sides of which consist almost entirely of suspended glass walls, has virtually no animation in itself but is enlivened by the wide river in front of it and the open country beyond, while the skyscrapers of Manhattan appear to counterbalance it. – An even more isolated building is the *Edificio Polar, Caracas* (1953–4, *ill. 307*), by

Martin Vegas Pacheco (born 1926) and José Miguel Galia. The four sides of the giant rectangular block, each of which are differently faced, project several yards beyond the lower storeys so that the building not only seems to stand freely within space but also to float on top of it. The principle behind this had been anticipated by Adler and Sullivan in their Guaranty Building, Buffalo. – Düsseldorf town centre is given a powerful emphasis by the *Phoenix-Rhein-rohr Building (ill. 308)*. Three slabs, a large central slab flanked by two smaller ones, offer a differentiated accent which has nothing oppressive about it because of the extraordinary lightness, almost transparency of the building's appearance. Bruno Taut's utopian vision of half-a-century earlier for a 'city crown' has at last become reality, although in a very much more sober and useful form. What the building as a whole lacks in movement is compensated by the very pleasing proportions and the excellent arrangement of the slabs. – The same elements were used by the Finnish architect Viljo Revell (born 1910) and John B. Parkin Associates to give a meaningful climax to the centre of Toronto in the shape of the *City Hall* (1958–65, *ill. 310*). On a relatively small site of *c.* 200 × 300 m two slab-shaped office blocks of different heights are wrapped around a low circular conference hall, echoing its circular movement. The powerful, smoothly ribbed, vertical ends of the office blocks and the broad horizontal bands halfway up and along the top give the impression of a firmly composed architectural unit and at the same time provide a lively articulation.

Town planning

In the last few examples, we have touched upon a problem to which we have unfortunately not been able to give special consideration in this study, namely the problem of town-planning. We saw how in the middle of the eighteenth century, John Wood father and son designed sites in Bath that stood in complete contradiction to the regularly laid-out and enclosed urban organisms of the Renaissance and Baroque periods. John Nash, with his proposed 'garden city' in Regent's Park, London, in the early nineteenth century, took a further step towards the dissolution of the enclosed settlement. However, the principle has only been realized in its entirety during this century in numerous developments on the fringes of already existing towns, or even in the centre of towns where these have been destroyed. The ideas prefigured in 1927 in a relatively small development, the Weissenhof Estate, Stuttgart, with the cooperation of the most advanced international architects of the day (Behrens, Gropius, Le Corbusier, Mies van der Rohe, Oud and others), were repeated on a very much larger scale in the *Hansa Quarter, Berlin* (1957, Interbau Exhibition, *ill. 311*). A number of architects from all over Europe and the rest of the world cooperated in this venture, and created a prototype whose viability has been proved. The basic approach was the same as that which Wright, Rietveld, Le Corbusier, Mies van der Rohe and others brought to the design of the villa for the smallest communal unit, the family, which Gropius brought to the working community in his factory at Alfeld, and which Aalto brought to the community of the sick at Paimio, and there are many other examples. In this case, it involved the functional arrangement of a larger section of an urban community. Indispensable conditions in such an arrangement are generous use of space and the provision of ample light to achieve an unity between interior and exterior space. Here the openness and permeability which had been achieved in individual buildings had to be applied to the structure of an entire district.

In view of the mass production of extremely boring housing and office blocks today, the question which arises most urgently and most often is whether this world-wide uniformity will kill the creative personality in man. However, rather than staring hopelessly at meaningless architecture, which is in the majority because it cannot be otherwise in a mass society, we should concentrate our attention on those solutions which rise above the ordinary and which are therefore alone of importance. The mass society is a fact, and the technology and bureaucracy which lie behind it, a necessity. How this situation can be altered in the future, we do not as yet know. But, it is equally obvious that this mass society would not have become possible and will not continue to be possible without the help of the creative spirit in its various manifestations, including those of architecture. The responsibility of the architect, in fact, is greater today than it has ever been before.

Glossary

Abacus: The topmost member of a capital, a plain square slab in the Greek Doric style, but in other styles often moulded or otherwise enriched.

Acanthus: Plant with thick fleshy leaves reproduced in carved ornament of Corinthian capitals.

Aedicule: Framed niche set in a temple.

Apse: Semicircular niche containing an altar, usually at the eastern or chancel end of the church.

Aqueduct: Structure adapted for the transportation of water, consisting of a pipe or channel or a bridge.

Arcade: Two or more arches with their supporting pillars or columns, taken together and considered as a single architectural feature.

Arcaded arch: Arch at the point where vault meets wall.

Architrave: Usually a supporting beam above columns.

Atrium: The principal room or a small court in the middle of a Roman house. Also the court in front of an Early Christian basilica.

Attic: Usually a low strip of blank wall above a cornice.

Balcony: Small open gallery built out from a wall, usually supported by corbels or brackets.

Baldacchino: Canopy over throne, tomb or altar.

Balustrade: Parapet or low screen consisting of balusters carrying a rail.

Baptistery: Building used chiefly for baptismal services.

Base: The lowest part or lowest main division of a pillar, column, tower, etc.

Basilica: 1. In Roman architecture, an oblong building with double colonnades inside and a semicircular apse at the end. 2. In Early Christian and Medieval architecture, an aisled church.

Bay: Unit of space between the supporting columns or piers of a church. Also a vertical unit of a façade.

Blind arch and Blind arcade: Arch or series of arches applied to the surface of a wall without openings.

Bracket or Corbel: Small supporting projecting piece of stone, often carved with scrolls or volutes.

Buttress: Mass of masonry or brickwork abutting a wall inside or outside a building to give additional strength.

Caldarium: The hot-room in Roman thermae.

Campanile: Bell tower of a church, standing more or less completely separate from the rest of the building.

Capital: The topmost part of a column, if separated from the rest of the column by distinct architectural treatment.

Cardo: North-south axis of a Roman legionary camp.

Cella: The inner sacred chamber of a Greek or Roman temple.

Centralized structure: Building in which all the principal axes are of the same length.

Chancel: The eastern part of a church comprising the choir and sanctuary.

Channel or Flute: Vertical groove in a triglyph or column.

Chevet: The French term for the east end of a church comprising apse and ambulatory with or without radiating chapels.

Choir: The part of a church where divine service is sung.

Choir-screen: Partition between the nave and choir of a church.

Clerestory: That part of the nave of a church which rises above the side aisles and contains windows.

Clustered or compound pier: Pier composed of a number of column shafts grouped together, usually around a larger central core.

Coffered ceiling: Ceiling divided into square or octagonal recessed panels.

Colonnade: Passage lined with columns bearing a straight entablature.

Colossal Order: Any order whose columns rise from the ground through several storeys.

Column: Free-standing upright supporting member with circular section.

Composite capital: Capital combining elements of various orders into a congruous whole.

Conch: Half-cupola, usually above an apse.

Corbel: see Bracket.

Cornice: The topmost part of an entablature, or any horizontal projecting ornamental member crowning a wall or part of a wall.

Crossing or Intersection: The open square formed where a transept crosses the nave and chancel.

Crypt: Room beneath the pavement of a church, containing relics or a tomb.

Decumanus: East-west axis of a Roman legionary camp.

Diagonal ribs: In a rib vault, the intersecting ribs extending from one corner of the compartment to that diagonally opposite.

Dipteros: Temple surrounded by a double row of columns.

Domical vault or Cloister vault: Vault rising directly from a square or polygonal bay, the curved surfaces separated by groins.

Dowelling pin: Small pin or similar projecting member made of bronze or wood to connect two parts together.

Drum: Cylindrical shell supporting a cupola or dome.

Dwarf-gallery: Wall-passage with a low arcade on the outside of a building; usual in Romanesque architecture, especially in Italy and Germany.

Echinus: The circular cushion-like member in Doric capitals below the abacus.

Enfilade: The alignment of the doors of a number of adjacent rooms on the same axis so as to produce a vista.

Engaged column: Column applied to the surface of a wall or arranged round a core (as part of a Clustered column).

Exedra: Recess, usually semicircular, containing raised seats, or any apse or niche or the apsidal end of a room.

Facing: Finishing of different material applied to the inner or outer surface of a building.

Fan-vaulting: Vaulting with ribs springing from one point in the shape of a fan.

Flamboyant: Late phase of Gothic architecture in France, named after the window tracery which was carved in the shape of flames.

Fluting: see Channel.

Flying buttress: Arch or half-arch transmitting the thrust of a vault or roof from the upper part of a wall to an outer support or buttress.

Freestone: Any limestone or sandstone or very homogeneous stone that can be worked freely in any direction.

Frigidarium: The cold-room in Roman thermae.

Gable: More or less triangular superstructure above doors, windows, etc., in Gothic architecture, or the triangular upper portion of a wall carrying a pitched roof.

Gallery: Passage, arcade or platform above a side aisle or ambulatory, or a decorative arcade or blind arcade running along the top of a façade.

Greek cross: Cross with four arms of the same length.

Groin: The curved ridge formed where two vaults intersect or two surfaces of a vault meet.

Groin vault or Cross vault: Compound vault in which two or more tunnel vaults intersect, forming groins.

Hall-church: Church with nave and side aisles of the same height.

Hypostyle: Hall or other large space over which the roof is supported by massed rows of columns giving a forest-like appearance.

Impluvium: Rainwater basin in the atrium of a Roman house.

Incrustation: The covering of wall-surfaces with some precious material.

Intercolumniation: The space between columns.

Intersection: see Crossing.

Keel arch: Arch which in profile resembles the cross-section of the lower part of a ship's hull, showing the keel and bilges.

Lantern: Any structure rising above the roof or dome of a building and having openings in its sides to admit light to the interior of the building.

Lintel: Horizontal beam or stone bridging an opening.

Mastaba: In Egypt, a tomb built above ground, usually with a very plain exterior, rectangular in form and with a flat roof.

Mausoleum: A large and splendid tomb or cenotaph.

Megaron: Large oblong hall in Creto-Mycenaean and Greek architecture.

Metopes: Slabs of stone, either smooth or decorated with reliefs, placed above the architrave of a Greek temple and filling the space between triglyphs.

Module: 1. In classical architecture, half the diameter of a column at its base. 2. In modern architecture, any unit of measurement which facilitates prefabrication.

Monolith: Member consisting of a single block of stone.

Moulding: Narrow projecting band of stone running along a wall or around a column or pillar.

Mutule: Projecting square block above the triglyph on the underside of a Doric cornice.

Naos: see Cella

Narthex: In Early Christian and Byzantine architecture, a large porch or vestibule at the end furthest from the altar and sanctuary.

vault: Vault of which the ribs form a network of lozenges.

Offset: Surface or piece forming the top of a horizontal projection on a wall.

Paradise: In Early Christian and Medieval architecture, a court or atrium in front of a church.

Pendentive: A concave spandrel leading from the angle of two walls to the base of a circular dome. It is one of the means by which a circular dome is supported over a square or polygonal compartment, used in Byzantine, occasionally in Romanesque and frequently in Renaissance, Baroque and later architecture.

Peripteros: Temple surrounded by a single row of columns.

Peristyle: An open space enclosed by columns.

Piano nobile: The main floor of a house, containing the reception rooms. It is usually higher than the other floors, with a basement or ground floor below and one or more shallower storeys above.

Pier: Heavy, solid masonry support, often consisting of a central core with engaged columns or pilasters.

Pilaster: An engaged pillar projecting slightly from the wall.

Pillar: Free-standing upright supporting member with a square or polygonal section.

Pinnacle: Vertical, tapered structure of masonry crowning a buttress or gable in a Gothic cathedral.

Portico: Open vestibule or ante-room covered by a roof supported on columns on at least one side or merely an entrance porch.

Pylon: Rectangular, truncated, pyramidal towers flanking the gateway of an Egyptian temple.

Quadriga: Four horse chariot, used as a triumphal motif in sculpture.

Refectory: The dining room of a convent or monastery.

Reinforcing arch: Arch to reinforce a tunnel vault.

Rib vault: Vault constructed on a square or polygonal ground plan, where the panels are supported by a skeleton of ribs erected before the vault head.

Rustication: Masonry cut in massive blocks separated from each other by deep joints, employed to give a rich and bold texture to an exterior wall and normally reserved for the lower part of it.

Sanctuary: Part of a church in which the main altar is situated.

Sexpartite vault: An ordinary quadripartite vault divided transversely into two parts so that each bay has six compartments.

Spandrel: Space between the shoulder of an arch and the surrounding rectangular moulding or framework, or between the shoulders of adjacent arches.

Springer: The stone at the point at which the curve of an arch or vault leaves the upright.

Stellar vault: Vault where the ribs are so arranged as to form star shapes.

Stucco: Plaster mixture used as covering for walls.

Tepidarium: Lukewarm room of Roman thermae.

Terracotta: Fired but unglazed clay.

Thermae: Roman public baths.

Tholos: Circular domed building sometimes surrounded by a circle of columns.

Tracery: The ornamental intersecting work forming the upper part of a window, screen or panel, or used decoratively in blind arches and vaults.

Triconchal structure: Arrangement of three semicircular or polygonal terminal apses around a chancel end or on the chancel end and transept arms.

Triforium: A arcaded wall-passage facing on to the nave of a church above the nave arcades and below the clerestory windows.

Triumphal arch: In Roman architecture, a monumental arch usually erected in honour of a victorious commander.

Tunnel vault or Barrel vault: The simplest form of vaulting consisting of a continuous vault of semicircular or pointed section.

Tympanum: The area between the lintel of a doorway and the arch above it.

Velarium: Large tent-like arrangement drawn up over an amphitheatre to protect spectators from the sun.

Vestibule: A passage or ante-room intermediate between the entrance and the interior of a building.

Viaduct: Structure bearing a roadway over a valley.

Volute: Spiral scroll of an Ionic or Corinthian capital.

Westwork: The west end of a Carolingian or Romanesque church, consisting of a low entrance hall and above it a room open to the nave and usually flanked or surrounded by aisles and upper galleries. The whole is crowned by one broad tower, and there are occasionally stair turrets as well. In the main upper room there was usually an altar.

Ziggurat: A stepped pyramid in Mesopotamian sacred architecture.

Index of Personal Names

Aalto, Aino 289
Aalto, Alvar 289, 292
Abadie, Paul 276
Abramowitz, Max 291
Adam, Robert 260
Adler, Dankmar 277, 292
Agrippa, Marcus Vipsanianus 37
Alberti, Leon Battista 125, 126–27, 230
Alexander the Great 31
Amenhotep III, Pharaoh 13
Angilbert III, Abbot 68
Antelami, Benedetto 105
Anthemius of Tralles 58
Antiochus IV, King of Syria 32, 33
Apollodorus of Damascus 40
Arévalo, Luis de 248
Arras, Matthias von 114
Attalus II 33
Augustus, Emperor 34, 42, 47, 127
Aurelius, Marcus 229

Ballu, Theodore 270
Barelli, Agostino 247
Barma 61
Barry, Sir Charles 269
Behrens, Peter 283, 284, 285, 286, 292
Berlage, Hendrik Petrus 279–80, 281
Bernard of Clairvaux 82
Bernini, Gian Lorenzo 233, 240, 241, 242, 244, 250, 253
Bentheim, Lüder von 236
Bernward, Bishop 69
Boffig, Guillermo 110
Boffrand, Germain 254
Bon, Bartolommeo 112, 115
Bon, Giovanni 112, 115
Borromini, Francesco 239–40, 242, 246, 247
Boullée, L.E. 260, 261
Bramante, Donato 57, 225, 226–27, 228, 230
Breton, Gilles le 233
Brodrick, Cuthbert 276
Brongniart, A.T. 265
Brosse, Salomon de 244
Brunelleschi, Filippo 124–25, 126
Bullant, Jean 234
Burlington, Earl of 255
Burnham, D.H. 277
Busketos 77
Butterfield, William 269

Calderini, Giuseppe 275
Callicrates 29
Cambio, Arnolfo di 111
Cambyses 16
Campen, Jacob van 243
Cannevale, Carlo 247
Caratti, Francesco 247
Chalgrin, J.F.T. 249, 259, 260
Charlemagne 63, 64, 68
Charles V, Emperor 230
Clairvaux, Bernard of, see Bernard of Clairvaux
Coducci, Mauro 225
Compte, Pedro 119
Conrad II, Emperor 75
Constantine the Great 45, 50, 53, 54
Cortona, Domenica da 232, 233
Cortona, Pietro da 240–41
Costa, Lúcio da 291
Cubitt, Lewis 272
Cuijpers, P.J.H. 275
Cyrus, King of Persia

Darius I, King of Persia 16
Demmler, G.A. 271
Dientzenhofer, Christoph 247
Dientzenhofer, Johann 67
Dientzenhofer, Kilian Ignaz 247
Diocletian, Roman Emperor 45
Domitian, Roman Emperor 42
Ducerceau, Jean 233

Ensingen, Ulrich van 109

Fancelli, Luca 127
Ferstel, Heinrich von 270
Fischer von Erlach, Johann Bernhard 249–50, 251
Fox, Charles 272
François I 232–33
Frederick II, Emperor 106
Frei, Otto 291
Fuga, Ferdinando 254
Furness, Frank 277

Gabriel, Jacques-Ange 244, 255
Galia, José Miguel 292
Garnier, J.L.C. 274
Gärtner, Friedrich von 264, 265
Gau, F.Ch. 269
Gaudí, Antonio 277, 280–81, 285

Gibbs, James 248
Gilly, Friedrich 262, 263, 264
Giotto 112
Gratianus, Roman Emperor 51
Gropius, Walter 284, 285, 286, 292
Guarini, Guarino 246, 247, 250
Guimard, Hector 282

Hadrian, Roman Emperor 32, 37, 42, 47
Hamilton, Thomas 265
Harrison, Wallace K. 291
Hatshepsut, Queen of Egypt 12
Hawksmoor, Nicholas 251
Henderson 272
Henry IV, Emperor 75
Henry VII of England 118
Hermogenes 32
Herostratus 31
Herrera, Juan de 234
Hildebrandt, Johann Lucas von 247, 250, 251, 252
Hippodamus of Miletus 33
Hoffman, Josef 282, 284
Holl, Elias 235, 239
Hontañón, Juan Gil de 119
Horta, Victor 280, 281, 282
Hugh, Abbot 80

Ictinus 29, 30
Innocent II, Pope 89
Isodorus of Miletus 58

Jones, Inigo 237, 239, 255
Julius II, Pope 227
Justinian, Emperor 54, 58, 61
Juvarra, Filippo 127, 226, 251, 254

Karaindash, King of Warka 15
Kent, William 255
Kikutake, Kiyonori 291
Klenze, Leo von 262, 264

Labrouste, Henri P.F. 271, 272, 273, 280
Langhans, Carl Gotthard 260
Latrobe, Benjamin H. 261, 265
Laugier, Marc-Antoine 259
Laves, G.L.F. 271
Layens, Mathias de 120
Le Corbusier (Charles Edouard Jeanneret) 286, 288, 291, 292

Index of Buildings